Values and Vision
in Primary Education

Values and Vision in Primary Education

Edited by Kathleen Taylor and Richard Woolley

Mc Graw Hill Education Open University Press

Open University Press
McGraw-Hill Education
McGraw-Hill House
Shoppenhangers Road
Maidenhead
Berkshire
England
SL6 2QL

email: enquiries@openup.co.uk
world wide web: www.openup.co.uk

and Two Penn Plaza, New York, NY 10121-2289, USA

First published 2013

A catalogue record of this book is available from the British Library

ISBN-13: 978-0-335-24666-3
ISBN-10: 0-335-24666-4
eISBN: 978-0-335-24667-0

Library of Congress Cataloging-in-Publication Data
CIP data applied for

Typeset by Aptara, Inc.

Praise for this book

"This book reaffirms in a very readable and engaging way the liberal, humane values that have informed, and still inform, the work of so many primary schools and teachers. It challenges its readers to engage personally with both values and vision. This is particularly necessary in the current context where primary education is in danger of being replaced by primary schooling through government diktat. The book is part of the principled resistance necessary to combat this menace to English childhood and teacher professionalism."
Colin Richards, former senior HMI and Emeritus Professor, University of Cumbria, UK

"A book putting children at the centre of education is a rare delight. It sloughs away the boredom of government directives and the 'compliant culture' (Compton) that follows. Chapters begin with eye-catching vignettes about learning. The text is evocatively written and, like a good novel, has memorable nuggets at regular intervals: e.g. Taylor's 'curiosity is all about possibilities.' The book delivers practical approaches for student teachers from practitioners. It is refreshing in its willingness to articulate values. Kimaliro and Woolley present the challenge for us all: 'how can teachers make possible the dreams that are to shape tomorrow's pathways?'"
Dr Trevor Kerry, Emeritus Professor, University of Lincoln, UK & Visiting Professor, Bishop Grosseteste University, UK

"This book enters the initial teacher education field like a breath of fresh air because it reminds us of children and their worlds. The contributors tackle some of the 'big ideas' in education and provide a strong foundation for those students in initial teacher education who might be seeking to make sense of their emerging role as educators. Each of the chapters contextualises its theme within the recognisable curriculum orthodoxies of primary education but seeks to expand these margins and place children once again at the centre of the curriculum. The editors deserve congratulations in remind all of us about the purposes of primary education."
Dr Robyn Cox, Associate Professor Literacy Education, Strathfield, Faculty of Education, Australian Catholic University, Australia

For our students

Contents

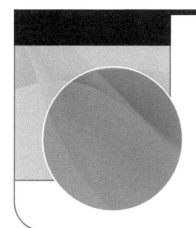

Editors and contributors

Editors

Kathleen Taylor is a visiting tutor at Bishop Grosseteste University where, for fourteen years, she led the BA (Hons) Primary Education and was Head of the Department of Undergraduate Primary Initial Teacher Education. Her specialisms include children's language and literacy, educational philosophy, science and design technology. Kathleen has worked as a consultant for overseas projects. Her PhD research is focused on ethos in teaching and learning interactions in a primary school.

Richard Woolley PhD is Head of Centre for Education and Inclusion at the University of Worcester. His interests include citizenship, children's spirituality, personal, social and emotional wellbeing, and religious education. He coordinated several subjects in primary schools and served as a deputy head teacher and special needs coordinator. Previously he worked at Bishop Grosseteste University, latterly as Head of the Department of Undergraduate Primary Initial Teacher Education.

Contributors

Ashley Compton is a Senior Lecturer in Primary Education at Bishop Grosseteste University. Ashley's specialisms include creativity in learning and teaching, mathematics and music. Her EdD research focused on creativity in primary teacher education and she is currently part of *Creative Little Scientists*, a European research project about creativity in science and mathematics in the early years.

Linda Cooper is a Senior Lecturer in Humanities at the University of Chichester and a former Senior Lecturer at Bishop Grosseteste University. Linda specializes in ICT and humanities in primary education.

Karen Elvidge is a Senior Lecturer at Bishop Grosseteste University and has been the Academic Coordinator responsible for the Flexible Route PGCE (Primary). She is the National Priority Thread Coordinator for SEN and Inclusion and the Diversity 'Champion' for the School of Teacher Development.

Nigel Hutchinson is a Senior Lecturer in Primary Education at Bishop Grosseteste University. His interests include mathematical and physical education. He previously taught in primary schools for twenty years including two headships.

Eunice Kimaliro is a teacher and educator with over 20 years' experience in the Kenyan school system. She has worked on a variety of projects including as an advisor. Eunice is currently based at the University of Worcester undertaking research on teacher identity in a Kenyan primary school.

Lindy Nahmad-Williams is a Senior Lecturer in Education Studies at Sheffield Hallam University. Previously at Bishop Grosseteste University, Lindy specializes in early years education, English and drama. Her PhD research explored issues in prison education.

Rachael Paige is a Senior Lecturer in Primary Education at Bishop Grosseteste University. She is a former head teacher whose specialist interests include language and literacy, education philosophy, the impact of social interactions (including behaviour for learning) and school improvement.

Mike Steele is a Senior Lecturer in Primary Education at Bishop Grosseteste University. Mike specializes in English, primary languages and investigation-based learning. He has served as a primary school head teacher.

Preface

This book grew out of the shared experience of working together in Higher Education, and Initial Teacher Education in particular. The contributors worked mainly on an undergraduate degree, the BA (Hons) Primary Education, within the School of Teacher Development at Bishop Grosseteste University, UK, part of provision that was rated as outstanding by the government's regulatory and inspection body, Ofsted. The focus on values-based education, helping students to develop personal philosophies of education, and emphasis on creativity and the arts provided a rich learning environment for both staff and students.

Each contributor to this book expresses their views in their own voice. Its strength lies in some of the diverse outlooks and passionately held opinions. Our intention is that the format of each chapter provides a degree of consistency for the reader, as will the shared vision for primary education. Each chapter opens with a 'vignette' – a short account of practice or experience to which we return at some point in the chapter. Boxed text features provide the opportunity to *pause for thought, reflect on research* and consider *case studies*. Each chapter concludes with suggestions for *developing practice*, which you will want to evaluate in the light of your own context, experience and vision for primary education.

Acknowledgements

This book grew out of its contributors' shared experience of working in Primary Initial Teacher Education at Bishop Grosseteste University, UK. We express our gratitude to colleagues, both students and staff, for their support during this project and to the Research Centre, which provided funding to facilitate two study days to develop the plan for this book.

Bishop Grosseteste University marked its 150th anniversary in 2012, and this book seeks to capture some of the philosophy and ethos within its rich tradition to celebrate a commitment to inspirational Initial Teacher Education. This is our way of marking the anniversary and sharing our experience of a values-based approach to learning and teaching.

It goes without saying that all shortcomings in the text are our own. Every effort has been made to contact copyright holders for their permission to reprint material in this book. The publishers will be grateful to hear from any copyright holder who is not acknowledged and will undertake to rectify any errors or omissions in future editions.

Finally, our most sincere thanks are expressed to all the students, teachers, colleagues, children, carers and parents who have shared their learning, insights and experiences with us. Without their input this book would lack some of its reality. Where appropriate their contributions have been anonymized.

1

Curiosity

Kathleen Taylor

> 66 What is it about these small conker parcels, some wrapped, some bare, that evoke such excitement and joy in the children? The hustle and bustle under the [Horse Chestnut] trees led me to look closer and to something more beautiful than I had remembered. Not just the shiny nuggets but the powerful protective atmosphere under the tree's branches. I became aware of the secrets of the tree, the crevasses, the leaves, brown sticky things I had never noticed before. All this fascinated me. I was hooked and wanted to discover more.
>
> *Eme, student BA (Hons) Primary Education,*
> *Bishop Grosseteste University* 99

Introduction

Eme's account shows her seeing things as if for the first time. She has walked past the trees every day at the university campus while studying for her degree but on this occasion she stops to dwell, and by dwelling all that had been invisible to her becomes visible. She re-discovers the richness of the natural environment through childhood memories and finds something more beautiful that motivates her to discover more.

Curiosity is all about possibilities and what might be discovered. Like Eme, children the world over have an innate fascination for the world around them and an insatiable natural curiosity – this is the natural disposition from which children start to learn. When children are given a forum, such as those who gave evidence for the Cambridge Primary Review in England, they identify the value of lessons that spark their curiosity and encourage them to explore (Alexander 2010).

This chapter considers children's curiosity and the things that interest them as a starting point for learning and teaching. It explores the emotional and interpersonal experiences that lie at the very heart of learning by considering important aspects such as choice and a sense of purpose. The tensions facing teachers for managing and facilitating child-led learning when the focus remains on measurements and comparisons of children's academic performance are also considered. So, too, are the complexities in teaching, such as knowing what experiences stimulate curiosity rather than providing fleeting encounters for the child. Questions are asked about providing and managing first-hand experiences, providing time for children to explore, knowing when to intervene and scaffolding learning without taking over, how to deal with the unknown, and fundamentally believing the child will make new discoveries.

Curiosity as a starting point for learning

When I first read Eme's writing as part of a student teacher's first year module called 'Learning How to Learn', I could not help but think of Caitlin, a 5-year-old child I encountered in a Foundation Class in a rural Lincolnshire school. Caitlin joined a small group of other five-year-olds on a mini-beast hunt around the school grounds. As soon as she stepped outside she spotted her first mini-beast – or rather mini-beasts, as there were hundreds of what seemed to be little red 'spiders' dashing about the brick wall that formed the entrance to the school. Questions followed rapidly not only from Caitlin but from other children who were capti-vated as much by Caitlin's running commentary as by the 'spiders' themselves. One of her first responses was to compare them to a town where all the people dash about, hurrying and scurrying from one place to another. Her analogy was perfect, but how had she linked what she was seeing to the idea of a bird's eye view of a town. What experiences was she drawing from? These small children quickly took over the teacher's role by asking questions and developing Caitlin's analogy, one child saying, 'it's as if they're in cars', and contradicting each other's explanations, such as Thomas who expressed doubts about our calling these tiny mini-beasts spiders saying, 'we don't know that's what they are'.

I had neither envisaged a mini-beast hunt centring on the school's wall nor a response from the children that was so sophisticated, intellectual and richly dia-logic. However, the teacher was open to following up children's responses at this preliminary point in the overall planning of the project. It was a scene of children pursuing their interests through asking questions, making comparisons, mak-ing connections, offering suggestions, arguing, and contradicting one another. In every sense, the children were engaged in the pursuit of learning. Their natural disposition of wanting to find out was in action, their curiosity was aroused, and I have no doubt the teacher's plans were somewhat out of kilter. It seemed to me that in those moments the teacher had found the children's place to learn, a place that teachers strive to find but all too often fail to do so. A further question I asked myself was how would the teacher maintain this high level of initial curiosity, and that the greater challenge lay in the nurturing of curiosity, as important if not more important than the arousing of it.

The point of the following discussion is to examine the ingredients of motivating teaching and learning and what it means to manage and sustain motivating teaching and learning experiences for children. However, such a discussion is bound to reveal the inconsistencies, complexities, tensions, and dilemmas that teachers have to deal with on a daily basis in their pursuit of inspirational and thought-provoking contexts for learning. There are some striking similarities in both the student's and the children's experiences that are worth examining more closely so as to begin to uncover some of the motivational factors that encourage children to want to learn. As the title of this chapter indicates, curiosity is at the heart of both.

Choice and talk

Both the student and the children have chosen and are pursuing what interests them. Immediately this poses a dilemma for teachers who know it is impossible to offer individual choice to every child all of the time in school. However, a closer look reveals the teacher's role and influence. In the case of the student, Eme, she was asked by her tutors to look carefully at the local natural environment and choose an intriguing and evocative part of it for further investigation. In the case of the children, the teacher has joined in and grabbed the moment, rather than moved the children to other more vegetated places around the school, which was the intent. In each case, the teachers have embraced choice. Choice is an important motivating factor because it heightens awareness of what might be possible (Donaldson 1978). Also, the context for choice matters, so that learners can make important choices rather than trivial ones, the former leading to more significant judgements and discernment (Taylor 2010). In both cases, the situation from which the student and children can choose has been well thought out by the teachers, to be seen as guidance and facilitation, rather than contrived or imposed. It is the teacher's way of giving an opportunity to the learner to take ownership of their interest and learning.

Choosing is not without its demands for the learner, be it student or child, and if in the hands of a teacher who values talk for learning provides a context for using the discourse associated with how to learn. In the first instance, the learner considers what is involved in making a choice; it may not be straightforward, the learner might not know what to choose, thus decisions have to be made. Most decisions involve some form of internal dialogue, or in-the-mind reasoning, where consequences as well as possibilities are considered, but for a young learner being shown how to make reasoned decisions through talk, and especially talk that involves questions and considering alternative perspectives, is an essential part of learning about how to learn. In these conversations, child and teacher – and child and child – are *thinking together* where each is acting as a guide and model for using language as a tool for thinking (Mercer and Littleton 2007). While the children in the scenario described earlier were very good at talking, many children lack experience of talk or holding conversations. Mercer and Littleton make the same point when they argue that children may well not have a 'propensity for reasoned dialogue', but in seeing and experiencing reasoned dialogue can be 'explicitly inducted into ways of talking' (2007: 68), which is exactly what was happening with the children examining the behaviour of the 'spiders'. Eme, on the other hand, has the means to recount her thoughts through writing, which in itself is a reflective meta-cognitive process, whereas children thinking together through talk, especially with the aid of an experienced adult or indeed child, as in the case of the children examining the behaviour of the 'spiders', is the main conduit for reflection and meta-cognition.

Criticism in the late 1960s and 1970s focused on post Plowden Report (1967) child-centred learning and Piagetian ideas of children learning as 'lone scientists' (Alexander 2004: 10). The belief was that stimulating environments where children could interact with materials and resources were sufficient for cognitive development to occur forming the basis of constructivist theory. Undoubtedly children need appealing and exciting learning environments to stimulate the mind, time to explore, find out, and play. (For further discussion, see Chapter 7, *Environment*.) However, the work of Vygotsky (1962) and Bruner (1963), who identified the significance of social interaction in cognition and which formed the basis of socio-constructivist theory, gained momentum in the 1980s, fuelling greater educational debate for more social interaction in classrooms. In recent years, the idea that knowledge is co-constructed has become more embedded in pedagogy through an emphasis on meta-cognition, learning how to learn, the basis of teaching materials such as those of Smith and Call (1999), Clarke (2008) and Wallace (2001). Recent developments such as dialogic teaching, an approach to teaching advocated by Alexander (2004), go further, making clear the real need for teachers to engage with children's comments, responses, and answers. Scaffolded talk that is dialogic supports cognition because it provides a model of how the mind works; in other words, dialogue demonstrates meta-cognition (Alexander 2000, 2004; Mercer 1995; Mercer and Hodgkinson 2008; Mercer and Littleton 2007). Effective dialogue between the teacher and the child, between child and child, extends thinking and, when used as a tool for teaching, provides a model for other children to use in their dialogue between themselves and the teacher and also between themselves and other children. The internal dialogue to which I referred earlier, through which reasoned thoughts emerge, is made visible in dialogic teaching.

Purpose

Another similarity is that both scenarios depict learners engrossed in thinking, busy with their thoughts, having time to dwell and time to share their thinking either through writing, as in the case of Eme, or talking, as with the children. There is a real sense of purposefulness and self-direction. Thus the question to be addressed is how has this been achieved? Essentially, the importance of having time to dwell, or thinking time, cannot be overestimated. It is a special sort of thinking time where the learner has time to absorb what is new and, most importantly, emotionally and intellectually engage with the new. The thinking time to which I refer is similar but not the same as 'thinking time' or 'wait time' in lessons where children, in response to their teacher's questions, are given time to think things out and think aloud (Alexander 2004: 19). Rather, it is dwelling time, the necessary personal space children need to mentally explore a new experience without prompting. When there is a shared sense of dwelling between teacher and child, and child and child, hierarchical structures disappear, both parties silently appreciating the shared moment. Such experiences can be likened to reading where the inference of what is not said between the lines carries the meaning. Essentially, a teacher who values such spaces will substitute prompts for expectations, knowing the shared experience carries possibilities and ideas. The argument is not without precedence, for lying at the heart of Dewey's educational philosophy is the idea that to engage in an experience is to engage with ideas and possibilities and in so doing 'awaken anticipation and initiate action' (Pugh and Girod 2007: 12).

Both scenarios reveal learners driving their learning through a natural entwining of dwelling and dialogue in the mind, demonstrated in Eme's writing, and dialogue through talk, demonstrated in the exchanges between the children. This is especially the case for the children, where dwelling and dialogue are entwined naturally because both are driven by the children. Neither case is dominated by organizational features; on the contrary, the emphasis is on the learner's pace to learn.

Perhaps Margaret Donaldson's description of a school courtyard at the beginning of her seminal work *Children's Minds* (1978) captures best the notion of learners' pace and a scene not dominated by organizational features but rather underpinned by them. It is a scene of children pursuing their own interests, watering flowers, referring to books, drawing and making notes of the world around them (Donaldson 1978). She suggests anyone seeing this would think they had found Utopia and goes on to ask what goes wrong in schooling. I have already referred to the criticisms made against child-centred learning of the 1960s and 1970s and while this scenario typifies such learning, there is much to be learned from it for today's children. I am not suggesting that children today are any different to the children in the courtyard, or that times were different then, but that the scene is a reminder that children are capable of dwelling, concentrating, and playing for long periods when their interest is captured, like today's hi-tech savvy children who are equally predisposed to spend considerable time using computerized technology. It is what lies behind the courtyard scene that reveals the skill of the teacher in creating an autonomous learning environment, the hidden organizational features, and what that means to the children.

The teacher, in creating autonomy for children, removes organizational constraints enabling each child to pursue his or her own interests independently and purposefully. The ease with which children experience accessing and using resources frees their minds to experience learning through the senses and to intellectually and emotionally engage with the experience. A modern-day version might include cameras, video cams, digital recorders, and iPads, all now as familiar to the child as drawing tools, notebooks, and books. It is in these experimental situations where children are in effect playing that connections are made, as for example in the courtyard scenario where the children made connections between plants and water, pencils and drawings, books and reading, and a more modern technical scenario between icons and images, switches and actions. Indeed, another student James, studying sunflowers as part of the module 'Learning How to Learn', drew upon his skills in photography to 'capture the beauty' of a sunflower and by comparing one picture with another identified 'distinct differences between sunflowers'. Being familiar with the camera enabled James to experience both the beauty and complexity of the sunflower and increase his motivation to engage with it. In the same way, the familiar features of the natural and constructed local environment of the courtyard provided a platform from which to learn independently and in which to feel secure to discover new things, learn new skills and, most importantly, make connections.

Pause for thought

Two aspects emerge as significant from the courtyard scene. First, the sense of security the children feel in their familiar setting partly achieved by the autonomous environment created by the teacher and, second, the new skills children are learning. However, a closer look reveals hidden complexities.

Consider the courtyard scene:

- What has the teacher to do to maintain autonomy and a sense of purpose?
- How will the children learn new skills?
- What might the teaching look like?

A sense of security

Curiosity does not come without a certain sense of anxiety, which, in the natural course of events, serves to safeguard us from dangerous consequences. However, anxiety can obstruct curiosity. The sense of not knowing can immobilize the curious spirit, thus in creating an autonomous environment the teacher is in effect removing some of that anxiety for the child.

In the same way, some students experience the task of finding an intriguing starting point from which to explore learning how to learn as onerous, so seek out analogous experiences from childhood in an attempt to create familiarity where they feel there is none. Their first emotional response is anxiety, thus situating the unfamiliar into something familiar is all part of establishing a more secure platform from which to discover new things and new skills like the children in the courtyard.

Eme, in making connections to her own childhood, sets the mood for her journey into experiencing learning like a child, a prerequisite for learning about learning and, for that matter, learning about life. Her context under the trees is particularly evocative of childhood, while the children's courtyard context *is* childhood. Another student, Matthew, in the same university campus, came across the lavender borders and wrote, 'I had flashbacks as it brought back childhood memories of the lavender that used to grow in my grandmother's garden', while Richard wrote, 'I love the smell and taste of apples, reminding me of home-made apple crumbles'. From a starting point that engages them emotionally, the students are able to identify with the basic human need for meaningfulness, intrinsic to which lies purpose. Furthermore, in rekindling the feeling of a child-like curiosity for the world around them, they discover new things about the tree, lavender, apple, and open up possibilities for discovering new things about themselves as learners and future teachers.

The emotional connection the students make through their learning reveals their personal life narratives, which become another meaningful factor contributing to a sense of purpose and intent. Of course we cannot see into the minds of the children playing in the courtyard but we know from research into child development, and our own experience tells us, that children's natural disposition to invent imaginary worlds and stories is a way of projecting purpose into their play (Taylor 2010). Real or imaginary, their narratives serve to contextualize their learning, making it meaningful to them. Writing about curiosity, Bruner suggested little is known about how to support a child to become master over their own attention but that there is much to be learnt from children's prolonged attentiveness when being told stories and asks if there are comparable properties between the internal sequence of story and those which sustain a child's curiosity beyond a moment's vividness (Bruner 1982). Caitlin's analogies of the insect world to her own would suggest her first response was to make a story of what she was seeing, placing the new encounter in the context of the familiar and known, and then to continue to draw upon the analogy to explain the insects' motives for their movements. Revealed in the children's and students' responses is their personal dialogue in-the-mind that fuels their curiosity, which Bruner described as talking to oneself through a sustained sequence (Bruner 1982). I ask that we merely remember what it is like to be a child and to re-connect with our in-the-mind narratives that sustain and motivate because it is these child-like narratives that lie at the heart of learning. (Chapter 2 on *Narrative* explores this issue further.)

Eme's sense of purpose to 'discover more' is driven by the emotional and intellectual connections she has made to the learning environment under the trees. Her curiosity engages both the affective and intellectual domains simultaneously, each fuelling the other and providing the motivation to drive her to want to learn. Whatever way curiosity is stirred into action, the learner's emotional connection to the starting point is a major driver for sustaining curiosity and managing anxiety. Curiosity-led learning is an emotional experience and not one bound solely by the intellect. In a sense, Eme and the other students are finding ways to personalize their experience. In the early twentieth century, Dewey explained the need for teachers to connect subject matter with experience, suggesting it induced a 'vital and personal experiencing', or in other words, living with their ideas (Pugh and Girod 2007: 16). Personal experiencing is one way for the learner to sustain curiosity and establish a sense of purpose.

New skills

Curiosity undoubtedly drives enquiry, as with Caitlin and Thomas one question follows another. However, the teacher invariably asks where are these questions leading to and in effect exercises some judgement over the enquiry to facilitate learning as opposed to frustration, which is the alternative. She knows children need a variety of appropriate skills to further drive enquiry and that the enquiry has to have a purpose, which lies in the questions the children ask, for example Thomas's query suggesting he is not convinced the mini-beasts on the wall are spiders. Examining how the teacher facilitates Thomas's query may reveal the identity of the new skills.

Pause for thought

- Consider how you would support Thomas in finding out if the mini-beasts on the wall were spiders or not.
- If not, what could they be and how would you help him find out?

Initially, the teacher involved the whole group in helping Thomas find out by providing them with magnifying glasses. She suggested they think like detectives by taking a closer look at the mini-beasts, and demonstrated how to use the magnifying glasses. This may seem an obvious thing to do but it is important to recognize the significance of teaching how to observe. Often, we rely on recognition alone, so for example we see all birds as birds without necessarily seeing the differences between them. Rather than distinguishing between a blue tit and a great tit, we draw upon what we recognize as stereotypically a bird.

Looking without seeing is something of which we are all guilty. Often the busy lives we lead prevent us from seeing the finer detail in the world around us and it is as if we have become acclimatized to looking but not seeing. It is only when our attention is drawn to something that we begin to see. Caitlin was instrumental in drawing the teacher's and other children's attention to the swarm of mini-beasts on the school wall, which they had not seen and so readily ignored. By likening what she saw to human social constructs, she revealed her deeper perception. By encouraging the children to look more closely, the teacher attempted to deepen their understanding of what they were seeing. She further encouraged them to capitalize upon Caitlin's metaphor of the town, which drew them to proffer analogies about the mini-beasts 'looking like cars' and 'running like lots of people in a hurry'. The teaching and learning scenario constructed by the teacher is particularly powerful because children are being helped to expand their perception, a concept discussed by Pugh and Girod in relation to Dewey's ideas about the way in which art encourages us to re-see what might be considered ordinary. Pugh and Girod (2007: 19) suggest that teaching to re-see and using metaphor are two significant teaching methods for the expansion of perception.

In subsequent lessons, the teacher provided opportunities for children to draw and photograph the mini-beasts. She taught skills for drawing with pencils, particularly suited to capturing detail and form, and photography using digital cameras. In the same way, students in university are taught drawing skills using pencil, pen and ink, charcoal, pastel and other artistic skills using paint, clay and working with textiles. Such skills provide not only the means for recording what is seen but enhance perception of what is seen. Dewey believed art teaches perception, so by providing the means to respond artistically to what is seen has the potential to deepen perception and open up more possibilities. It is important to recognize the transforming effect in uniting science and art. Instead of recording mini-beasts purely to teach the concept of 'insect' or 'spider', the teacher provides the means by which children can respond to the mini-beasts, thus prolonging their fascination for the creatures while simultaneously prolonging a fascination for the new skills and tools.

Rather than instigating a web search to find out what the mini-beasts were, the teacher arranged for the children to make some comparisons through more teaching and learning outdoors examining other mini-beasts. Children with the help of other adults collected different kinds of mini-beasts in bug boxes and were encouraged to look for similarities and differences. It was at this point that the children were able to sort and group mini-beasts deciding upon their own criteria, such as *slithery* mini-beasts, *flying* mini-beasts, all of which aligned well to scientific enquiry, but more significantly to the learning process itself. The children were captivated by the idea of finding patterns and making links and connections. On one child finding a red beetle, and another finding a bush covered in butterflies – Red Admirals and Peacocks – the search was intensified to find other red mini-beasts, raising questions about where they were found and suggestions about why they were red. The children's sense of tenacity was tangible, and while tenacity is considered contingent to a state of curiosity, to see this with children as young as four and five was thought-provoking, because of its implications for teaching (Schmitt and Lahroodi 2008).

Finding patterns and making connections is central to curiosity and is not restricted to science enquiry but to any enquiry. Feynman ([1997] 2007) would say that mathematics is patterns and mathematics is looking for patterns. In my capacity as a primary teacher teaching reading, I would say language is patterns and reading is looking for patterns – phonic patterns, syntactic patterns, and semantic patterns. While the children are playing detectives in the scientific arena of the natural world, detection work and detection skills cross subject domains. In trying to comprehend their investigation of mini-beasts, the children are learning the skills of how to learn and it is these skills that are transferable. To provide opportunities for the children to talk about their skills for learning, the teacher videoed the investigations and used them in the classroom to promote talk about learning. The viewing of the videos promoted as much interest as did the investigations, the children curious to see themselves as detectives. In this situation, it was straightforward for the teacher to ask questions about the skills they had learnt and to provide opportunities to talk about the usefulness of such skills in other aspects of their learning.

The point where children were making connections between form and function formed a natural conclusion to the children's investigations. Liam said, 'why haven't they all got lots of legs and then they could run more quickly like centipedes', while Caitlin, still drawing upon her analogy of the town, said, 'I think they're shopping for food'. Thomas's query remained a query for some time during the project, although when closely observed he was convinced they were insects because they had six legs. More importantly, he was able to draw on his existing knowledge to form his own conclusion that 'spiders' make webs, which would be a good way to know if they were 'spiders' or not. Thomas's puzzlement had pushed him to offer a plausible suggestion, which was a very sophisticated skill for such a young child. This type of situation is what Piaget refers to as a point of *cognitive conflict*, where something that cannot be easily explained may stimulate the child to develop more powerful ways of thinking, as in the case of Thomas (Adey et al. 2003). It can also be a point of frustration for the child, and the demands upon the teacher are complex in steering the enquiry to a satisfactory conclusion. Such a situation highlights the difference between child-led enquiries that can give rise to the unexpected as opposed to teacher-led activities over which the teacher has much more control.

Pause for thought

- Consider why the teacher did not choose to use the internet as a source of information straight away.
- Can you see a role for using information technology and what would be the advantages or disadvantages?

The big ideas

Case study

Another student Marie, studying a sunflower, was puzzled by the arrangement of the petals, so compared the sunflower with other daisy-like flowers, such as asters, Michaelmas daisies, and white field daisies. She hypothesized each would have a similar number of petals. Although the number of petals varied, she found a pattern. At the time she did not know her pattern fitted a pattern in nature described as a Fibonacci pattern after the mathematician who formulated it, and in some respects it didn't matter for she had discovered a pattern.

There is something deeper within the human psyche at work when we begin to examine the world around us. It is our engagement with the bigger human quest for finding meaning about the big ideas that perplexes us. Unfortunately, wondering about the big ideas might remain just that, for wonder is not the same as curiosity and is more easily suppressed. Some would argue that curiosity does not necessarily fix our first attention but rather grows out of what has fixed our attention, mainly driven by a desire to know (Schmitt and Lahroodi 2008). As a consequence, curiosity drives the process of enquiry.

To examine the enquiry process in more detail, let us take a closer look at the notion of students and children engaging with big ideas. Dewey said that too often 'we teach concepts instead of engaging our students with ideas' (Dewey 1933, in Pugh and Girod 2007: 14). Marie's initial curiosity, outlined in the case study, grew into puzzlement, the beginnings of which can also be seen when Eme writes about the brown sticky things she had never noticed before. In studying the lavender, Matthew becomes puzzled as to why, at times, the smell is stronger than at other times and wants to find out why this is. Richard sees the flesh of the apple deteriorate from an appealing pale green to a less appetizing brown and is similarly motivated to find out what is happening. Such questions draw the students to engage with the 'big ideas' in nature. The sticky buds, lavender, and apples have the potential to reveal, for example, ideas about nature's inter-dependency and inter-connectivity between the plant and animal world, and form and function as the children discovered. The students' quest is no different to the children's, who might ask why sand runs like water or why insects have six legs. Neither are such questions different to those that fuelled the greatest scientists to discover and unlock the patterns, principles, and laws of nature we know today. It was those early scientists like Aristotle who, in discovering patterns and making connections about the universe, revealed the process of enquiry. The namesake of the university where I teach, Robert Grosseteste, later translated and added to Aristotle's ideas about scientific method in the twelfth century when he wrote, 'the natural way for us to arrive at knowledge of principles is to go from the whole objects which follow the principles, to the principles themselves' (Crombie 1953: 55). His translations and writings were further developed by Roger Bacon who, like Grosseteste, drew upon Aristotle's work, and set out points developed by Grosseteste establishing induction, which is the building up of generalized rules, and experiment, together with the use of mathematics, as the means for demonstrating connections between occurrences in nature (Crombie 1953). Crombie suggests Grosseteste was the first medieval writer to set out a systematic and coherent theory of experimental investigation and rational explanation, which we recognize today as modern experimental science. However, writings about Grosseteste reveal not only a logical mind at work but also a mind that is driven by an appetite for knowledge and one who finds great pleasure, in those 'situations that reveal general laws', when the patterns connect (Southern 1986: 144). Grosseteste, according to Southern, continued his early habit of considering small things in nature in great detail from which to draw the widest conclusions (Southern 1986). In respect to buds, lavender, and apples, these are the natural objects from where we start to make links to the big ideas or the principles that govern the universe, such as Marie's example when she established a numerical pattern for the sunflower petals and in so doing uncovered a principle for growth represented mathematically by a Fibonacci series of numbers. In recognizing the resemblances between the different daisy-like flowers, Marie was driven to finding a common pattern that linked them together and this she did. The patterns that connect are all around us and constitute the 'big ideas', so a child making a connection between the symmetry of a human face and the symmetry of a butterfly is in effect assimilating the 'big ideas' in nature. In his book *Mind and Nature: A Necessary Unity*, which primarily addresses knowledge and learning, Gregory Bateson presents the case for teaching about patterns that connect (Bateson 1980: 16). Perhaps his case is even more relevant in today's climate where interrelationships between human and nature are paramount if we are to understand, for example, the effects of our actions upon the environment, a current and highly significant 'big idea'. (See also Chapter 7, *Environment*.)

However, as stated earlier, not every child's question can be followed through by the teacher, which poses dilemmas concerning what to pursue and what not to pursue. It is important to recognize in the examples presented in this chapter that the students' task is designed specifically to reveal the enquiry process embedded in the school curriculum and underpinning learning theories, particularly Bloom's taxonomy (Bloom et al. 1956, 1964). Also, to gain further knowledge of the starting point itself. While in school, experiences and objects are offered to children as starting points for exploring specific curriculum content as well as learning how to learn. So, in the school situation children are likely to ask questions about sand within a topic about materials, and similarly about insects in a topic about minibeasts. In this way, the teacher can prepare for possible lines of enquiry while also preparing the journey for the children to travel the enquiry process.

The enquiry process

In past years, the enquiry process has been embedded in the National Curriculum for England (DfEE/QCA 1999) and Curriculum Guidance for the Foundation Stage (DfE 2012), and explicit in the Excellence and Enjoyment (DfES 2004) curriculum guidance Learning to Learn as well as the National Curriculum for Wales, Skills Framework (DfCELLS 2008) and should not be viewed as something special but rather an entitlement. Whatever the curriculum domain, enquiry skills permeate the field. It might therefore be more helpful to focus on pedagogy for enquiry to illuminate a process that is unequivocally at the heart of a creative and engaging school curriculum.

Observation is generally recognized as an essential skill for enquiry, and I have already discussed the skills the teacher needs to draw upon to teach observation, the need to teach re-seeing, and the need for the child to engage aesthetically and emotionally with what is being observed. However, observation is not limited to the sense of sight, rather it is multisensory, so listening to leaves rustling, touching grass, tasting apples, and smelling lavender are fundamentally observational. It is important to consider how teaching may be skewed so that children rely heavily on one sense over and above another and why this should be. Furthermore, while observation may begin a process of enquiry, it also underpins an enquiry throughout. Indeed, the skills aligned to enquiry are recursive, and it is in this way that the child gets better at using them.

So, asking questions, finding patterns, making links and connections, making suggestions, and proffering predictions permeate enquiry and are refined as the enquiry proceeds. The teacher's skill in supporting children to refine a question without undermining it is complex and often difficult, especially for beginner teachers. It is in situations where children are experimenting with their questions and ideas that their curiosity is at its most vulnerable and can easily be quashed by a passing comment that closes down a possibility. This is exemplified in the case study that follows.

Case study

In an older class in a Lincolnshire school a group of children studying insects were discussing whether or not insects could think. One child suggested flies do not think because their response to being swatted was a reflex action, therefore deducing flies could not think. Another child suggested insects could think because some hunted for food, and whereas the fly's reaction to the swatter was defensive and might be a reflex action, hunting for food was aggressive and therefore required thinking. Rather than intervene with deductions of her own that might favour one idea over another, the teacher asked the children to suggest ways in which to sort out their conflicting ideas. One way she suggested was to gather together their reasons for and against thinking and non-thinking insects on a big sheet of paper she provided, and to think of as many alternative explanations as they could. Leaving them with the intriguing question, could there be more than one explanation? Later she organized for the children to present their arguments through a dramatized courtroom where the jury voted for what they considered to be justified or unjustified arguments. The teacher drew upon her bank of pedagogical tools to extend enquiry learning, and in so doing, highlighted the difference between merely knowing the ingredients of enquiry learning as opposed to putting them into practice.

Reflecting on this case study, consider:

- The pedagogical techniques that could be used to extend enquiry learning.
- What is the process for sharing teaching techniques in schools you have experienced?

Another older group of children were debating whether or not there were male and female flies. The idea had developed from noticing some differences in coloration. Rather than immediately directing the children to the internet to find out, the teacher engaged the children in dialogue that helped them clarify their thinking, asking questions about what they might expect to happen in one experiment that had been suggested, separating the flies to see which laid eggs, and why they thought certain things might happen. Alexander (2004: 27) describes this type of extended questioning as 'cumulative where teachers and children develop coherent lines of thinking and enquiry', which he argues is demanding on the teacher's professional skills and subject knowledge as well as insightful into the capacities of the children. To take children's thinking forward requires time for the teacher to think and, as Alexander suggests and as I mentioned earlier, the notion of a lesson's 'pace' requires some re-assessment if cumulative dialogue is to become common practice (Alexander 2004: 46). The teacher also asked questions about the children's experimental design, asking how their experiment might be improved and what modifications they might make and why, as well as asking about other ideas for ways to test their suggestions. While her discerning, quietly enthusiastic interjection fuelled enquiry thinking, her empathy with the children as detectives and scientists fuelled their tenacity and their appetite for finding out. Just as learning demands the engagement of both the cognitive and affective domains, so too does teaching, each are reciprocal.

Developing practice

To develop effective practice we need to consider:

- how our pedagogy nurtures children's curiosity;
- what opportunities we create for children to engage emotionally in their learning;
- how we sustain curiosity through enquiry processes and by making connections to big ideas;
- how we understand and value the nature of dialogue for thinking in our classrooms;
- how we respond to children's ideas, imaginings, inventions, and discoveries;
- how we share in the child's world of possibilities.

Conclusion

Perhaps one point, more than any other, is worth revisiting, and that is the vulnerability of a child's curiosity, if only to show how precious a gift it is. Undoubtedly, being curious serves as a starting point for learning. However, curiosity alone is not enough. It requires nurturing by a caring other person that appears a fairly straightforward if not a simple requisite, but it is far from simple. Curiosity can just as easily be neglected, dismissed or totally quashed.

To explain this further, take the scene from the children's book *The Whales' Song* by Dyan Sheldon and Gary Blythe (1991), where Lilly is sitting on her Grandmother's knee talking about the magical idea of whales singing. The scene is reminiscent of the dwelling time I referred to earlier. But, the moment of shared ideas and possibilities is savagely interrupted by Uncle Frederick who *stomps* into the room and kills the preciousness of the situation with his words of fact and logic: whales were important for their meat, bones, and blubber (Sheldon and Blythe 1991). I have often paused when reading this to children, picking up on their knowing looks and their recognition of the way Lilly is left feeling disillusioned and humiliated.

Children know as well as adults what it feels like to have questions and ideas destroyed, and the knowing looks of the children tell you this. Fortunately, children are invariably resilient and as with other stories based on a similar pretext, for example 'True Adventures of a Boy Reader' in Laurie Lee's *I Can't Stay Long* (1975), Lilly pursues her curiosity to hear whales singing. While many stories are based upon the transforming powers of determination, and gallantry of the human spirit, this may not be the case for many real-life situations. Children may well begin life with a determined and noble spirit, but it may not be possible for all children to hold onto this; on the contrary, where curiosity is constantly put out eventually even the brightest and most optimistic children become subdued or learn to manage their curiosity. Such management manifests itself in the variety of defence mechanism children adopt to avoid ridicule or being ignored, mainly not asking any questions. This is reason alone for ensuring children's curiosity is nurtured and valued. As teachers, surely our goal should be that all our children leave school with the tenacity for continuing learning.

References

Adey, P., Nagy, F., Robertson, A., Serret, N. and Wadsworth, P. (2003) *Let's Think Through Science: Developing Thinking with Seven and Eight Year Olds*. Windsor: NFER Nelson.

Alexander, R. (2000) *Culture and Pedagogy: International Comparisons in Primary Education*. Oxford: Blackwell.

Alexander, R. (2004) *Towards Dialogic Teaching: Rethinking Classroom Talk*, 3rd edn. Thirsk: Dialogos.

Alexander, R. (2010) *Children, Their World, Their Education. Final Report and Recommendations of the Cambridge Primary Review*. London: Routledge.

Bateson, G. (1980) *Mind and Nature: A Necessary Unity*. Glasgow: Fontana/Collins.

Bloom, B.S., Krathwohl, D.R., Engelhart, M.D., Furst, E.J. and Hill, W.H. (1956) *Taxonomy of Educational Objectives: Cognitive Domain*. London: Longman.

Bloom, B.S., Krathwohl, D.R. and Masia, B.B. (1964) *Taxonomy of Educational Objectives: Affective Domain.* London: Longman.

Bruner, J. (1963) *The Process of Education.* New York: Vintage Books.

Bruner, J. (1982) *Towards a Theory of Instruction.* Cambridge, MA: Belknap Press of Harvard University Press.

Clarke, S. (2008) *Active Learning through Formative Assessment.* London: Hodder Education.

Crombie, A.C. (1953) *Robert Grosseteste and the Origins of Experimental Science 1100–1700.* Oxford: Oxford University Press.

Department for Children, Education, Lifelong Learning and Skills (DfCELLS) (2008) *Skills Framework for 3 to 19-year-olds in Wales.* Cardiff: Welsh Assembly Government.

Department for Education (DfE) (2012) *Statutory Framework for the Early Years Foundation Stage.* Runcorn: DfE.

Department for Education and Employment/Qualifications and Curriculum Authority (DfEE/QCA) (1999) *The National Curriculum: Handbook for Primary Teachers in England.* London: DfEE/QCA.

Department for Education and Skills (DfES) (2004) *Excellence and Enjoyment: Learning and Teaching in the Primary Years. Learning to Learn: Progression in Key Aspects of Learning.* London: DFES.

Donaldson, M. (1978) *Children's Minds.* London: Fontana.

Feynman, R. ([1999] 2007) *The Pleasure of Finding Things Out.* London: Penguin Books.

Lee, L. (1975) *I Can't Stay Long.* London: Penguin.

Mercer, N. (1995) *The Guided Construction of Knowledge: Talk amongst Teachers and Learners.* Clevedon: Multilingual Matters.

Mercer, N. and Hodgkinson, S. (2008) *Exploring Talk in School.* London: Sage.

Mercer, N. and Littleton, K. (2007) *Dialogue and the Development of Children's Thinking.* London: Routledge.

Plowden Report (1967) *Children and Their Primary Schools.* Report of the Central Advisory Council for Education in England. London: HMSO.

Pugh, K.J. and Girod, M. (2007) Science, art, and experience: constructing a science pedagogy from Dewey's aesthetics, *Journal of Science Teacher Education*, 18: 9–27.

Schmitt, F. and Lahroodi, R. (2008) The epistemic value of curiosity, *Educational Theory*, 58(2): 125–48.

Sheldon, D. and Blythe, G. (1991) *The Whales' Song.* London: Red Fox Books.

Smith, A. and Call, N. (1999) *The ALPS Approach: Accelerated Learning in the Primary School.* London: Continuum.

Southern, R.W. (1986) *Robert Grosseteste: The Growth of an English Mind in Medieval Europe.* Oxford: Oxford University Press.

Taylor, K. (2010) Exploring media and materials, in A. Compton, J. Johnston, L. Nahmad-Williams and K. Taylor, *Creative Development.* London: Continuum.

Vygotsky, L.S. (1962) *Thought and Language.* Cambridge, MA: MIT Press.

Wallace, B. (2001) *Teaching Thinking Skills Across the Primary Curriculum: A Practical Approach for All Abilities.* London: NACE/Fulton Publications.

Narrative

Rachael Paige

"" James climbed onto the seat beside me and balanced the large Life Book on his lap. The excitement of my anticipated visit was clear from the moment I arrived as I saw his face at the window and then James running to the door to greet me. He ushered me straight into the lounge to show me his new possession. The looks between the adults told a silent story of current worry and concern for the small child only just discovering an early part of his life. 'This picture is funny, I was a funny baby.' His mum sat down and started to provide a narrative gathered from information established from the social worker and collated in the Life Book. 'That is your birth mummy and there you are as a little baby.' I offered what I interpreted as supportive embellishment, 'Oh yes, there you are playing with your toys', and I looked carefully at the pictures and descriptions provided. But a little hand wanted to turn the pages quickly and was keen to move to the more familiar pictures of him meeting (adoptive) mum and dad for the first time and more recent pictures of his birthday and holidays. The exchange lasted no more than a few minutes but it allowed James to begin to explore his story. ""

Introduction

Each of us is a living story, a culmination of experiences and influences sculptured by circumstance and our own response and interpretation of our life events. For us all, personal storytelling is part of the process of making some sense of our experiences and creating our own identity. For children, creating opportunities for storytelling and guiding them in developing the skill of storytelling enables expression in a deeper form and nurtures the joy of sharing with others. To experience the pleasure of making someone else laugh through our narrative, or evoke an emotional response in the listener is a significant and gratifying experience that can motivate children in understanding a key purpose of story. Not only that, but the human need to connect with others can be significantly satisfied when presenter and audience meet each other through inferred meaning, or a shared understanding of character motivation. To recognize the importance of the telling of the story, why it is told, and how it is expressed is very important. It is these elements that are enveloped to create the narrative, and this key aspect needs to be given a place within our curriculums appropriate for such a significant human trait.

This chapter considers how narrative can be developed with children in different contexts to enable expression of ideas, thoughts, and emotions. The importance of encouraging children to create their own narrative will be explored, together with how teachers can impact not only on the skills and knowledge of storytelling but contribute to the emotional wellbeing of the children in their class by facilitating opportunities for children to make sense of their world and experiences, respect and value their own 'voice', and respond appropriately to other people's narratives. Within the chapter, the emphasis is upon the telling of a story, rather than the reading aloud of a storybook, and how the author controls the narrative creating specific emphasis through differing techniques, such as specific word choice or intonation. Four significant themes will emerge relating to why story, and more specifically the narrative, is significant and important:

- to enable us to make sense of our own world;
- to develop our own 'voice' and sense of identity within our social world;
- to understand that our own 'conceptual world' (Bruner 1986) influences our understanding and perception;
- to create a connection with others. This may be through shared understandings within a story or enjoying the collective experience of hearing, reading or telling established or traditional stories thus creating a shared culture and community.

Pause for thought

Think about the little boy, James, presented in the opening vignette. He is 5 years old and has been with his adoptive parents for just over a year. Using these prompt questions, consider how story and language impact James's view of himself and his place within the world:

- Consider why James was keen to move to the more familiar pictures in his Life Book.
- What do you think may have influenced his understanding of the purpose of the Life Book and his choice of language when describing the type of baby he wanted to

present to the audience? Does it relate to what he would like them to admire in the present and the need for high self-esteem?

• As a teacher, how would you respond to a young child who was learning about a life before the one they have established with their adoptive or foster family?

Life Books

I recall the first time I was introduced to the concept of Life Books. It was early in my career and I was working in a small rural school. Three siblings joined the school, newly adopted into a local family. The oldest sibling, Hannah, was assigned to my class and from that first day her Life Book came to school weekly. She would sit with me at any opportunity and show me her pictures and tell me stories, she would join groups of children in the playground and convey events using the collection of information and artefacts within her book to instigate memory. Any opportunity for 'show and tell' and the Life Book would emerge and the same stories were re-told. For her classmates it became tedious and while they usually remained polite, an audible groan by the braver among them occasionally could be heard. However, for Hannah language became so important in enabling her to understand not only the events that had happened to her but also to acknowledge, and on some level accept, how these events impacted her own sense of self.

Due to the collaborative working of the social worker and adoptive family, Hannah was in a place where she was able to begin to explore her story. She was able to understand that she had two mummies whom she loved, and that was acceptable. 'Birth mum' could still be an acknowledgement and a part of Hannah's identity, a contributing factor to the young lady she was becoming, while 'mum' loved her in the present and enabled her to allow her story to be heard. As a young teacher, my initial response was to try to repress some of the concerning stories the child would tell me. My own ideals of what childhood should be led me to believe that ignoring anything that did not gratify my idealistic perception of children was the best approach. Through experience I began to realize the importance of giving children the opportunity and space to make sense of their world, to feel accepted within the social world whatever their background. The importance of allowing children to verbalize their thoughts and feelings became important to me in supporting each child in creating their own sense of identity.

Life Story therapy, of which establishing a Life Book is a key element, is used with children who have encountered difficult life events, usually resulting in adoption through the care system, similar to Hannah's experience. Perry (2012, cited in Rose 2012: 10) acknowledges the negative impact upon those who do not have the security of their life story: 'Without a life story, a child is adrift, disconnected and vulnerable'. Having a story to tell offers a sense of personal security in understanding our own constructed self-identity, it connects us to other people within our desire to belong in community (Rose 2012: 19), and it impacts upon our future possibilities and successes. Our past is part of our story and contributes to the choices, attitudes, and decisions we adopt in the present and future. All children need the opportunity to tell their story. [For further reading on Life Books, see O'Malley (2011) and the websites www.adoption-works.com and www.bemyparent.org.uk.]

Our truth

We have already established the importance of being able to verbalize our story and we have identified some of the tools currently available in a social care system to enable children to acknowledge their story so far. As with James in our introductory vignette, it is interesting to consider the parts we include, or omit, and the language we choose to express meaning. The words and phrases we select give some insight into our understanding of the world, our values, and our expectations. They can also provide evidence and understanding as to the stage of acceptance or understanding the teller is experiencing at the point of that particular telling (McDrury and Alterio 2003). Teachers spend a significant part of their time managing problems and issues between children, making judgements about who is 'right' or relaying the most accurate information. Within the wider school community, senior leaders spend much of their time listening to a range of different perspectives and attempting to establish some sense of 'truth'. As educators we need to acknowledge that our social world is not absolute. There are many interpretations and perspectives that cause us all to draw conclusions. Bruner (1986: 122) refers to this as our 'conceptual world', a constructed interpretation of what we have experienced, influenced by our own beliefs about how the world works linked to the values we have adopted.

Within my own headship, phrases such as 'from my perspective . . .' and 'I acknowledge your interpretation but my understanding is . . .' were not just people management tools but a real shift in my own understanding that we all have our own truth. More importantly, that we are all entitled to our own truth and have the right to express it appropriately. When we consider our whole school values and philosophies do we make space for different interpretations and varying opportunities to enact those underlying principles that complement the individual's constructed understanding? Within our classes do our children have the opportunity to evolve their understanding of the shared values and how these relate to their circumstances? Many misunderstandings and miscommunications stem from different interpretations of the same concept or idea. Perhaps there is a place for narrative here in creating shared understandings and enabling vision for school communities.

Creating a shared story to develop a school community

Sullivan (2000, cited in Rutherford 2002) identifies that common language shared within an institution evokes a common understanding of what it means to be a part of that context. Within my own small-scale study focusing on staff perceptions of how values are shared within the school context, all participants except one chose the word 'family' as a suitable description of the whole staff team. Interestingly, when I joined the school myself I was introduced to this concept of 'family' and although the school had passed through many changes, this concept had remained. Within the study, participants were then asked to identify key values they felt were expressed throughout the school. Even within the exploration of values the constructed view of the supportive family was further developed. This was the school's story and during observations I saw this underlying principle enacted. I heard the sentiment reflected in the language from the parents/carers and the governors, and in the behaviours of the children.

There are, of course, issues when shared metaphors have negative connotations for participants within the group and when we do not allow our story to change and the way we represent that story to evolve. However, our shared language is so important in bringing together a shared story. Many schools already create their vision for improvement through the use of effective tools and a further emphasis on creating a shared story is possible. A SWOT (Strengths, Weaknesses, Opportunities, and Threats) analysis (Fine 2010) or the TOWS matrix (Weihrich 1982) can effectively provide the opportunity for a shared expression of the school community's profile and this is common practice as a school improvement approach. However, it can also be a significant time to value all that has occurred previously, influencing what is happening now and into the future. Churches and Terry (2007: 167) explore the idea that we can influence our future story by acknowledging our current 'state' and identifying what we want from our future 'state'. This is a technique effective for school improvement but also a principle we can adopt for developing an ethos with our children where they understand how acknowledgement of our past can help influence making good and effective choices for our future.

Pause for thought

Take a moment to reflect upon the key principles that underpin your own evolving educational philosophy. It may be helpful to record your thoughts as you think about the following and then return to them at a later point. These questions could also stimulate discussion with colleagues:

- How important is it for the teacher to structure opportunities for children to tell stories from their own life experiences?

- How can the teacher develop an environment where children feel safe to share their ideas, thoughts, and experiences?
- Do children gain anything of value listening to each other's narrative?
- Are there approaches we can embed within our classrooms to support children in understanding that they can make choices that impact their future success and happiness? How do we promote this philosophy?

By taking time to think carefully about our own values around the significance of supporting children in telling their story, we begin to challenge some of our own practices. Within our curriculums we need to make the space and time to allow children to explore their own style and voice. The emphasis upon teaching story structure has its place, but to learn the art of storytelling can evoke enthusiasm and creativity, a far more effective way to raise standards. Rosen's (1988) work with groups of boys aged 8–18 offers an example of giving children and young people the opportunity to develop their own storytelling skills, using borrowings and models from fiction to refine their telling. Rosen identifies a shift in her own pedagogical approach. Although in preparation for each session she would rehearse a story to tell, often the increased confidence of the students resulted in them telling their own story. Rosen (1988: 11) acknowledges, 'The first resource of the classroom was not what I brought but what was brought by the pupils'. Each student's retellings of known stories incorporated their own emphasis and elaboration reflected experiences, interests, and ideas unique to the individual. Within a 1980s classroom it may be that the curriculum was flexible enough to incorporate time for storytelling with older pupils and perhaps the reality for teachers in a twenty-first century classroom means that there is a conflict between our desire to use storytelling in a less formal way and the pressures of an extensive curriculum. Rosen found that her approach enabled the students in other curriculum areas and this implies that story can be used as an effective tool to support children in more abstract and complex ideas.

While Rosen was working with older children, Fox (1989) noticed how preliterate children were able to express their ideas and emergent understanding of aspects within wider areas such as mathematics, science, and even ethics through the use of story. Young children were able to express their understanding of mathematical concepts, for example, without the prompting of the teacher, whereas within a more formal subject-specific lesson this freedom may have been repressed. Both Rosen (1988) and Fox (1989) raise an interesting thought for us as teachers relating to our role in the classroom. The children in Fox's study were not prompted for stories relating to specific subjects, and the stories were not scaffolded by the teacher (Fox 1989). Similarly, Rosen found that the students were refining their own storytelling through practice and listening to each other, not necessarily using a very structured model from the teacher. In both of these studies, the teacher learnt a great deal from listening and observing the students. Rosen was able to create a completely new climate for learning and develop her own understanding of what these particular children needed to enable great success. Starting from the pupils' stories was important and developed an environment where all present could be included because each child had a story to tell and 'is subject to the narrative of his own living' (Rosen 1988: 13). All the pupils could gain a sense of belonging by connecting with aspects of other people's stories, which resonated with the listener and aspects they could acknowledge as different, demonstrating we are all individuals.

Telling our story

Case study

David, a student teacher, reflects on his experience of a storytelling project:

'On my first telling of the personal story I had made notes of the key events and I used these to structure my narrative. I felt very uncomfortable and kept returning to my notes to help me. I told the story but sensed from the audience that I had not engaged them beyond the events. On my second retelling to another audience I felt more relaxed and more familiar with the actual events. This time I incorporated some of my personality, selecting words and phrases which embellished the true story but created humour. I also integrated a sense of "reveal" at the end of the story where I gave little clues as to the ending during the telling. This time I gained a better rapport with my audience and the reveal at the end of the story was greeted with a warm acceptance bringing the group together because many had used the inferred meaning to predict the end. There was a good feeling at the end of the story and I felt good about myself because I had engaged all those people in my story.'

We may already value the importance of storytelling and understand the benefits of becoming familiar enough with a story that we can tell it with the added intonation, building of suspense, and embellishment that can really enthuse the listener. However, for many trainee teachers it is the building of confidence in the art of storytelling that appears to be a risk too far. Before we expect children to develop as storytellers we, as the leaders and role models in the classroom, need to develop our own confidence and style in telling stories. Rosen (1988: 8) witnesses the transformation into a 'new dimension' when the teacher closes the book and really interacts with the listeners on a more significant level. The feedback at the end of the story is deeper and goes beyond hearing a story to internalizing significant aspects and messages, creating a deeper understanding of the rhetorical and inferred.

Within the Waldorf-Steiner education system, storytelling is a key aspect of the learning opportunities presented to children. Teachers are expected to tell stories, rather than read them to the children (Steiner 1974: 48). This encourages the teller's own individuality to emerge (http://www.waldorfcurriculum.com) and provides opportunities for the connection between teller and listener to develop. Storytelling is taken even further by Waldorf-Steiner teachers, who ideally progress with the same class throughout their education, in returning to stories to further develop opportunities for learning in a moral context and using stories as illustrations used for real life (Steiner 1974: 49). The account of David, outlined in the case study, provides an example of how a teacher is starting to develop such skills and gaining a greater awareness of the power and possibilities of storytelling.

Stories from our childhood

In creating our own storytelling style, we are influenced by many factors that culminate in our own preference. The influences of our early experiences related to story are very important in creating the initial approach to our own storytelling and narrative style. Some of this style is through copying phrasings we have heard significant adults use or phrases from books we love. Those stories we connect with during our childhood somehow embed themselves deep within our subconscious. I did not realize how significant the early stories we engage with are until I stumbled across the *StoryTeller* series (Marshal Cavendish) on a video-sharing site. I had acknowledged that my love of stories had been encouraged by the commitment of my parents to purchase a weekly magazine filled with stories and poems read by actors and celebrities of the time but when I watched the presentation of the artwork from the stories and listened to the accompanying music composition, something was evoked on an emotional level within me.

In her study of children's storytelling, Fox (1993) highlights how children view stories they read and hear as metaphors for their own lives, incorporating their concerns and own emotions. What was it about Gobbolino, the witch's cat (Moray Williams 1942) who journeys from place to place becoming a kitchen cat, a ship cat, a show cat among her many guises in pursuit of a place to belong that I identified with as a child? Already, my emphasis upon Gobbolino's journey and search for a home reflects my somewhat nomadic childhood and desire to settle, alongside the common need in most of us to be accepted. With adult perspective and insight I can make this connection because it is part of my story.

> **Pause for thought**
>
> Think about a story or storybook from your own childhood. Select the story based on whether it had an effect upon you, due perhaps to its content, context, or associations with the person with whom you shared the story.
>
> - Acknowledge how remembering that story makes you feel and who is associated with the story.
> - How were you introduced to the story? Did you enjoy the story when you accessed it on your own or was it a shared experience?
> - Think about which aspects resonated with you and whether these were connected to the metaphors identified by Fox.

Selecting a story

We all have our favourite stories that we enjoy and return to at intervals. Children especially love to hear a story again and join in those parts that have become familiar to them. For children it could be the repeating phrasings in stories such as *The Gruffalo* (Donaldson 1999) or the traditional tale of *The Little Red Hen* that engage them with the narrative initially. When a story is first read, curiosity and intrigue are drivers that can really engage the child in wanting to know what happens next and arouse interest (Medwell et al. 2012). It may even be the illustrations that spark enthusiasm for the story but what is it that moves a story from an enjoyable read to one that is returned to time and time again?

In her analysis of children's 'borrowings' from stories they have read or been told during their own storytelling, Fox evolves her interpretation using the term 'transformations' where real life and fiction are interwoven to create a new 'tableau' (Medwell et al. 2012: 12). What makes particular aspects significant is the link the child makes between the fictional story and their own experiences, which brings about an enjoyment or recognition personal to that child. For teachers there are many implications here. If there is a more significant and deeper level to storytelling and sharing stories, then there is a responsibility to exploit opportunities. Before children can tell their story they need to have the models and structure with which to affiliate their ideas. Here there is opportunity for the teacher to think about the type of texts that are used, those that are representative of diverse families, and introduce exploration of issues pertinent to the children in the class.

A teacher who knows their children well, who has taken the time to find out about their interests, worries, and circumstances can then make sensitive and informed decisions about which stories are shared within their class. The selection of stories is driven by the teacher's knowledge of what the class needs and this becomes an approach motivated by underlying values about what education really means. Woolley (2010) explores how this issue of using literature and story needs to be handled very sensitively with children who are facing challenging circumstances, such as those related to grief and loss. Children who are facing significant issues often feel they are isolated and find it difficult to believe that other people have experienced similar feelings (Woolley 2010). Within such circumstances, the expectations to voice their own story can be too complex for the child and therefore it can be useful to use a resource where the child can express their feelings and thoughts in a more detached way.

Teachers are not social therapists and it is important that a collaborative approach with appropriate agencies is instigated to support those children with complex emotional needs. However, when a child is ready and it is relevant, developing a narrative through the use of pictures, puppets or exploring an already established narrative as a way to explore new feelings and emotions can be helpful in these circumstances. For those children who would benefit from using story as a tool to enable them to explore issues or feelings from their own lives, two helpful resources have been created by a working party led by Morris and Woolley (2008). Although these are not exhaustive lists, they are very helpful and practical resources for use within our diverse classrooms.

Case study

Anna has been in the same class as her friends from joining school in the Reception class and now she is in Year 4 (aged 8 years). Her parents chose to send Anna to a small school because she was diagnosed with autistic spectrum disorder from when quite young and they felt this environment was the most appropriate. Anna's teacher noticed that at playtimes Anna walks around the outside of the playground and does not interact with the other children. Anna's teacher had heard of social stories (Gray 2010) and how these can be used to help children on the autistic spectrum interact with their peers. After an initial session looking at a social story relating to turn-taking and facilitating a group to play with Anna at breaktime, her teacher is confronted with Anna hurting another child during a turn-taking game. Anna's teacher encourages another group activity the next day where turn-taking is expected. There are no incidents during this playtime but Anna's teacher notices that she is very agitated during the next lesson and does not want to talk with other people.

Throughout this chapter, we have been considering the importance of giving children the opportunity to become a teller of their own story and also how story can be used to connect with others. For some children, like Anna in our case study, the innate desire and ability to fulfil these two aspects relating to self-identity and social interaction is hindered by the challenges around social understanding.

Social stories (Gray 2003) offer an opportunity for an adult to explore with a child a very specific social situation using a story as a stimulus to discussion. While some stories have pictures of scenarios to stimulate exploration, social stories can also be created with the child as the central character (see http://www.machkovich. com/Cory/AutismRecovery/SocialStories/index.htm#). Social stories create a process for an adult to engage with a child and understand their perspective while offering a model of common social responses to a situation (Gray 2003). This use of story is not about modifying behaviour but is about connecting with the child and understanding their perspective while enabling them to begin to understand some of the socially acceptable behaviours and norms within a society that will help them develop skills to relate to others.

Pause for thought

Explore some of the resources recommended around social stories and consider Anna's situation. Once again, these questions can stimulate some discussion and debate with colleagues. Your response to these questions may also give you some further insight into your own philosophy of education and your values and beliefs about inclusion.

- Do you agree with the teacher that Anna needed to be directed to interact with other children at breaktime, or as some professionals suggest, should Anna be permitted to have time to be quiet on her own before the social pressure of the classroom environment?
- Some professionals feel that social stories need to be in a context the child has experienced. Do you think the approach taken by Anna's teacher was effective or should social stories be used as an exploration of the incident in the playground?
- Why do you think Anna was agitated after the second playtime with the turn-taking game? How could the teacher have developed a greater understanding of Anna's perspective and of her feelings?

Using artefacts to instigate narrative

Using pictures and artefacts within the classroom is another way to stimulate interest and curiosity. In Chapter 1, Kathleen Taylor explores how objects can be a starting point in children's discovery and how this approach can provide the opportunity to develop key skills in exploration, investigation, and experimentation. Within the context of developing storytelling, we may encourage children to ask questions and build a story around a stimulus we have chosen. As part of my own practice with Year 6 children (aged 10–11 years), I often used picture cards or objects to instigate ideas for story, reflecting some of the statutory assessment test format with story starters or pictures. However, by giving children the opportunity to choose their own stimulus immediately, we are shifting the emphasis from creating a narrative based on the teacher's resources to taking ownership of the narrative themselves. By selecting a photograph or object the child is expressing what is important or significant to them. By observing and listening to the children's narrative we can again hear what is important to that child, or identify how the child is interpreting the world around them. This also offers the opportunity for natural narrative to emerge expressing genuine ideas, thoughts, and feelings. This approach may also be beneficial for a child on a journey through the process of grief or loss.

On a recent visit to my father's home, we ventured into the attic to look at some old photographs. An intended few minutes to retrieve some photographs evolved into a few hours as objects stored in the loft instigated 'do you remember when' stories. These genuine stories were not rehearsed but flowed very naturally with an array of emotions expressed. We enjoyed recalling some of our expeditions and humorous events associated with our travels stimulated by the trinkets we had brought back with us. We remembered people from our past captured in photographs and pondered where life had taken them now. We sensitively recalled the last days with my mum looking at her personal belongings preserved carefully and handled respectfully. That opportunity to use story allowed me to connect with my emotional self and with the person sharing that moment with me, to express how I felt through a story, from my perspective, filling in the narrative with my own thoughts and feelings. When we listen to children's natural narrative we can learn so much about their understanding of the world around them.

Developing practice

To develop effective practice, we need to consider:

- how well different cultures, communities, faiths, family groupings, and lifestyles are represented in school library collections;
- the types of stories and picture books available to support children when facing challenges and difficult circumstances;
- how we signpost children appropriately so that they can make their own choices accessing these resources;
- how artefacts can be used to stimulate expression and ideas;
- how we create opportunities for children to use these objects in creating a narrative;
- how to create a learning environment where story is valued through display, a diverse choice of story and picture books, and time in the curriculum to develop storytelling opportunities;
- practising telling our own stories in preparation for creating a culture of narratives.

Conclusion

Throughout this chapter, we have addressed the value in using narrative as a tool for expression and exploration of ideas. A key theme has been how narrative can enable an individual to develop confidence in expressing their thoughts, feelings, and experiences (these ideas are considered further in Chapter 9, *Voice*). The use of established stories, artefacts, or simply the opportunity to tell a story has been highlighted alongside established processes such as Life Story therapy. Underpinning the practical suggestions has been the key principle that that we live within a 'conceptual world' (Bruner 1986) where our interpretation of events is influenced by many factors. The challenge for educators is to create an environment where the child's voice and perspective is respected and heard, which involves the teacher passing the control to the learner. The opportunity to tell our own story builds confident, self-assured individuals who can express their own needs in a healthy way.

References

Bruner, J. (1986) *Actual Minds, Possible Worlds*. Cambridge, MA: Harvard University Press.
Churches, R. and Terry, R. (2007) *NLP for Teachers: How to be a Highly Effective Teacher*. Bancyfelin: Crown House Publishing.
Donaldson, J. (1999) *The Gruffalo*. London: Macmillan Children's Books.
Fine, L. (2010) *The SWOT Analysis: Using Your Strengths to Overcome Weaknesses, Using your Opportunities to Overcome Threats*. Sine loco: Kick It, LLC.
Fox, C. (1989) Children thinking through story, *English in Education*, 24(2): 25–36.
Fox, C. (1993) *At the Very Edge of the Forest: The Influence of Literature on Storytelling by Children*. London: Cassell.
Gray, C. (2003) *My Social Stories Book*. London: Jessica Kingsley.
Gray, C. (2010) *The New Social Story Book*. Arlington, TX: Future Horizons, Inc.
Marshal Cavendish (1982) *The StoryTeller Series*. Available at: http://www.youtube.com/watch?v=9FrdmTlCzpo (accessed 14 June 2012).
McDrury, J. and Alterio, M. (2003) *Learning through Storytelling in Higher Education: Using Reflection and Experience to Improve Learning*. London: Kogan Page.
Medwell, J., Moore, G., Wray, D. and Griffiths, V. (2012) *Primary English: Knowledge and Understanding*. London: Sage.
Moray Williams, U. (1942) *Gobbolino, the Witch's Cat*. London: Kingfisher Classics.
Morris, J. and Woolley, R. (2008) *Family Diversities Reading Resource*. Lincoln: Bishop Grosseteste University Colege. Available at: http://www.bishopg.ac.uk/?_id=10679.
O'Malley, B. (2011) *LifeBooks: Creating a Treasure for the Adopted Child*. Winthrop, MA: Adoption Works.
Rose, R. (2012) *Life Story Therapy with Traumatised Children*. London: Jessica Kingsley.
Rosen, B. (1988) *And None of it was Nonsense*. London: Mary Glasgow.
Rutherford, D. (2002) Changing times and changing roles: the perspectives of primary headteachers on their senior management teams, *Educational Management Administration*, 30(4): 447–59.

Steiner, R. (1974) *How to Create, Tell and Recall a Story* (trans. H. Fox), lecture 4 in *The Kingdom of Childhood*. London: Rudolf Steiner Press.

Weihrich, H. (1982) The TOWS matrix: a tool for situational analysis, *Long Range Planning*, 15(2): 54–66.

Woolley, R. (2010) *Tackling Controversial Issues in the Primary School: Facing Life's Challenges with Your Learners*. London: Routledge.

Websites

Cory's website. The following site has some real examples of how creating social stories specific to the child can support them in their social development: http://www.machkovich.com/Cory/AutismRecovery/SocialStories/index.htm#

Gray, C., *Social Stories*: http://www.thegraycenter.org/social-stories/. This website also includes a video clip of Carol Gray talking about the use of social stories.

Johnson, M., Waldorf Steiner curriculum: http://www.waldorfcurriculum.com (accessed 1 July 2012).

Marshal Cavendish (1982) *StoryTeller* series: http://www.youtube.com/watch?v=9FrdmTlCzpo.

CHAPTER

3

Creativity

Ashley Compton

> I was teaching my class of 9- to 11-year-olds about equivalent fractions and making a whole through addition of fractions but found that most of the children were really struggling with these concepts. In music we were working on different rhythms so I decided to combine these lessons. In North America, note lengths are described as fractions – so a crotchet is called a quarter note, a quaver is an eighth note, a minim is a half note, and a semi-breve is a whole note. In the next maths lesson we started by clapping different rhythms in 4/4 time notated on cards. The children suggested some rhythms, which I wrote on the board, and then we all clapped them. Next, I clapped one of the rhythms and the children had to identify which one it was. We looked at some printed music and identified different patterns. We spent most of the lesson exploring different ways of making up one bar of music and what this told us about equivalent fractions.
>
> The following maths lesson the children had to compose sixteen bars of music, using any combination of notes that would make four beats in the bar. Keyboards were available to those who wanted to consider tune as well as rhythm. Most of the children attacked the activity with enthusiasm and understanding. A few of the children understood some ways of making four beats but included others that were too short or too long. Some children composed their pieces very quickly and then spent time refining them, ensuring they had the right number of beats but also making them more musically pleasing. The culmination of the lesson was to perform the pieces. This was hugely popular and we had to continue into playtime to get through them all. The following lesson we went back to more traditional fraction work where the children had to find combinations of halves, quarters, and eighths to make a whole. This had been disastrous when previously attempted but this time the majority of children understood the work and completed it easily.

Introduction

In this chapter, we will focus on creative teaching, teaching for creativity, and what creativity is. Was there creativity in the vignette above? Was the teacher being creative? Were the children being creative? I think there was teacher creativity in making connections between different aspects of the curriculum and taking an unusual approach to teaching mathematics. These approaches proved valuable because my observations showed the children were engaged with their work and my assessments indicated that the children had made considerable progress. I think the children were creative mathematically because they were investigating patterns and creative musically because they were composing. In both aspects, they were making choices and had some autonomy in their work. However, you might interpret creativity differently and therefore come to different conclusions.

One of the difficulties with research into creativity is that there is no agreed definition that states precisely what creativity is. Davies (2006: 40) claimed that creativity is 'often misconstrued, misunderstood and plainly misused'. Mindham (2005: 82) examined many definitions of creativity and determined that 'none seem to be entirely relevant or sufficiently specific to be of help in the classroom'. In this chapter, you will be encouraged to develop a definition of creativity that will be relevant and helpful in the classroom.

The nature of creativity

In ancient Greece, creativity was perceived as being dependent on divine or mystical inspiration, with the nine muses presiding over the arts and literature, inspiring favoured mortals to create works of genius. Millennia after the Greek gods have ceased to be worshipped, some artists today still refer to their muse as being responsible for providing inspiration. In the Jewish, Christian, and Islamic traditions there is a divine Creator, while the Earth and all that is in it are the great Creation. Lubart (1999) describes Western creativity as linear, mirroring the gradual creation of the universe; however, Eastern creativity is circular, reflecting beliefs about reincarnation, with destruction of the old before creation of the new.

These ideas about creativity, which relate to genius and divine inspiration, are not particularly relevant to the classroom but do shape many people's perceptions of creativity. Research on creativity in ordinary people, rather than geniuses, began in the 1950s with a particular emphasis on divergent thinking. Divergent thinking links to the use of 'brainstorming' and open-ended questions in schools. These allow children to challenge themselves by thinking of unusual solutions or multiple answers and are used in various subjects, such as mathematics and science. Unfortunately, some teachers find this sort of open-ended enquiry difficult because they do not know how to respond to unexpected answers and feel safer when they can prepare a script of the lesson (Inoue and Buczynski 2011; Moyer and Milewicz 2002).

Boden (2004) describes three types of creativity:

- *exploratory*, in which you explore what can be done within the rules of the domain or subject;
- *combinational*, in which you combine old ideas in new ways and make links between different areas;
- *transformational*, in which you know the rules fully so now you can break them and create your own rules.

While transformational creativity is more relevant to genius level creativity (like Debussy who broke the musical rules by using running fifths, Newton who invented calculus because the existing mathematics was not sufficient, and Fosbury who changed high jumping with his revolutionary Fosbury Flop), the other two types are definitely applicable to children and non-genius adults. Boden's exploratory creativity is particularly relevant to learning and is related to playfulness aligned with judgement. Combinational creativity has particular relevance to cross-curricular work that encourages children to think about how different aspects of a topic relate to each other, rather than studying each subject in isolation. Combinational creativity benefits from a broad curriculum from an early age because wide exposure to many subjects increases the number of possible connections that can be made. These two forms of creativity are combined in Craft's (2005) suggestion that creativity and learning are closely related in a constructivist model because learning involves exploring and making connections between ideas in order to make them meaningful.

Another definition of creativity that is particularly relevant to education is Craft's (2003) 'possibility thinking' and little c creativity. These involve questioning, thinking 'what if', and making choices. Craft has researched this approach to creativity in the early years of childhood in particular but applies it to all ages, seeing it as leading to self-actualization. Craft has a broad view of creativity that also includes problem solving and having novel and valuable ideas.

The idea of novelty is common to many definitions of creativity, although Craft (2008) worried that an emphasis on novelty can lead to a throw-away culture. Often this novelty is at two levels: new to the individual and new to the world. Children in primary school, and their teachers for that matter, are unlikely to come up with anything that is completely new to the world, so it is the individual level of novelty that is primarily relevant to schools. Kaufman and Beghetto (2009) delineated four levels of creativity. They split 'new to the individual' into two layers: Mini-C, which is creativity in the learning process and involves exploring, questioning, and imagining; and Little-C, which is personal creativity. These levels could apply equally to pupils and teachers. However, before the Big-C genius level creativity they added Pro-C, which is professional level creativity. This provides scope for teachers to use their professional skills and imagination to come up with teaching approaches or resources that are new to their colleagues, school or even Local Authority, although they might not be completely new to the wider educational world.

While Bowkett (2005) just required the idea or product to be novel, Cropley (2001) required that it was effective and ethical as well. This means that Cropley would not consider a new safe-cracking device or biological weapon creative because of the destructive intent. Weisberg (2006) demanded that the originality had to be intentional rather than accidental but did not feel that value should be a consideration, partly because of the problem of who determines the value. By contrast, Boden (2004) and the National Advisory Committee on Creative and Cultural Education (NACCCE 1999) included valuable as a necessary characteristic of creativity. This does not have to mean a monetary value but means the idea or product must be useful or important to someone. However, it is not clear who determines this value. These ideas of intent and value are particularly relevant to education. When a very young child does some finger painting and produces artwork that is similar to some in the Tate Modern art gallery in London, is it creative? Did the child intend to make that particular painting? Was there meaning behind the painting? Is it valuable? And if so to whom? How is the value of a painting actually determined?

Case study

The Reception class was trying to answer the problem 'How can we find the container which holds the most water without measuring it?' The containers were all different shapes and sizes so it was difficult to compare them. Julia suggested pouring the water from the different containers down a hill and seeing which travels the farthest. She was able to talk about how they could make the test fair and then she carried out her idea.

- Is Julia's idea original? Is it valuable?
- In what situations and subjects are children encouraged to have original ideas?
- How does originality fit with the curriculum?
- What originality is required from teachers and who judges its value?

In a UK Government commissioned report, *All Our Futures*, NACCCE (1999) devised a definition of creativity for education that was based on four characteristics of creative processes: imagination, purpose, originality, and value. The committee felt strongly that creativity was accessible to all. Their concept of creativity included both the arts and problem solving but was not restricted to these. According to NACCCE, creativity requires a balance of skills, knowledge, and understanding combined with the freedom to experiment. Their definition is summed up in the statement: 'imaginative activity fashioned so as to produce outcomes that are both original and of value' (NACCCE 1999: 30). This definition was used by the Qualifications and Curriculum Authority (QCA) from 2003 and was influential in English primary education.

Cochrane and Cockett (2007) found a range of definitions in school with head teachers, men, and science teachers emphasizing critical thinking, while women and art teachers were more focused on self-expression. Since the majority of primary teachers are women, this could mean that a self-expression view of creativity dominates in primary schools, which could be a problem since Ofsted (2003), the government school regulation and inspection body in England, found that an over-emphasis on self-expression often resulted in insufficiently challenging, superficial work. However, there is no reason why critical thinking and self-expression cannot be combined to produce challenging, original outcomes.

In these definitions I have not questioned whether or not creativity is a 'good thing' in education. However, in an Austrian study, Brandau et al. (2007) found that high scores on a creativity test related to high levels of disruptive behaviour and hyperactivity. Their conclusion was that 'lively' behaviour should be seen as creative potential rather than viewed negatively and punished. Aljughaiman and Mowrer-Reynolds (2005) also found that the teachers they questioned viewed creative traits in a negative light, even though the teachers said they supported the development of creativity. As part of his characteristics of creative people, Lucas (2001: 38) said: 'Creative people question the assumptions they are given. They see the world differently, are happy to experiment, to take risks and to make mistakes'. Having pupils question your teaching can be quite threatening. Even just seeing the world differently can cause difficulties in a prescriptive curriculum where success as a teacher is judged on the pupils' ability to complete standardized tests.

Pause for thought

- What does creativity mean to you? Does it apply to adults and children equally?
- Where are you creative in your own life? Can you apply this to your teaching?
- What role, if any, do you think creativity should have in education for pupils and/or for teachers?

Table 3.1 Comparison of UK government publications

Hadow (1931)	Plowden Report (1967)	Excellence and Enjoyment (DfES 2003)	EYFS (DfE 2012)
Enquiry	Enquiry	Enquiry	Curiosity, investigate
Experiment			Experiment
		Problem solving	Think about problems
Creative imagination	Imagination		Being imaginative
		A way of learning	Characteristic of effective teaching and learning
The arts	Learning through the arts	The arts	Expressive arts
Play	Play	Play	Playing and exploring
Cross-curricular projects	Cross-curricular projects	Cross-curricular projects	Interconnected areas of learning and development

Creativity in education

Creativity is not a new feature in English education. Aspects related to the definitions of creativity already discussed have been prominent in several government documents, starting with the 1931 Hadow Report on primary education. Many terms related to creativity were present in the primary and early years curriculum at the beginning of the twenty-first century. They are still present in the Early Years (DfE 2012), although it is not yet known how prominent they will be in the new primary curriculum.

The similarities among these documents (Table 3.1) could lead you to think that there had been a consistent message about creativity and teaching since 1931. However, in between these reports there have been backlashes against creativity. These have been related to:

- economic factors,
- curriculum factors,
- a lack of understanding about creativity, and
- a technicist view of teaching.

Limited funding and resources for schools can lead to creativity being seen as an unaffordable luxury. An overemphasis on English and mathematics and a back-to-basics mentality can threaten creativity, especially when this comes with the prescriptive climate of a detailed, subject-based curriculum and an emphasis on testing. This does not mean that teaching basic skills in English and mathematics automatically opposes creativity. Indeed, many authors believe that creativity needs to be grounded in skills and knowledge (e.g. Boden 2001; NACCCE 1999; Ofsted 2010; Roberts 2006). This is true for teachers as well as for pupils; Edmonds (2004) found that teachers who lacked confidence in science subject knowledge were less creative in their approach to science teaching. Ofsted (2010) also found that a lack of teacher subject knowledge resulted in pupils having fewer opportunities to be creative, not just in science but across the curriculum.

There has been concern in the past decade that teachers are being viewed as technicians who deliver pre-packaged materials rather than as thinking, questioning professionals (Burnard and White 2008; Craft 2005). The proliferation of government-produced schemes of work and lesson plans related to the Literacy and Numeracy Strategies in England promoted the teacher as technician model. It has promoted a compliant culture where teachers have come to expect to be told what to do and our student teachers are surprised, and often dismayed, if they are not given detailed schemes of work to use on placement. Based on research with teachers from eleven European countries, Davies (2006) determined that for creative teaching teachers needed to have freedom to innovate, feeling they had control over the curriculum they taught. This will not occur with a technician model of teaching. To be creative teachers need to reclaim their professionalism, developing their own values and vision.

Conditions for creativity

Having identified some of the threats to creativity, we need to think about some of the conditions that promote creativity. Some of the factors we need to consider include:

- where it happens;
- when it happens;
- what resources you have;
- whether alone or with someone else;
- whether it is for yourself or for someone else;
- whether someone or something has inspired or influenced you;
- whether it is your choice or something required of you.

Unfortunately, factors that promote creativity for one person might inhibit it for someone else. On a degree course on which I work, we have a group placement where several students work together in a single classroom. Some students find that this promotes creativity because they are able to bounce ideas off each other and come up with lessons they would not have thought of on their own.

Other students have reported that they find working in a group inhibits their creativity because they do not feel comfortable voicing their ideas or because they have to make compromises with the others, unless they have a particularly compatible group. Although these were adults, I have had similar experiences with children and group work, particularly when composing in music.

Case study

Rebecca, a student teacher, was leading the class into the gym for a carefully planned ball skills lesson in PE. When they arrived at the gym they discovered that in the past hour someone had set up the staging for the school play, filling at least a quarter of the gym, so her lesson would not be possible. Faced with this unexpected situation Rebecca froze and could not think of what to do next. The class teacher volunteered to take over and led the children into the gym for an impromptu aerobics lesson, with the teacher and various children taking turns to lead the session from the stage. They were faced with the same physical conditions but only the class teacher was able to react creatively. However, there were some differences in the internal conditions. The class teacher felt less pressure to succeed and also had a greater wealth of knowledge and experience upon which to draw.

If different people react differently to these conditions, is there any point in considering them? This is where formative assessment – not of subject knowledge but of how children learn and react to different conditions – is important. Flexibility is also important. Do the children all have to work in the same way or can there be a mixture of approaches within a lesson? The example of Rebecca, in the case study, suggests that both confidence and experience can be significant factors in providing opportunities for creativity.

Aside from the physical and situational conditions, Lucas (2001: 39) came up with a set of four key conditions for creativity:

- the need to be challenged,
- the elimination of negative stress,
- feedback, and
- the capacity to live with uncertainty.

In the above example, the negative stress proved too much for Rebecca and prevented her creativity. The role of formative assessment is clear in these conditions, both in providing feedback and in judging what level will be challenging without being overwhelmingly difficult.

Harrington (1990) came up with a 'creative ecosystem'. Many of these classroom conditions relate to ideas discussed in other chapters, including Chapter 1 (*Curiosity*) and Chapter 13 (*Values*):

- a safe atmosphere so children feel free to take risks and where mistakes are valued as learning opportunities;
- an environment where differences are respected;
- children given opportunities to play, with exploration and experimentation encouraged;
- activities presented in exciting or unusual ways so that children are engaged;
- children allowed ownership of their learning and given choices about resources and methods;
- children encouraged to come up with new ideas knowing that these ideas will be welcomed;
- a supportive environment but one which encourages critical reflection.

Case study

The Reception class was studying mini-beasts. Phillipe was outside when he spotted a spider's web at the edge of the awning. He told the teacher that he wanted to look at it closely but it was too high up for him to see clearly. The teacher asked him what he could do about that. He decided to use the large wooden blocks to construct a set of stairs he could stand on. Once completed, he climbed up the steps with a magnifying glass and studied the web. Other children noticed Phillipe on the stairs and wanted to join him. Phillipe said it would be too crowded and would not let them come up. The teacher asked them how they could make it safe for more people to look at the spider's web. When Phillipe finished observing the web, he worked with the other children to extend the stairs so that they could go up one side and down the other. The children then decided to make railings along each side to make it safer. Phillipe added arrow signs to show in which direction to go. Throughout the remainder of the lesson, a number of children climbed the stairs, some stopping to observe the web, others just enjoying going up and down the steps. The usual classroom rule was that all constructions should be taken apart before lunchtime. In this case, however, the teacher asked the children if they would like to keep it to the end of the day. They wanted to and so they made some 'closed' signs and put traffic cones at the end of the stairs to prevent children playing on them during the lunch break.

The story of Phillipe and the spider's web demonstrates a creative ecosystem. This is clearly a classroom where play and exploration are encouraged, where children have ownership of their learning and where their ideas are welcomed. He was able to pursue his idea, using resources that were available to him. The teacher did not give answers but challenged with questions. Children were aware of dangers but able to manage risk. These are all aspects of the Early Years Foundation Stage curriculum in England (EYFS; DfE 2012), so it may not be surprising to encounter creative practice in a Reception class. Are these same conditions present in Key Stage 1 and 2 classes (for children aged 5–7 and 7–11 years)?

Which subjects are creative?

While the EYFS emphasizes that all areas of learning should be integrated and interconnected, learning at Key Stages 1 and 2 is more likely to be presented in discrete subject areas. Therefore, it is pertinent to consider the creative potential of different subjects.

Think of a famous person who makes their living out of being creative. It is very easy to think of people from the arts who create things – authors, poets, playwrights, composers, artists, choreographers, directors, architects – and those who perform things – actors, musicians, dancers. There is a strong link between creativity and the arts and some people, including some in government, limit their definition of creativity to the arts. However, you might have thought of a famous person from a different category – an inventor like James Dyson, an entrepreneur like Anita Roddick, a theoretical physicist like Stephen Hawking. If creativity relates to coming up with original and valuable ideas and products, it is certainly not limited to the arts but extends to all aspects of life.

Studies of teachers and student teachers have presented a mixed picture. Kampylis et al. (2009) found that Greek teachers and student teachers believed that creativity could be associated with many subjects but they listed the arts subjects as having the most creative potential. They stated that Greek teaching was dominated by textbook use in many subjects and they noted that the subjects deemed most creative were those that did not use textbooks. Davies et al. (2006), who used a range of research approaches with student teachers at several institutions, reported similar results for England. One group of students had to choose two subjects for lesson observations, one that they expected to be creative and one they expected not to be creative. Mathematics was chosen as the subject least likely to be creative by 73 per cent of the students, while art was chosen as most likely to be creative. The students explained that art allowed self-expression and there were no right or wrong answers, while they saw maths lessons as tightly structured and full of closed questions with one correct answer. However, more than a third of the students were surprised at the level of creativity actually present in the 'non-creative' subject they observed. Although teaching in England is less textbook-dominated than teaching in Greece, there is heavy textbook or 'scheme' usage in mathematics so this could be a factor in the English results. Another group of student teachers was asked 'Draw a Creative Person'. Most of the drawings showed people from the arts, surrounded by equipment related to the arts.

In my own research, I asked our student teachers to describe their most creative lesson from recent placements. English was the most frequent subject identified, with science next, followed closely by art. Mathematics and history also had a good collection of examples. English, maths, and science may well have been represented because they may have been taught more frequently than other subjects, so the students had more opportunities and/or confidence to be creative in these subjects. I was surprised that only one student nominated music, although several of the lessons described involved music in the service of another subject. It could be that the music lessons the students had been involved in had not been creative, with students following a purchased scheme and pupils performing uniformly rather than creatively. When teaching music education to a group of teaching assistants, several of them expressed surprise that music lessons could be creative and fun. Several of them regularly taught music lessons to the children during the class teacher's non-contact time, but they just followed the prescribed scheme and found the lessons regimented and uninspiring. I have also seen art lessons that were similarly uncreative, with children copying rather than creating. Therefore, arts lessons are not necessarily creative but all subjects have the potential to be creative.

In a study by Robson et al. (2008), the student teachers did not believe creativity was about specific subjects but about the way they were taught. Some concepts they identified in creative teaching were making it interesting, engaging, being flexible, adapting, and experimenting. These fit well with Harrington's (1990) creative ecosystem model.

Teaching creatively/teaching for creativity

NACCCE (1999) distinguished between creative teaching and teaching for creative learning, although Jeffrey and Craft (2004) felt that the distinction between the two is not as relevant as the relationship between them. It is possible to have creative teaching, such as a teacher going into role, but the children are passive observers and are not being creative themselves. In the case study of Phillipe, there creative learning was going on but the teacher was not being particularly creative herself. However, the two often go together as in the vignette at the beginning of the chapter. There is also some evidence that student teachers need to experience creative lessons as learners before they can be creative as teachers (Robson et al. 2008).

NACCCE (1999: 103) state that teaching for creativity is a demanding and complex process but set out three 'tasks' involved in it: encouraging, identifying, and fostering. The encouraging task is about getting children to perceive themselves as creative, as well as developing attitudes, such as persistence and resilience. Identifying is about recognizing that creativity is generally domain specific and then helping children to discover the domain in which they are most creative.

Table 3.2 School factors and personal factors that promoted creative teaching in student teachers

School factors	
Resources	Having sufficient resources and space
Atmosphere	An atmosphere that supports creativity and risk-taking
Time	Flexible timetable; having sufficient time
Staffing	Help from other adults
Curriculum	Interesting topic; cross-curricular planning
Children	Behaviour; enthusiasm
Mentor	Being observed/not being observed; supportive mentor; given freedom and flexibility; positive feedback
Personal factors	
Confidence	General self-confidence; confidence in subject knowledge; confidence in teaching ability; confidence in behaviour management
Preparation	Thorough planning; having ideas; subject knowledge; knowing the class well
Own attributes	Enthusiasm; perceptions of own creativity; positive mood; energy and good health

An analogy might be helping young people to find the totems that will be their driving force in life. The examples given for the final task, fostering, include stimulating curiosity and developing memory but also include learning about the creative process itself. While agreeing with these three tasks, Jeffrey and Craft (2004: 84) determined from their research that there was a fourth task: 'the inclusion of the learner in decisions about what knowledge is to be investigated, about how to investigate it and how to evaluate the learning processes'. This essentially amounts to pupil ownership.

Just as there are conditions for creativity for the children, my research identified school factors and personal factors that promoted creative teaching in student teachers (Table 3.2). The mentoring factor is interesting because it is the only one where there were distinct differences of opinion. Most of the student teachers found it easier to be creative when they were not being observed but several felt they were more creative when being observed because they were trying to rise to the challenge. Fear of Ofsted can inhibit creativity in teachers. However, Ofsted have produced several reports about creativity that encourage teaching for creativity. They warn that just leaving children to follow their own interests is not sufficient to promote creative learning. They produced a description of effective teaching for creativity:

> Teachers were seen to promote creative learning most purposefully and effectively when encouraging pupils to question and challenge, make connections and see relationships, speculate, keep options open while pursuing a line of enquiry, and reflect critically on ideas, actions and results.
>
> (Ofsted 2010: 5, 6)

Making connections

One of the factors that teachers need to work with is the curriculum. In the past decade, teachers have begun to talk about the creative curriculum. Wilson (2007) described the creative curriculum as involving cross-curricular planning, assessment for learning, good questioning skills, and dialogue. Cross-curricular planning or topic work had been a feature of teaching in the 1970s following the Plowden Report (1967) but gradually became discredited, partly due to topics that involved very tenuous links. A cross-curricular approach relates to Boden's (2004) combinational creativity because it is about making connections. When considering these connections, it is useful to think about the definitions of creativity discussed earlier. Are these connections new to the pupils, new to the school or new to the world? Are the connections commonplace or unusual? Are the connections valuable in that they will enhance the children's learning? Do the children have sufficient knowledge and skills to make the connections?

Case study

Debbie was teaching about electricity in science and the Tudors in history. She decided to connect these by getting the children to make electric torches that were decorated with one of Henry VIII's wives.

Sam was teaching about the local area in history and geography, three-dimensional (3D) shapes in maths, non-fiction writing in English, and drawing in art. He created a cross-curricular project where the children went on a trip around the local town, taking photographs of landmarks. When they returned to the classroom, they built and evaluated a junk model of a local landmark, constructing their own nets for the 3D shapes. They put the various models together in their relative positions to make a 3D map of the town. They made sketches of the landmarks based on their memories and the photographs and then used these as illustrations for the brochures they wrote, which explained the historic significance of each landmark.

Use the following questions to evaluate these examples:

- What scope is there for cross-curricular planning in the current curriculum and climate?
- What are the advantages and disadvantages of a cross-curricular approach?
- How can you ensure progression in subject-specific skills and knowledge when using a cross-curricular approach?
- Do some subjects or topics need to be taught discretely?

Pupil choice and autonomy

Pupil ownership was a factor in Harrington's (1990) creative ecosystem and Jeffrey and Craft (2004) saw it as part of teaching for creativity. What does pupil ownership mean in the classroom? The Royal Opera House in London runs an educational project called 'Write an Opera'. The children form an opera company, come up with a theme and plot for the opera, create the characters, the script and the music. As well as performing, they are in charge of the budget, advertising, set design and construction, costume, make-up, lighting, prompting, backstage, and front of house. The teachers are only in charge of casting, directing, and panicking. This is an extreme level of pupil ownership but it was a powerful experience both for myself as the teacher and my 9- to 11-year-old pupils when we created and performed *Going, Going, Gone?* It was frightening to give that much control to the children but the growth in their self-confidence, as well as development of their skills in many subjects was dramatic.

The issue of pupil choice and autonomy can be found in the difference between experiments and investigations in science. Lindsay planned a science lesson for her Year 2 class (age 6–7 years) where they performed an experiment on materials. She was particularly focused on teaching the idea of a fair test. Individually, the children had to undertake an experiment in which they had to test what material soaked up the most water. They had to make it a fair test by using the same amount of water and the same amount of material each time. They measured the water, then they each tested cotton wool, paper towels, kitchen roll, plastic bags, and sponge, marking each out of three on effectiveness. The children were all involved and Lindsay noted that it helped them to become interested in science. Emma planned an investigation about what light travels through for her Year 2 class. She provided a range of light sources and materials. The children were able to explore their own choice of items and make their own decisions about how they would conduct the test. They were excited and motivated to find out more and planned further investigations about light. In both examples, the children are motivated and actively involved in their learning. However, in the investigation they have much greater ownership. This could result in deeper learning about scientific processes but could also be seen as problematic because they might not be learning about the teacher's chosen objective.

Developing practice

To develop creative practice, we need to:

- develop our own definition for creativity;
- consider how to establish conditions for creativity in our own classrooms;
- evaluate our own practice for creative teaching and opportunities for pupil creativity;
- reflect on how much choice and autonomy the pupils are given;
- consider the role of formative assessment in creativity.

Conclusion

This chapter considered various definitions of creativity but focused in particular on ideas of originality, value, exploration, and making connections. These apply equally to teachers and pupils, although the level of originality might be different. Teachers can use these ideas to teach creatively but also need to think how they relate to teaching, which develops creativity in the children. Although each of these can be done separately, they are stronger when done together. If the children experience the teacher modelling creativity, there is more likely to be an atmosphere that supports creativity and encourages them to take risks in being creative themselves. However, modelling creativity and giving the children ownership of their learning is only part of teaching for creativity. Through questioning and challenging, providing resources and opportunities, encouraging perseverance and tolerance of ambiguity, the teacher can support the children in their explorations and creations.

There is considerable emphasis on summative assessment and accountability in English education. This performativity culture results in considerable stress on teachers, which can lead to teachers playing safe, avoiding risk, and being less creative (Ellis et al. 2007; Fisher 2004). In contrast, formative assessment supports creativity. It allows teachers to identify children's approaches to learning and set appropriate levels of challenge. It supports risk-taking through providing feedback and an emphasis on learning from mistakes. Self-assessment practices can help with the evaluation of new ideas and products to test their originality and value. This self-assessment also relates to teachers evaluating their own practice for creativity and overall effectiveness.

According to Sternberg (2006: 97), 'creativity is in large part a decision that anyone can make but that few people actually do make because they find the costs to be too high. Society can play a role in the development of creativity by increasing the rewards and decreasing the costs'. Teachers need to regain their professionalism and confidence so that creativity is seen as a risk worth taking for their own sakes and for the sake of the children.

References

Aljughaiman, A. and Mowrer-Reynolds, E. (2005) Teachers' conceptions of creativity and creative students, *Journal of Creative Behavior*, 39(1): 17–34.

Boden, M. (2001) Creativity and knowledge, in A. Craft, B. Jeffrey and M. Leibling (eds.) *Creativity in Education*. London: Continuum.

Boden, M. (2004) *The Creative Mind: Myths and Mechanisms*, 2nd edn. London: Routledge.

Bowkett, S. (2005) *100 Ideas for Teaching Creativity*. London: Continuum.

Brandau, H., Daghofer, F., Hollerer, L., Kaschnitz, W., Kellner, K., Kirchmair, G. (2007) The relationship between creativity, teaching ratings on behaviour, age, and gender in pupils from seven to ten years, *Journal of Creative Behavior*, 41(2): 91–113.

Burnard, P. and White, J. (2008) Creativity and performativity: counterpoints in British and Australian education, *British Educational Research Journal*, 34(5): 667–82.

Cochrane, P. and Cockett, M. (2007) *Building a Creative School*. Stoke-on-Trent: Trentham Books.

Craft, A. (2003) Creative thinking in the early years of education, *Early Years*, 23(2): 143–54.

Craft, A. (2005) *Creativity in Schools: Tensions and Dilemmas*. London: Routledge.

Craft, A. (2008) Tensions in creativity and education, in A. Craft, H. Gardner and G. Claxton (eds.) *Creativity, Wisdom, and Trusteeship: Exploring the Role of Education*, Thousand Oaks, CA: Corwin Press.

Cropley, A. (2001) *Creativity in Education and Learning*. London: Kogan Page.

Davies, D., Howe, A., Fasciato, M. and Rogers, M. (2006) *Creative Teachers for Creative Learners: Project Overview*, Teacher Education and Training Effective Practice Guides. Available at: http://www.ceruk.ac.uk/ (accessed 21 March 2009).

Davies, T. (2006) Creative teaching and learning in Europe: promoting a new paradigm, *Curriculum Journal*, 17(1): 37–57.

Department for Education (DfE) (2012) *Statutory Framework for the Early Years Foundation Stage*. Runcorn: DfE.

Department for Education and Skills (DfES) (2003) *Excellence and Enjoyment*. London: DfES.

Edmonds, J. (2004) Creativity in science: leaping the void, in R. Fisher and M. Williams (eds.) *Unlocking Creativity: Teaching across the Curriculum*. London: David Fulton.

Ellis, S., Barrs, M. and Bunting, J. (2007) *Assessing Learning in Creative Contexts*. London: Centre for Learning in Primary Education.

Fisher, R. (2004) What is creativity?, in R. Fisher and M. Williams (eds.) *Unlocking Creativity: Teaching across the Curriculum*. London: David Fulton.

Hadow, W. (1931) *Report of the Consultative Committee on the Primary School*. London: HMSO.

Harrington, D.M. (1990) The ecology of human creativity: a psychological perspective, in M.A. Runco and R.S. Albert (eds.) *Theories of Creativity*. London: Sage.

Inoue, N. and Buczynski, S. (2011) You asked open-ended questions, now what? Understanding the nature of stumbling blocks in teaching inquiry lessons, *Mathematics Educator*, 20(2): 10–23.

Jeffrey, B. and Craft, A. (2004) Teaching creatively and teaching for creativity: distinctions and relationships, *Educational Studies*, 30(1): 77–87.

Kampylis, P., Berki, E. and Saariluoma, P. (2009) In-service and prospective teachers' conceptions of creativity, *Thinking Skills and Creativity*, 4: 15–29.

Kaufman, J. and Beghetto, R. (2009) Beyond Big and Little: the four C model of creativity, *Review of General Psychology*, 13(1): 1–12.

Lubart, T. (1999) Creativity across cultures, in R. Sternberg (ed.) *Handbook of Creativity*. Cambridge: Cambridge University Press.

Lucas, B. (2001) Creative teaching, teaching creativity and creative learning, in A. Craft, B. Jeffrey and M. Leibling (eds.) *Creativity in Education*. London: Continuum.

Mindham, C. (2005) Creativity and the young child, *Early Years*, 25(1): 81–4.

Moyer, P. and Milewicz, E. (2002) Learning to question: categories of questioning used by pre-service teachers during diagnostic mathematics interviews, *Journal of Mathematics Teacher Education*, 5: 293–315.

National Advisory Committee on Creativity and Cultural Education (NACCCE) (1999) *All Our Futures*. Available at: http://sirkenrobinson.com/skr/pdf/allourfutures.pdf (accessed March 2013).

Ofsted (2003) *Expecting the Unexpected*. London: Ofsted.

Ofsted (2010) *Learning: Creative Approaches that Raise Standards*. London: Ofsted.

Plowden Report (1967) *Children and Their Primary Schools*. Report of the Central Advisory Council for Education in England. London: HMSO. Available at: http://www.dg.dial.pipex.com/plowden02.shtml (accessed 7 April 2005).

Roberts, P. (2006) *Nurturing Creativity in Young People: A Report to the Government to Inform Future Policy*. London: DCMS.

Robson, C., Patterson, R. and Kidd, D. (2008) *Planning for Creativity in the Curriculum of Initial Teacher Education*, TDA Case Studies. Available at: http://www.tda.gov.uk/ (accessed 19 April 2010).

Sternberg, R. (2006) The nature of creativity, *Creativity Research Journal*, 18(1): 87–98.

Weisberg, R. (2006) *Creativity: Understanding Innovation in Problem Solving, Science, Invention and the Arts*. New York: Wiley.

Wilson, R. (2007) *The Creative Curriculum*. Wakefield: Andrell Education Ltd.

CHAPTER

4

Play

Linda Cooper

> Three children – Elouise, Nathan, and Sarah – were playing in the gar-
> den on a sunny afternoon. Nathan and Sarah had recently moved into
> a new house and had invited Eloise around to play. After briefly explor-
> ing the house the children went to the garden, which was quite large, but
> overgrown and rather unkempt. These three children, being old friends,
> routinely played outside together, but this usually involved familiar play
> objects associated with childhood. They were used to equipment like tram-
> polines, netball/basketball posts, ball-game equipment, and a much loved
> play house, which used to sit at the end of the children's previous house.
> All this equipment was still packed, however, and the garden was relatively
> empty. Nathan felt a bit despondent in the empty garden and was heard
> to declare that he 'felt bored'. There was 'nothing to do' he complained, 'as
> there was nothing to bounce on'.
>
> Sarah had a different attitude to the environment. She did not see the
> situation in terms of a deficit, preferring to see the possibilities. The chil-
> dren wandered around chatting for a while, until Sarah initiated a search
> in the long, uncut grass. The children started to find objects that belonged
> to the last residents of the house. They found some small plastic balls and
> a wooden stick and deduced from this that a young child and a dog had
> lived there. Sarah also saw the perfect opportunity for some fun and an
> impromptu game ensued in which one person batted, another bowled, and
> the third fielded. The children tried, as much as possible to adhere to the
> rules of the game called 'rounders', which they played at school, but other
> rules were introduced as well. The children experimented with the problems
> and outcomes of whacking a plastic ball with less than ideal equipment and
> enjoyed the way the ball pinged off the stick in a very unpredictable manner.
> Much delight ensued with lots of laughing and whooping and the children
> were lost in the game for a least an hour until they were called in to tea. The

game had meandered through many permutations of the original premise and the children were keen to resume the game after their meal. In the end, they played through until it was time for Eloise to go home. 🙶🙶

Introduction

Education should seek to produce learners that are curious, creative, imaginative, motivated, enthusiastic, and prepared to take risks. It should develop aspirational, self-assured, flexible, and resilient human beings who not only can answer questions independently, but seek to raise their very own questions and hypotheses as well. It should be a liberating and empowering experience where children find out what they are good at and are given the time and space to explore aspects of learning that intrigue them. Education should allow children to not only produce products, but also to luxuriate in and dwell on the process of the learning journey.

As Rose (2009: 94) notes, 'Play is not a trivial pursuit', it is a vital part of the cognitive development of the young child. Play is the mechanism by which so many ideals for education, as expressed above, are encountered by young learners. Bruce (2001) strikes a similar chord to Rose (2009) when she notes that the ability to adapt to a changing world, to respond creatively to new ideas, feelings and relationships require intelligences; 'play helps children to be flexible' (Bruce 2001:10) and so develops their intelligence.

We may as well say that play helps children acquire the skill and love of learning and this chapter will explore some of the themes associated with the creation of 'good' learners. In particular, we shall look at how the complex and multidimensional activity that is play, helps children to develop in this way. Practitioners have long identified play as a desirable ingredient in education, but actually defining its role can be difficult. As Orr (2003: iv) notes, 'play is not a comfortable subject. For a century at least play has been hotly debated among researchers, practitioners, parents, politicians and policy makers'.

Johnston and Nahmad-Williams (2009) also debate the intricacies of play and its associated vocabulary. Terms like 'well-planned play', 'directed play, 'play for learning', and 'free-flow' play can be difficult to resolve into a coherent theory of play. These authors argue that the vast number of terms used to describe play can be confusing because of the different understandings and interpretations current among practitioners. They conclude that the terminology and rhetoric connected to play ultimately conceals, or even reveals, that a good understanding of its 'value' in learning needs to be established. We have, at least, some way to go before we can claim consensus on this question.

This chapter concentrates on just a few themes that make up the huge topic of play but the main thrust of it will be to follow the argument suggested by Johnston and Nahmad-Williams' (2009) rationale. This is used as a lens that might clarify our view of the 'value of play' for a child's holistic development.

To emphasize the importance of play, the term 'play' must first be defined.

Just defining the term play is a subject rich in ambiguity. Smith (2010) draws on Fagen's (1974) work that observed animal behaviour. Fagen (1974) defined play structurally and functionally.

- The structural approach to defining play emphasizes the behaviours or 'signals' associated with play situations. These signals might consist of laughter in children or an expression that has been characterized as 'an open mouthed play-face'. Play can also be made up of a sequence of behaviours, for example running, jumping, rolling, and leaping that are applied in a certain manner so that they might be considered 'playful'.
- The functional approach to defining play relies much more heavily on the wider context in which these behaviours are encountered. Play is therefore viewed as an activity performed and enjoyed for its own sake, and not for any external goal. As such, if an external goal is present, then this can be considered not to be play. Play, therefore, has no consequences and is very much associated with the process, not a product or final goal.

The concept of play has been continuously redefined and updated. When unravelling what she calls 'the mystery of play', Moyles (1989) notes among other features that:

- play must be accepted as part of a process, not necessarily with any outcome but capable of one if the participant so desired;
- play is always structured by the environment, the materials or the contexts in which it takes place;
- play is necessary for both children and adults (this theme is to be returned to);
- play is not the obverse of work; both are parts of all our lives (again, we will return to this idea later in the chapter);
- play is potentially an excellent learning medium.

These might be taken as qualifications or extensions of the more traditional definitions, and other authors have taken this process even further in attempting to establish hard and fast rules that can be applied to judge whether any given activity qualifies as play. Bruce (2001), for example, defined twelve rules that characterize play. When playing children will:

- use first hand experiences from life;
- make up rules as they play so as to keep control;

- symbolically represent as they play, making and adapting play props;
- choose to play – they cannot be made to play;
- rehearse their future in their role play;
- sometimes play alone;
- pretend when they play;
- play with adults and other children cooperatively in pairs or groups;
- have a personal play agenda, which may or may not be shared;
- be deeply involved and difficult to distract from their deep learning as they wallow in their play and learning;
- try out their most recently acquired skills and competences, as if celebrating what they know;
- coordinate ideas and feelings and make sense of relationships with their families, friends, and cultures.

Pause for thought

- Return to the vignette detailed at the start of this chapter. Given the above characteristics and definitions of play, can you categorize any of the actions described therein as play?
- Are the any descriptions given above that might lead the reader to think that this situation should *not* be defined as play?

Defining play is a tricky business and could certainly fill the rest of this chapter. In the first vignette, the play is rule bound and goal oriented, which might lead some to remove it from the 'category' of play and place it in the realm of sport – or competition – instead. The fact that many of the rules were used to lend structure to and prolong an activity that was deemed enjoyable for more intrinsic reasons, invites us to consider how rules and goals can themselves be redefined and acquire meaning within the wider context of play. Recalling the structuralist definition encountered earlier in this chapter, we might pause so as to account for the viewpoint of the protagonists, the children themselves.

For a child, one activity might be interpreted in different ways. For example, the simple activity of washing up the dishes could have several alternative outcomes. Being asked to wash up by an adult as part of the fulfilment of chores would not be considered an invitation to play. An adult might try to make the activity fun by introducing some frivolous elements and the child might find the process more enjoyable and not begrudge the time they spent carrying out the activity but the child would probably still not label this as 'playing'. However, a child that initiated washing up as part of a larger play scenario and who spent time playing with objects in the water, blowing and popping bubbles might consider this as 'play'. The children in the vignette that opened the chapter would have certainly described their activity as 'play', and for the purposes of this chapter we shall take this wider subjective approach to defining our subject.

Play in the curriculum

Although it is difficult to settle on a definition for play, the practitioner will also find that the status of play within the curriculum from which state schools work keeps shifting. In England, the Curriculum Guidance for the Foundation Stage (QCA/DfEE 2000: 25) acknowledged the importance of play when it stated that: 'well planned play, both indoors and out, is a key way in which children learn with enjoyment and challenge'.

The Early Years Foundation Stage Framework (EYFS; DCSF 2008b) was more rigorous than the previous statutory document when stipulating what should be provided by educational establishments in relation to play. In particular, it stated that:

> Play underpins the delivery of all the EYFS. Children must have opportunities to play indoors and outdoors. All early years providers must have access to an outdoor play area which can benefit the children.
>
> (DCSF 2008a: 7)

In particular, this document heavily advocated child-initiated play. It stated that:

> Providing well-planned experiences based on children's spontaneous play, both indoors and outdoors, is an important way in which practitioners support young children to learn with enjoyment and challenge.
>
> (DCSF 2008a: 7)

Moreover, in the assessment of children against the Early Learning Goals in the EYFS, DCSF (2008b: 16) stated that judgements 'should be made from observation of consistent and independent behaviour, predominantly [from] children's self-initiated activities'.

The most recent curriculum document for the early years has a different approach to play and slightly shifts the emphasis between child initiation and adult-directed activities. From September 2012, the Statutory Framework for the Early Years Foundation Stage (DfE 2012: 6) details that, 'Each area of learning and development must be implemented through planned, purposeful play and through a mix of adult-led and child-initiated activity'. This document places the decision for the balance of adult- and child-led activities into the hands of the practitioner, who should make the decision about this based on the needs of each individual child. It does, however, state that as children get older, the balance would be expected to shift towards adult-led activities to prepare children for more formal learning in Year 1 (from age 5 years) (DfE 2012).

The debate between the right mix of child-led and adult-directed activities will no doubt continue. What is important here is that children get access to a good combination of both types of play and practitioners have enough pedagogical understanding to be aware of the difference between the two. In play situations, adults can help to extend the thinking of children and to expand the experience thus allowing pupils to consider a wide range of possibilities. Adults must also realize, however, that they can bring their own agendas to the play situation that may not match that of the children involved. It is important that the adult does not distort the play so that it moves into the direction the adult wants it to go. Orr (2003) notes that play is often mistakenly interpreted as adults showing children how to play through modelling rather than providing opportunities for children to engage in their own play. As Smidt (2011: 2) argues, children should be able to 'own' play and that 'the child is in control of what to do and how to do it'.

Most children will play differently when adults are involved. When I look back on play in my own childhood, it was something that certainly remained in the realm of the child and childhood friends and it was not something I wished adults to be involved in. Play consisted of adventure and fantasy play situations that would persist over long periods of time. Play scenarios one day could be left and picked up again the next without the effort of explanation for what had taken previously. Adults slowed the pace of the play down and they had to be scaffolded into the experience. If I was playing on my own, I might seek company in the form of an available parent. However, if younger company were available, I would usually always pick a child over the adult to continue the play. Indeed, in these situations I would be rather surprised if adults wanted to participate and I recall feeling a little annoyed that I felt obliged to let them join in the games.

Types of play

Because of the ambiguous nature of play, it is often categorized into different sorts. To help us to continue to understand the complexities of play, it is useful to review a taxonomy of play types provided by Hughes (2002). Hughes identified sixteen different types of play:

- symbolic play – play where objects or symbols are used to represent people or ideas;
- exploratory play – play that is to do with 'finding out', e.g. stacking bricks;

- object play – problem-solving play that involves examining objects regardless of what their proper use might be;
- rough and tumble play – physical play with others;
- socio-dramatic play – acting out imaginary or real-life social experiences;
- dramatic play – recreation of scenes from others' lives, e.g. the recreation of a scene from a TV show;
- social play;
- communication play;
- creative play – play that enables new connections to be made;
- deep play;
- fantasy play;
- imaginative play;
- role play;
- locomotor play – physical play;
- mastery play – play related to the natural environment, e.g. digging holes, damming streams;
- recapitulative play – play that might involve dressing up in historic clothes, creating language and religions, re-enacting wars.

Having tried to define play, we turn to calculating the value of play. To study the holistic benefits of play, this theme will be explored from the cognitive, social, and emotional as well as the physical level.

Cognitive benefits of play

Play is a liberating activity that allows children to explore their world without risk of failure and herein lays its value. 'Formal learning' or goal-oriented activities like 'worksheets' produce a very different approach to learning. In such learning, a child may be limited by a variety of issues, the most immediate of which would be their inability to decode and interpret text as well as mark making. This produces a situation where a child has a potentially negative and de-motivating learning experience and one where they could easily fail. Play allows children to approach scenarios in a manner of their own choosing. This, in turn, helps children to access desirable learning outcomes such as discovery, experimentation, problem solving, making connections, and risk-taking at their own pace.

Early educational theorists noted the link between play and cognitive development. Piaget (1896–1980) observed children playing to develop his theory of cognitive development. He concluded that play provides children with a multitude of opportunities to interact with materials and construct knowledge about the world. For Piaget, play was one of the primary contexts in which cognitive development could occur (Singer et al. 2006).

Vygotsky (1978) understood the role of play as a vehicle for cognitive development, but also emphasized the role of the 'other' in the process. During play, children interact with others and from this they can potentially extend their learning. Vygotsky emphasized pretend play and its importance in developing a child's understanding of symbols and social conventions. For instance, being able to pretend a stick is a sword to create a meta-representation shows a child's capacity for more advanced, abstract thought (Alexander 2009).

Convergent and divergent thinking

Play resources that are offered by practitioners can produce a range of responses and can encourage cognitive development. Froebel (1782–1857), one of the first pioneers of play, realized the importance of play objects. He developed a set of play materials that were called 'gifts' through which children could be inspired to enter into a process of exploration. He believed that children should not be taught by rote, but via self-expression and through exploratory play resources to aid cognition (Pound 2008).

The play environment can be used to promote different thinking outcomes. For instance, some materials can promote convergent thinking where the play is used to problem solve to arrive at single solution (e.g. jigsaws). Divergent thinking is enhanced by materials that do not have one way of using them, but instead offer a range of possibilities (Hughes 2010). The acquisition of both convergent thinking and divergent thinking skills is important in learning. However, play materials that are open-ended have often been associated with encouraging children to be more creative, a very desirable learning outcome (Hughes 2010).

Block play is one example of a type of play material that might encourage the development of divergent thinking in young children. Blocks are versatile and offer the sort of play that can be returned to time and again. With each experience the outcome of the play may be different. On one occasion the blocks might be put together to form a bridge over a shark-infested river, on another they might be used to make a shelter for a favourite toy. As well as being thoroughly absorbing, block play offers numerous benefits with regard to cognitive development. While playing with blocks children are simultaneously learning about space and measurement principles. They are learning about the concept of equivalency: that a certain number of units of one size correspond to a different number of units of another size. In addition, children learn about two-dimensional and three-dimensional spaces, the concepts of area and volume, and the spatial skills of visualization and mental rotation (Hughes 2010).

Good early play experiences, in well-resourced play environments, can therefore be linked to the production of creative learners who show persistence, flexibility, independence, and the ability to try new approaches to problems should a first attempt not succeed. They also provide a wealth of personal experiences that can be drawn on by children later in life, to provide context for abstract concepts they are learning. In fact, many experiences of creative play in early childhood can have delayed benefits for older children and adults. If we return to the vignette at the start of the chapter, Sarah, by inventing a game out of a stick and a discarded plastic ball, showed much evidence of being creative. In addition, she showed persistence and the capacity to discover possibilities in scenarios that for other children appeared limited; this creative approach to her play will help her to succeed later in life. (For further discussion of the nature of creativity, see Chapter 3, *Creativity*.)

Case study

Sally was a Year 7 child (aged 12) who had been set the task of making a model of a castle for her history homework. The castle she chose to reproduce required that she combine a variety of materials to make a replica model that contained a moat, a keep, walls with castellation, a bridge, a portcullis, and a gatehouse. This was made out of a variety of materials that she found around the home. The castle was finished with effects achieved through the use of pens and paints for decoration and ornamentation, sand to add texture, and PVA glue to add a shining glimmer to the blue paint that was used for the moat. The castle was made over a period of an afternoon.

Although this exercise was not a play experience and was approached as homework, her mother saw and understood how this child drew on her many early play experiences to help her achieve the task. Sally knew from years of experience of playing with a variety of materials how to combine objects to make an appealing model. Sally required little help and was aware of what materials she needed to make the castle and how to use them. From her years of experimenting in less formal and structured activities, she knew how to roll card to make a convincing turret, as well as layering materials to make a 3D object. She knew how to combine sand and paint and glue to produce a magnificent grass effect. She also knew how to position materials to show the right dimensions and proportions particular to the castle. While undertaking this task, Sally showed persistence, determination, and the ability to think around a set problem. For a child who had never had the opportunity to explore materials in this manner before, the activity would arguably have been much harder.

There are many aspects of play and cognitive development that could be explored, but in this chapter there simply isn't the space to do so. However, before moving on to discuss play aiding social and emotional development, one more fundamental aspect of play should be considered. Put very simply, it should not be forgotten that play is enjoyable and makes cognition and learning fun! When children play, as in the vignette at the beginning of the chapter, they get lost in the experience and, at times like these, learning is an incidental but beneficial result of the occasion. Play can be used as a vehicle to motivate and hook the interests of learners. If children can gain early experiences of being sustained in an activity, this can often help them with the attributes of persistence in later life.

Case study

As part of a 'Senses' topic, the Nursery and Foundation class were exploring touch. Prior to the activity, a mixing bowl had been filled with some plastic animals and frozen in water over several days. At the start of the 'touch' day, the ice block had been looked at by the class, then throughout the day it had been explored with children observing the melting process and the animals slowly emerging from the ice.

After lunch, the ice was again examined. Subsequently, two nursery-aged children, who only attended school in the afternoons, and who were often reluctant to engage fully with the rest of the class and preferred, instead, to play outside, started to explore it. One child had English as an Additional Language (EAL) (Child A), the other was a native English speaker (Child B). Once the rest of the class had moved on to free-flow play, the two boys went over to the ice and started to explore it independently. They had virtually no verbal communication throughout their exploratory play, but instead used a lot of non-verbal expression.

The pair started by rubbing their hands over the slippery surface and splashing in the melted ice. They then started getting the animals to jump through the water, taking great delight in splashing the water in the tray, at which point Child B was making appropriate animal noises, while Child A was grinning but remained silent. A horse was partly protruding from the ice block and Child A began using a dinosaur to 'jab' at the ice in an attempt to free the horse. Child B then joined in. Both boys spent the majority of the remainder of the afternoon hacking at the ice endeavouring to first free the horse, then a cow. Throughout the play, both boys remained completely immersed in the task. Two other children at different times went to explore the ice briefly, just wanting to smooth their hands over the block of ice. Towards the end of the afternoon, other children joined Child A and Child B and also started trying to melt the ice to free the animals, chatting while they were playing, but Child A and Child B remained non-verbally immersed throughout.

Many thanks to Tessa James (a Year 3 Initial Teacher Training student at Chichester University) for the above case study.

Play and social and emotional development

Play is considered important in the development of social skills. In particular, socio-dramatic play and fantasy play, in which children assume roles and engage in role play, have been associated with social and emotional development in children. When children are playing with others, they have to learn how to communicate in order to direct and extend their play. For the play to continue harmoniously, children have to learn to cooperate and compromise within a larger group. When playing with others, it is advantageous to learn quickly that they cannot always have their own way if they wish to remain in the game, as children who do not learn to compromise and cooperate frequently get left out.

Fantasy and socio-dramatic play, therefore, should be an important feature of a child's environment. Siegler et al. (2006) note that the amount of fantasy play that young children engage in is:

> positively related to their understanding of other people's thinking and predicts the children's later understanding of emotion ... Children who participate in greater than average fantasy play...tend to be relatively socially mature and popular with their peers.
>
> (Siegler et al. 2006: 269)

In addition, Hughes (2010) notes that dramatic play allows children to experiment with and 'try on' a variety of roles and therefore understand other people in order to see the world through the eyes of others. Play, therefore, helps children to decentre and appreciate the viewpoint of others.

Other types of play, such as rough and tumble play, can aid social and emotional development. Rough and tumble play is often dismissed as a valuable form of activity by teaching practitioners. It is often seen as too aggressive and a preemptive of real fights. Smith (2010), however, notes that this type of play helps children to understand emotional signals. To participate in this play, children need to accurately comprehend expressions such as happy, sad, angry, scared, and neutral. They need to have the emotional awareness to know when this type of activity could be continued by recognizing a 'play-face' as opposed to an expression that says 'I want to stop' (Smith 2010).

Play and physical development

Physical play helps children to acquire mastery and control over their body as well as develop muscle bulk, stamina, and endurance. Physical play helps to promote coordination and balance. Educational establishments need to provide indoor and outdoor play equipment for children to develop their gross, fine, and locomotor skills – the outdoor space being particularly important. Theorists have, for a long time, acknowledged the importance of the outdoor environment. For Froebel (1782–1857) an outdoor space and nature were seen as key to a child's development. McMillan (1860–1931) developed Froebel's emphasis on space and freedom by placing importance on creating large nursery gardens. Interestingly, McMillan's learning spaces were developed with large verandas and with windows that folded back so that the rooms were light and airy (Pound 2008).

Children's landscapes for play are changing and they often spend less time playing outdoors. Play, particularly that which takes place outside, needs to allow children the opportunity to challenge themselves by taking calculated risks. The resilience and confidence that was often developed when children spent time away from their parents/carers, undertaking activities like crawling through bushes, jumping fences, and climbing trees has declined. The reasons for this are diverse, but include safety issues that manifest, for example, in a fear of predatory adults, a high density of population resulting in overcrowding with fewer open spaces, changing leisure activities that rely on technology, and high traffic volumes that increase the risk of road traffic accidents. Educational establishments need to ensure that provision is made for opportunities no longer available to children outside of school. Provision of space should encourage free flow between indoors and outdoors. Physical play that involves all of a child's senses not only has benefits for the body, but also has knock-on effects for other areas of development:

> When children actively explore their environment, it has an impact on all areas of learning … they develop knowledge and understanding of the world in which they live. This then promotes increasing independence and significantly contributes to a child's social, emotional and intellectual development.
>
> (Johnston and Nahmad-Williams, 2009: 295)

Physical play is naturally very uplifting and helps children to feel happy. Other types of play need to be interspersed with physical play to allow children to use up excess energy. Smith (2010) argues that physical play encourages children to take breaks and prevents cognitive overload. As younger children have a shorter attention span, bouts of physical play help children 'space-out' the cognitive demands of school.

Developing practice

To develop effective practice, we need to consider:

- whether we understand the value of play;
- how we understand the vocabulary of play;
- how theorists valued the importance of play;

- that children get the opportunity to experience play that is both child initiated and which involves adults;
- that play materials can promote different types of cognitive outcomes;
- how play can promote creative thinkers;
- that play has both immediate and delayed benefits for learners;
- how play provision should include both the indoors and outdoors environment – and children should free flow between these areas;
- that plays benefits learners holistically.

Conclusion

Play is a subject that could take up a book of its own, not just one chapter. Play is full of complexities and is difficult to understand due to its ambiguous nature and due to the large amount of vocabulary associated with it. The character, types, and value of play have only begun to be unpicked in this chapter, which has selected just a few themes associated with play to expand upon; many others had to be omitted. What cannot be denied, however, is that play should be an important part of the curriculum for young children. Play not only helps young children learn but has delayed benefits that can be reaped in later childhood, adolescence, and adulthood. Play needs to be understood and valued by practitioners not only in the early years but in later primary stages as well. Both Rose (2009) and Alexander (2009) call for play-based learning to be extended from Reception into Key Stage 1 (for children up to 7 years of age). Play experiences count and develop attributes in young children that stay with them for a lifetime.

References

Alexander, R. (2009) *Children, Their World, Their Education. Final Report and Recommendations of the Primary Review.* London: Routledge.

Bruce, T. (2001) *Learning through Play.* London: Hodder & Stoughton.

Department for Children, Schools and Families (DCSF) (2008a) *Practice Guidance for the Early Years Foundation Stage.* Available at: https://www.education.gov.uk/publications/eOrderingDownload/eyfs_practiceguid_0026608.pdf (accessed May 2012).

Department for Children, Schools and Families (DCSF) (2008b) *Statutory Framework for the Early Years Foundation Stage.* Available at: https://www.education.gov.uk/publications/standard/publicationDetail/Page1/DCSF-00261-2008#downloadableparts (accessed May 2012).

Department for Education (DfE) (2012) *Statutory Framework for the Early Years Foundation Stage.* Available at: http://media.education.gov.uk/assets/files/pdf/e/eyfs%20statutory%20framework%20march%202012.pdf (accessed May 2012).

Fagen, R.M. (1974) Selective and evolutionary aspects of animal play, *American Naturalist*, 108: 850–8.

Hughes, B. (2002) *A Playworker's Taxonomy of Play Types*, 2nd edn. London: PlayLink.
Hughes, F. (2010) *Children, Play and Development.* London: Sage.
Johnston, J. and Nahmad-Williams, L. (2009) *Early Childhood Studies.* Harlow: Pearson Education.
Moyles, J. (1989) *Just Playing.* Buckingham: Open University Press.
Orr, R. (2003) *My Right to Play.* Philadelphia, PA: Open University Press.
Pound, L. (2008) *How Children Learn.* London: Step Forward Publishing.
Qualifications and Curriculum Authority/Department of Education and Employment (QCA/DfEE) (2000) *Curriculum Guidance for the Foundation Stage.* London: QCA.
Rose, J. (2009) *The Independent Review of the Primary Curriculum.* Available at: http://publications.education.gov.uk/default.aspx?PageFunction=productdetails&PageMode=publications&ProductId=DCSF-00499-2009.
Siegler, R., Delocahe, J. and Eisenberg, N. (2006) *How Children Develop.* New York: Worth Publishers.
Singer, D., Golinkoff, R. and Hirsh, K. (2006) *Play = Learning.* New York: Oxford University Press.
Smidt, S. (2011) *Playing to Learn: The Role of Play in the Early Years.* London: Routledge.
Smith, P. (2010) *Children and Play.* Chichester: Wiley-Blackwell.
Vygotsky, L. (1978) *Mind in Society: The Development of Higher Psychological Processes.* Cambridge, MA: Harvard University Press.

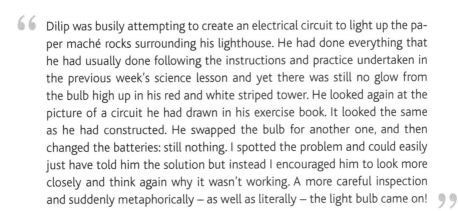

CHAPTER

5

Investigation

Nigel Hutchinson

> 66 Dilip was busily attempting to create an electrical circuit to light up the pa-
> per maché rocks surrounding his lighthouse. He had done everything that
> he had usually done following the instructions and practice undertaken in
> the previous week's science lesson and yet there was still no glow from
> the bulb high up in his red and white striped tower. He looked again at the
> picture of a circuit he had drawn in his exercise book. It looked the same
> as he had constructed. He swapped the bulb for another one, and then
> changed the batteries: still nothing. I spotted the problem and could easily
> just have told him the solution but instead I encouraged him to look more
> closely and think again why it wasn't working. A more careful inspection
> and suddenly metaphorically – as well as literally – the light bulb came on! 99

Introduction

Children continuously seek to make sense of the world around them, to find out
how things within it work, and to explore out towards the boundaries that seem
to contain it. Where they have ownership of this process and the tools, support,
encouragement, and guidance to equip them with the necessary skills and attitudes required on their own unique learning journey, it can develop into a personal voyage of discovery through school and in life.

In the very familiar opening scenario to this chapter it is all too easy to tell,
rather than allow, Dilip those opportunities for discovering, for himself, the answer.
Whether it is in a problem-solving situation such as this where Dilip was applying
his learning to an area of interest and his own creativeness, or a more open-ended
investigation with no definite intended outcome, the benefits to the child in the joy
of his realization were there for all to see. To the child who always asks 'why?' in
response to statements, the answer should always be 'let's see if we can find out'.

This chapter explores investigation, including the notion of investigations, and in particular the investigative process as an essential element of Primary pedagogy. Sometimes the enquiry will lead to known and prescribed truths and answers as the learner follows in the footsteps of their teachers and those who have gone before. On other occasions, however, the pathways will be new and forged by the child's own interests and lines of questioning. In each instance, irrespective of the final destination, if any, the aim should be that the investigative process produces the wonderment of the learner finding out something for the first time that is new to them.

In England, an established National Curriculum (DfEE/QCA 1999) has tended to result in a uniformity of purpose for many schools, whereby they teach only that which can be readily known and easily taught in the limited time they have available to them. This is despite many positive statements of intention within it, but is perhaps inevitable due to the concurrent testing and inspection regimes alongside it. Consequently, the efficient transmission or delivery of this material has been frequently subsumed into 'off the shelf' ready-made curriculum packages and standardized 'one size fits all' teaching strategies. Investigations, even when used in obvious areas such as mathematics and science, have been relegated to optional extras alongside 'safer' tried and trusted approaches. Unfortunately, subject drafts of the latest intended National Curriculum for England appear to accentuate and encourage these methods of teaching. Driscoll et al. (2012), among other educationalists, demonstrate that a more creative approach to the curriculum is possible.

Through analysis of the theoretical and practical benefit of using investigations and investigative techniques in the primary classroom, with many tried and trusted illustrative examples, this chapter argues for the centrality of an investigative pedagogy to be more prevalent in schools. It is not flagged as anything particularly new. Indeed, similar such approaches have been espoused at regular intervals and I owe much of my own philosophy to the inspiration of 'The enquiring classroom' (Rowland 1984). (For further discussion about how key concepts within the curriculum have remained constant in England over past decades, see Chapter 3, *Creativity*).

What is investigation?

Case study

The children hesitated at the classroom door as a huge notice proclaiming 'Crime scene – do not cross without permission' was draped across the glass door pane. A careful inspection of the now chaotic scene inside revealed the awful consequences of a break-in. 'Nobby' the class pet guinea pig was missing! A partially coded ink-written ransom note was pinned to the blackboard. Other potential clues to the perpetrator were strewn around the classroom. The investigation had already begun! Suspects were identified and considered for interview. Plans for forensic tests were drawn up. Would 'Nobby' be freed in time?

Before exploring the nature of investigation, it is important to consider one or two significant ambiguities that frequently lead to misunderstandings and confusion in any discussion around investigation due to a lack of considered distinction: first, between 'problem solving' and 'investigation', which are often used interchangeably, particularly within mathematics lessons; and second, and perhaps more significantly, between 'investigation' and 'investigations'.

In the next chapter, problem solving is discussed and defined: exact definitions are hard to delineate. I like to think of problem solving implying a need to arrive at a solution to overcome the problem. In contrast, investigation is, to a greater extent, more about a want, a desire to find out more, even if there is no overt reason to reach any type of solution or end point. Hayes (2006: 112), writing in the context of collaborative work, suggests specifically that: 'problem solving necessitates . . . conjecture . . . trial . . . and experiment until the solution to the problem is found or agreed', whereas 'investigation follows a similar procedural pattern . . . but end(s) with . . . pupils pursuing their favoured option'.

This leads to a similar justification for using investigation as a verb rather than a noun as the title of this chapter. Investigations as posed or undertaken clearly require investigation, but as Bird (1988: 7) points out: 'it is easy to say things like "I did an investigation with my class yesterday"', which often implies '"so I can carry on as normal for the rest of the week".' The emphasis in this chapter is very much that investigation is and should be a very normal way of working and learning in and out of the classroom. Therefore, it is as a process rather than as an event that our own investigation should focus. Investigation, then, is an approach, a tool, a technique, a pedagogic strategy, a way of learning about things which is either encountered naturally and spontaneously or, alternatively, presented by others deliberately to foster the development of investigative skills. The latter may nonetheless and without apology be labelled as investigations.

In the situation described at the beginning of this section, the 'crime' scene was ripe for investigation. The transference of police detective work and the traditionally glamorous but dangerous work of espionage into the children's everyday experiences was an instant motivator. Although a fictional and contrived situation, it was brought to life and transplanted firmly within the children's familiar environment. It needed very small leaps of imagination to situate the events leading up to the discovery of the circumstances before them into a very real and present world. For all intents and purposes, it was story as a starting point for the children but with the added incentive that the children themselves were now characters in the play that was developing from it. The children's curiosity to find out what had happened and who might be responsible knew no bounds that morning.

So let us consider some of the traits and characteristics that are present whenever investigation may be occurring, in the classroom or indeed elsewhere. This notion of children 'finding out' for themselves would seem to be a central and significant one. Kyriacou (2009) suggests that this involves children being handed over elements of initiative, autonomy, and responsibility. If children are always told about things, and how to go about tasks in prescribed ways, their learning may well be superficial rather than having any real depth to it. In mathematical contexts, Skemp (1989) regards this as leading to instrumental rather than the desired relational understanding of concepts. Children finding out for themselves does not, however, imply some wishy-washy, do-as-you-like, laissez-faire approach to learning. Indeed, the best teachers will sensitively guide and support children's inquiries, developing their repertoire of investigative skills and encouraging and reminding them to use those previously acquired. Seeking meaningful answers would seem to have a very different 'feel' to it than simply trying to complete a given task 'correctly'.

So what skills may be involved? One of the first I suggest is using the senses that many children are born with and develop well before school: seeing, hearing, smelling, tasting, and touching. The challenge for the teacher is to encourage children to continue doing what comes naturally by providing those safe investigative opportunities to do so. Yes, children will find limitations eventually in most situations and may then require much more sophisticated equipment and resources to take their investigation further. The senses, though not always sufficient, are the obvious and necessary starting point.

A multi-sensory approach is almost by definition an active one: learning through doing. Children will experiment, try things out for themselves, and engage in first-hand experiences. Another phrase that springs to mind here is that of 'discovery learning'. Dean (2009) suggests that primary teachers (should) work to create such situations. I believe that investigation implies taking this further in developing other personal skills and attitudes such as perseverance, judgement, and reflection.

The analogous links between investigation and exploration are very apparent. Indeed, many writers use the words interchangeably. Maybe the latter is more concerned with finding and the former finding out, but much is perhaps similar all but semantically. As Pagden (2012) points out, investigation in this loose context is exemplified in children's exploratory play. When exploring, you are not always sure where you are going or what you will find if and when you get there. What is found along the way will also often be unexpected. Although a course may be set in a certain direction, often you will change course through choice or because events dictate so. You may get lost or at least temporarily misplaced, either through accident or unforeseen circumstances. Mistakes will be made, although hopefully you will learn from them and be less likely to repeat them in the future. Arrival at a destination or successful end point should be greeted with pride from yourself and praise and recognition from others. What a worthwhile adventure! What a learning journey!

Pause for thought

Consider an occasion when you were learning a new skill. Reflect on:

- what contributed to aiding your learning and what led to frustration;
- whether your learning developed in a straightforward manner, or whether facing frustration and having to persist added to the experience;
- whether you learned what you expected or intended, or whether there were any surprises along the way.

Linked with curiosity, through investigation, questions have to be asked to determine a direction of exploration in the first place. Continued questioning is vital so that a personal focus is maintained. Inevitably, perhaps, the higher-order type questions that begin 'how' and 'why' will be those that dig deepest into uncovering what there may be to be found out. Enquiry, another word often used synonymously with investigation, can be considered as the pursuit of answering a question. In a scientific context, Goldsworthy et al. (2000) identified six forms of enquiry, some of which may be considered to be investigational in nature. Similarly, Halocha (2007) details many facets of enquiry that would apply equally to the term investigation. However we actually define the various terminology involved in this kind of learning and teaching, a question often lies at the forefront of an investigational approach.

In the course of any investigation, many decisions will have to be made. Some will be relatively easy and based clearly on the evidence found already – perhaps revealed through judicious use of the senses. Some choices will be made through reflection and recall of previous experiences, applying and building upon prior learning. Other evidence that emerges, however, may be ambiguous and contradictory in nature with no obvious single response materializing. It is then perhaps that intuition, the informed guess, or the balance of probabilities comes into play, not as a final incontrovertible resolution itself, but one to review and revise in light of the further investigation.

In many areas though, investigation is not about *what* is found out but also about determining and providing some personal or wider judgement as to the *value* of the outcomes. Some aspects may be felt to lack comparative value, perhaps because they are already known by the investigator and hence do not advance learning. Others may lack validity, reliability or certainty, since even in the more perceptibly objective fields of learning, not everything can be scientifically or mathematically proven. Some discoveries may be profound and potentially far-reaching but morally or ethically disturbing in their consequences. Investigation is not just a blind headlong quest to find out everything that can be discovered. It must also include an impassioned debate about the worth and value of that which is found.

Why investigation?

Case study

Paul, along with the rest of his class of 8- and 9-year-olds, was investigating polyominoes. Having found all the pentominoes he could, and having reasoned with me why he felt there were no other possibilities, he was eager to take the investigation further. So he began to explore the different hexominoes that he could find. I had already noted that he was using a much more systematic approach based on patterns and groups he had noticed while exploring the five-squared shapes. Knowing myself that there were many possibilities for this one, I told him not to be disappointed if he was still looking for some of them by the end of the lesson. He asked to take them home to see if he could find more. The following day he returned beaming from ear to ear with extra sheets of paper detailing not only the 35 six-squared shapes but all 108 different heptominoes as well!

This episode illustrates well many of the advantages of investigational work. The original starting point was simply to explore the possibilities of shapes made from two, three, four, and five squares: a well-known mathematical pattern family. Although the initial phase covered in this lesson is fairly closed in nature, it can move off into all sorts of different directions and aspects of mathematics. Sometimes we may even get concerned about the open-endedness of problems and investigations when in reality most investigations can be as variable in this property as we the teacher or they the learners wish them to be.

As a learning approach, an investigation such as this one into polyominoes caters for all abilities and styles of learners: from those who like the security of a definite procedure and finite solution to those who wish to create their own rules, parameters, and endings; from those struggling with number or language, to those who can cope with magnitudes heading towards the infinite and vocabulary and expression rich in meaning and explanation. There is scope for the visual learner and the kinaesthetic learner; for the quiet individual and the extrovert team collaborator; for the competitive personality and the more relaxed. Not only are various types of learners catered for, it also allows children flexibility to use whatever style they prefer to use at any given point within their investigation. This means they can begin to develop the necessary repertoire of strategies that will be the foundation of success in future learning for life.

The key factor in effective learning – motivation – as was clearly the case with Paul, can be harnessed with reference to the teacher's knowledge of the individual preferences of each child in the class. The child has the opportunity to take ownership of the learning, choosing the direction and extent of what they wish to investigate. In this way, all children have the potential to achieve satisfaction from the outcome of their labours irrespective of what that outcome is, as it can be personal to them. Of course, this is not to be viewed obtusely as a recipe for 'anything goes' in terms of learning. With skilful assessment and planning of future learning opportunities, there is scope for the teacher to creatively formulate a dynamic curriculum that is grounded firmly in constructivist principles. Proponents of alternative more prescribed, rigid, didactic, and worksheet-based approaches cannot in reality begin to cater for the differentiated individual needs of thirty children anywhere near as successfully because of the limitations of time and resources that would be required to support each child to the same level of educational effectiveness.

Of course, there are many other ways of beginning investigation as I illustrate later on and as Kathleen Taylor has already described in Chapter 1, *Curiosity*. Many of the early experiences children naturally encounter in everyday life are an opportunity for investigation in their own right. One role of the teacher is then to provide and facilitate those new environments and experiences that the child has not met at home and elsewhere outside of school time. Another vital function of the teacher is to lead and guide the child through the process of discovery through dialogic teaching or whatever pedagogy is appropriate to each situation. In this way, whether completely child-initiated or teacher-initiated, the child can extract and obtain the maximum personal ownership and meaning and relevance in a way that 'Today children we are going to learn this . . .' methods can never hope to engender or achieve. Through the most successful of these investigative adventures, a lasting personal narrative will also be created, one that in many cases will last a lifetime in its recall and retelling.

Pause for thought

Consider which of *your* childhood curricular experiences *you* remember the most vividly and with the most pleasure. Reflect on:

- what contributed to making this a special and vivid memory;
- how a teacher's approach, the resources used, and the organization of the classroom (for example, how children were grouped) enhanced the activity;
- whether the design of the activity, the particular curriculum subject area or other factors affected your experience.

Many children will derive an abiding affinity to the natural world itself, and increasingly in today's urbanized and sanitized and synthetic environments, the opportunities for really becoming at one with nature are diminishing. This presents a challenge, too, when faced with the limiting four walls of a built classroom. Fortunately there is a powerful movement towards outdoor classrooms, particularly in early years settings. Similarly there is growing demand for forest school type adventures and education, and field trips and residential experiences for older primary-aged children also remain high on most schools' agendas. Knight (2011) champions the use of heuristic play in the outdoor environment and links these imaginatively to the elements of earth, fire, air, and water as well as the more commonplace notions of seasonal variation. All of these offer such rich opportunity for investigation from first-hand experience which is rooted in our primeval past while examining global ecological dimensions that will become ever more pertinent for today's children as they grow up in tomorrow's changing world.

For other children, it is the hand-made and manufactured aspects of the world that provide their vocation in life and a means of fulfilling their intellectual and future entrepreneurial ambitions. How things are made and how things work are such vital areas for investigative work in both economic and humanitarian development terms, that again to overlook such practical experiences in school would seem to be folly. The precursor to problem-solving type design and construction (outlined in Chapter 6, *Problem solving*) must be the investigation of what has gone before. Personal narratives of taking clocks, radios, and other such worn-out household items apart just to see what made them tick both literally and metaphorically are part of my own learning heritage. Admittedly with new technologies – as there is perhaps less to physically see and discover – it may be less rewarding with up-to-date devices but the principles of levers, cogs, electric circuits, and the like are still fundamental to many engineering projects and need that exploration and discovery as well as later theoretical input. One story that brings that theme to life is that of *Miles and the Screwdriver* by Taffy Davies (1985). With its moral and religious dimensions, it also provides a pertinent link to my final area of discussion as to the necessity of investigation within Primary education

Children's notions of right and wrong are formulated at an early age and then refined and revised in light of new experiences and influences. Morality in all areas often comes down to making the right choices and decisions based on values that are held the most prominently at the moment of need. Societal and cultural views will be inculcated but the individual must investigate the value of these and the merits of the options on offer. In the classroom, many approaches to behavioural management emphasize the importance of the child making good choices and would appear to have more inherent worthiness over time than an unyielding and simplistic authoritarian regime. It also begins to address the ensnaring and insidious power of peer and media pressure throughout innocent childhood, confusing adolescence and complacent adulthood alike.

Investigation in the primary classroom (and beyond)

Opportunities for child-initiated investigation in an otherwise potentially teacher-led curriculum are limitless. The main ingredient in preparing for success is often simply some imagination on behalf of the teacher to create interesting starting points and provide the necessary resources. Then the learner has the opportunity to follow their own instincts along the path of finding out the things they want to, always guided by the skilful interventions of the teacher. Children will sometimes originate their own investigations based upon their personal experiences and interests, and the key skills of the teacher quickly then become those of adaptability and propitiation. The sections that follow detail some examples of how investigation as pedagogy can be incorporated into a variety of traditional curriculum subjects and areas of learning and indeed why it should be so in a particular case.

Cross-curricular: investigating the crime

The ideas surrounding this scenario presented earlier seem to have come into vogue – I have seen several versions in print and in the classroom in the past couple of years. I undertook this topic many years ago as a newly qualified teacher with a Year 4 class, devising a variety of activities linked to science (chromatography using ink from a felt-tipped pen), drama and English (writing and conducting interviews of suspects), and maths (using patterns to crack numerical codes). With the use of technology, the potential for much more sophisticated analysis is also available. Of course, the focus of such investigations needs to be age-appropriate as well as taking into account the interests of the children. (For further discussion of cross-curricular approaches to learning and teaching, see Chapter 3, *Creativity*.)

Geography: investigating a locality/settlements/maps

Practical fieldwork is at the heart of geographical enquiry and an investigation into a chosen local area is possible to arrange – whether it is the school environment, a whole village or a city centre. Opportunities for finding out why places developed as they did and how they might develop in the future are manifold. So many skills, ranging from mapping work to data surveys to documentary analysis, are possible with living real-life resources already prepared. Extensions into comparative studies across the world through use of media and secondary sources are also possible to set up.

History: investigating clues to the past/buildings

In many ways, this can be very similar to the previous investigation and is often combined into one holistic cross-curricular topic, the basis of which is visiting locations. Opportunities for observation and drawing, questioning and describing manifest themselves at every turn. What can we find out about that house? Who lived there? When? How do we know? Augmented by education departments and museum services, the phrase 'The past comes to life' becomes a reality for children.

Physical education: investigating equipment/inventing games

It is vital for children's development that they have the opportunity to investigate with equipment, with techniques, with tactics, with composition, with rules, in order to understand what works best and what doesn't work at all. I always allow children to explore new equipment to see what they can do with it before channelling them down more orthodox and potentially effective tried and trusted approaches. Similarly, rather than always introducing teacher-led, small-sided games practices, allowing children to create their own versions with choice of equipment, rules, and scoring enables them to investigate the wider, and also the common, structures and elements of competitive and collaborative physical activities.

Science: investigating materials/properties/uses

If any curriculum area lends itself more easily to investigation it is probably science. The cross over into experimentation is readily seen. When looking at the properties and uses of materials, for example, then exploring them with your senses is an obvious first step, before more formal testing and examination. The real advantage in this approach is the opportunity to query, to classify, to expand vocabulary, to compare and contrast, which in turn allows plenty of opportunity to uncover and correct misconceptions.

Mathematics: finding all the possibilities (seven-pin problem/inventing number systems)

Similarly, I contend that mathematics can be taught through a completely investigative pedagogy. Pragmatically the inclusion of at least some investigations into a typical sequence of work is at least a first step towards a more holistic investigative approach. Finding all the polygons that can be made on a hexagonal seven-pin (including one pin in the centre) arrangement immediately widens the study of shape beyond the usual regular 2D polygons, allowing further appreciation of concepts such as area/perimeter and symmetry. Narrowing and relaxing the rules as to how these shapes can be made (using pinboards) or drawn (dotted paper) allows for both closure and almost infinite creativity. Another fascinating activity that always works well and enables an understanding of our base 10 number system to be fostered is getting children to invent their own symbolic number systems, perhaps using Roman numerals as a starting point. Again finding all the possibilities of ways into a mathematical topic is limited only by imagination.

Art: paint mixing/clay techniques

To highlight the core dichotomy between investigative and instructional teaching and learning, I turn to the arts for illustration. Paint mixing appears, even to a novice lacking any semblance of talent in this area such as myself, to be an essential and crucial part of the creativity process. Yet how often is this overlooked for the conveniences of time or money in favour of instant and ready mixed varieties of paint? As a teacher I have been guilty of this, but as a reformed learner I have come to appreciate the connections between the paint and paper or canvas that can be made; and the representation of the imagination that can be displayed. All for an understanding of the subtlety of colour, viscosity, and texture through the mixing of powder paint.

Religious education: studying belief systems

It would seem a valid argument that in studying any religious belief system and hence the religion itself, some investigation into the nature of the beliefs – what they are and why they are held by adherents of a particular faith – are integral aspects of finding out about them (Webster 2010). Indeed without this kind of approach, any attempt to understand a religion is reduced to a mere recognition of actions (such as festivals and liturgies) or observation of artefacts (such as places of worship and sacred texts). One weakness of this watered down approach is the potential to cause confusion between both religious and cultural boundaries; another may be the opening of pathways to indoctrination and fundamentalism through lack of critical evaluation of information and persuasion. The consequences, then, of a knowledge-only, rather than an *empathetic*, understanding of different religions has the potential to lead to intolerance borne of easily perceived differences rather than the unity of the common spiritual bonds that join humanity together.

Personal, social and health education (PSHE)

A broad interpretation of this area of the curriculum includes opportunities for philosophical debate and thinking in all topics covered by its title. If we are not careful, then all we end up doing is imposing our world-view and values upon children only for them to rebel and reject them later in life. Investigating alternatives is a key component. Is it always right not to fight back? What exactly do we mean by healthy and unhealthy eating? Views in such areas are more open to personal interpretation than probably most other curricular areas and yet a legitimated orthodoxy often seems to emerge. Consider the implications when PSHE in particular – but education in general – is used solely as a form of social control.

Developing practice

To develop effective practice, we need to consider:

- the place, role, and nature of investigation, investigations, exploration, and problem-solving activities;
- how we can enrich the curriculum by providing learners with open-ended activities that encourage independent and imaginative thinking;
- how we can create opportunities which dove-tail with curriculum requirements, rather than being add-ons;
- whether we allow the possibility of child-initiated learning (for example, when a child brings a fascinating object into the classroom);
- the use of investigation to engage less motivated learners and to challenge the most able;
- how individual curriculum subject and cross-curricular projects can be enhanced by the use of investigation.

Conclusion

In this chapter, I have sought to consider and advance the purpose, benefits, and practicalities of an all-embracing view of investigation, as a powerful pedagogical technique in the primary school learning environment. More importantly perhaps are the repercussions for children's understanding of ideas, concepts, and issues if such an approach is neglected in favour of more traditional transmission and delivery models of teaching. If we are content with just being told what to do, we become merely empty and indeed vacuous vessels waiting to be filled as learners and technicians rather than professional decision makers as teachers. I believe the importance of questioning things, finding things out for ourselves, searching for the newest of ideas and the oldest of truths are vital elements of what makes us thinking human beings. This chapter provides an overview of some key concepts and ideas – please don't take my word for the value of investigative learning, go out and investigate for yourself.

References

Bird, M. (1988) *Beginning Investigations*. Slough: Foulsham & Co.

Davies, T. (1985) *Miles and the Screwdriver*. London: Scripture Union.

Dean, J. (2009) *Organising Learning in the Primary Classroom*. London: Routledge.

Department for Education and Employment/Qualifications and Curriculum Authority (DfEE/QCA) (1999) *The National Curriculum: Handbook for Primary Teachers in England (Key Stages 1 and 2)*. London: DfEE/QCA.

Driscoll, P., Lambirth, A. and Roden, J. (eds.) (2012) *The Primary Curriculum: A Creative Approach*. London: Sage.

Goldsworthy, A., Watson, R. and Wood-Robinson, V. (2000) *Developing Understanding in Scientific Enquiry*. Hatfield: ASE.

Halocha, J. (2007) Developing investigative work/enquiry, in J. Johnston, J. Halocha and M. Chater (eds.) *Developing Teaching Skills in the Primary School*. Maidenhead: Open University Press.

Hayes, D. (2006) *Inspiring Primary Teaching*. Exeter: Learning Matters.

Knight, S. (2011) *Risk and Adventure in Early Years Outdoor Play*. London: Sage.

Kyriacou, C. (2009) *Effective Teaching in Schools*. Cheltenham: Nelson Thornes.

Pagden, A. (2012) Continuity and progression from 3–11, in A. Cockburn and G. Handscomb (eds.) *Teaching Children 3–11*. London: Sage.

Rowland, S. (1984) *The Enquiring Classroom*. Lewes: Falmer Press.

Skemp, R. (1989) *Mathematics in the Primary School*. London: Routledge.

Webster M. (2010) *Creative Approaches to Teaching Primary RE*. Harlow: Pearson.

6 Problem solving

Nigel Hutchinson

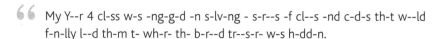 My Y--r 4 cl-ss w-s -ng-g-d -n s-lv-ng - s-r--s -f cl--s -nd c-d-s th-t w--ld f-n-lly l--d th-m t- wh-r- th- b-r--d tr--s-r- w-s h-dd-n.

James and Matthew were closing in on the answer and a smile of triumph was beginning to spread across their faces when suddenly . . .

Uif dpef dibohfe! Uif dvstf pg Tlvmm Jtmboe ibe tusvdl bhbjo!

Quickly Sarah and Becky took advantage recognizing the change in direction of the wind in their sails and so applying a new strategy . . . the finish line beckoned . . .

20,8,5,14 20,8,5, 2,5,12,12 18,1,14,7

Introduction

For the child growing up in a fast changing world, everyday life can present itself as a set of problems to be solved. Whether, for example, these are basic developmental tasks such as feeding oneself successfully with a spoon, or more complex social challenges like working with friends to organize and undertake a visit to the cinema, the child will be working within wide learning parameters. How best as teachers to build on a child's natural instincts to know and understand the present world around them, and then equip them for the anticipated future challenges ahead, is a problem in itself.

In the classroom described above, the situation may to the outsider have been contrived, but to our pirates Matthew, Sarah, James, and Becky, the quest was vivid and real. They along with their classmates had been poring over coordinates and symbols on maps, delving into the history of explorers and privateers, hearing and producing their own tales of adventure and derring-do on the high seas, for the best part of that week's lessons. Their honour and the prized riches that went with it depended on their being the first to solve the Mystery of Skull Island. The series of ever changing problem-solving activities had led the children ever closer to the treasure. Little did they know that a few moral conundrums as to what they would actually do with their new found fortune still lay ahead.

This chapter seeks to identify and justify a rationale for the inclusion of a problem-solving dimension in both the primary school curriculum and its attendant pedagogy. It argues for an approach that, irrespective of a subject-based or a creative cross-curricular framework, is geared to the lifelong learning needs of individuals and communities working both independently and collaboratively to create better futures for themselves and others. It incidentally and unashamedly also suggests that such learning can and should be fun.

What do we understand by problem solving?

Case study

Ann tucked her chair under the table and skipped excitedly towards the cloakroom. 'Is it coats today?', she aimed shrilly in my direction. 'Is what coats . . .?', I replied in genuine if naive puzzlement. 'Do we have to wear our coats this playtime?', her friend Beth persisted somewhat more articulately. 'Oh, I see, well is it cold outside? Is it raining?' Now it was the children's turn to look confused by what I had thought was a rather obvious response. Anxious to avoid wasting any more of her precious playtime, Ann turned to Beth and announced, 'Oh come on I'm wearing mine. I don't want whoever's on duty telling us off for not having one on'. A quick grab from their respective coat pegs and they were gone.

My introductory premise presupposes that as interested and well-educated teachers we have a shared meaning of what problem solving actually encompasses and what it practically looks like in action within the primary classroom. However, we as individuals hold specific personal assumptions regarding the term 'problem' and how we use it in our everyday lives. As can be seen in the simple exchange outlined above, I, as a new teacher in a school bound by arbitrary rules, was not aware of what the question was asking, let alone that it should be an issue. That, as far as shared communication between teacher and pupil is concerned was clearly also a problem in itself. Moreover, academic and professional literature provides a range of nuances in eliciting a generally agreed definition of problem solving within the context of education. Although there is common ground, there are also some very differing viewpoints and theoretical foundations.

De Bono (1972) argues that problem solving may be seen as a specialized part of thinking. Fisher (1987) suggests that problem solving involves thinking and doing, which implies it goes beyond the mere acquisition of knowledge and skills, entailing also the application of these for a particular purpose. Gardner (1983) maintains that problem-solving skill is tied to different styles of learning.

Discussion of problem solving within the curriculum often centres on the subject of mathematics, which is a very limited approach. In the school system in England, the Cockcroft Report (1982) is often quoted and best remembered for pronouncements such as: 'The ability to solve problems is at the heart of mathematics' (para. 249). In contrast, a report from Her Majesty's Inspectorate of Schools (HMI) provides a more rounded view stressing that 'in real life, mathematical solutions to problems often have to be judged by criteria of a non-mathematical nature, some of which may be political, moral or social' (HMI 1987: 41). Barmby et al. (2009) warn that taking only a 'real-life' view of problem solving would negate the inclusion of many types of problem and therefore a broader perspective should be maintained. Burton (1984: 1) believes 'that problem solving is only real when pupils take responsibility for their own mathematical thinking'.

Where, then, does that leave us in analysing the essence of problem solving? In one sense, whatever definition is used is fairly irrelevant in practical terms in the classroom, since once an individual identifies something as a problem there is a potential solution to be found. If child and teacher have a shared recognition of this, then both have the opportunity to move forward in their learning, albeit with one participant perhaps facilitating more of that learning through being more developed in their own knowledge understanding and problem-solving skills. However, some factors seem to be the basis of common ground when thinking about problem solving.

First, it is clear that the problem itself is of importance. If any possibility or occurrence is then to be recognized as a problem, to some extent it must be from the perspective of those who may then either choose or be required to solve the problem. In other words, some form of ownership of the problem would seem to be a necessary requisite. A protestation that 'I can't see what the problem is' could be interpreted either as someone distancing themselves from any emotional involvement in an issue, or alternatively as a genuine lack of identification with the purpose of a given task. The source of the problem then becomes a key factor. Is it something that has naturally been encountered within the would-be solver's own journey of discovery? Or is it an artificial obstacle that has been deliberately thrown into their pathway that may simply be ignored or circumvented? The source then will be a significant motivating factor or otherwise in a child's desire to solve the problem. They need to see the purpose and point of the task.

Another issue is the level of difficulty of the problem itself. If it is seen as insurmountable because of the child's lack of prior knowledge and understanding, this could result in withdrawal from the challenge either immediately or later, or even eventual failure with the resultant loss of self-esteem. Similarly, if a problem is too easy, it may not be recognized as a problem at all or be dismissed as valueless. Part of the difficulty with identifying, accessing, and then processing a problem may be in its presentation. How readily a child can identify with it and understand what may be required to solve it may also be an issue. This could again be whether it builds on a child's previous experiences, be they naturally encountered or scaffolded by others. Or it might be connected with the way it is packaged, how a word problem is phrased, or how familiar the surrounding context is. Polya (1945: 6) summed this folly up succinctly when he wrote, 'It is foolish to answer a question you do not understand. It is sad to work for an end you do not desire'.

Secondly, the context plays an important part in the purpose of the problem-solving activity. A consideration of context then appears fundamental in attempting to gain an understanding of problem solving. It is all too easy to fall into the over-simplified dichotomies that may exist on the surface in this area: real-life or manufactured, knowledge-based or child-centred? A much more reasonable stance would be to consider how much of various elements are contained within any problem. Or how far along the spectrum between any two extremes a problem is situated. The very complexity of many problems would point to a complexity in the constitution of the context itself. To delineate this further, it would also require eliciting definitions of other terms, such as what we mean by 'real life'. More importantly, it would seem to be the perception and connection of the child towards any given problem that would be significant in any judgement of the worth and validity of the context in which it was set.

Thirdly, the outcome or solution will have some intrinsic or extrinsic value. The motivation to build on what is learnt through any problem-solving activity and then perhaps to solve further problems would also seem to be a product of the outcome of the process. Was the final solution worth finding out having got there? Was there some kind of pay-off in terms of what was gained against the effort involved in solving it? Answers to these questions can only be realized after some kind of reflection and evaluation by the child, or alternatively through assessment by the problem setter in a more structured educational context. Therefore, the existence of some kind of intrinsic or extrinsic value at the end of the process would seem vital. Some of this may be included in what may be considered straightforward, all-encompassing educational practice: the provision of rewards, praise, and an increase in self-esteem. Others may simply be by-products of the learning process: an increase in knowledge, skills and understanding, and a desire to extend this learning further. Whether a creative solution to an open-ended problem has been achieved or the only correct answer to a closed question has been found would hopefully lead to this increase in motivation to ask further questions or apply the learning in other situations.

Finally, the processes involved can develop the solver's learning. This then would give the impression of being the fundamental value of problem-solving activities and approaches. How it has aided a child's learning and development is paramount. In other words: the furtherance of knowledge; the improvement of attitudes; the increase in skills; and the development of understanding. All of these may be within either the social or cognitive domain and lead us to an examination of the point of problem solving in the next section. It may also begin to address the optimist's view that there is no such thing as a problem, only an opportunity.

What is the point of problem solving?

Case study

Emma brought the piece of paper up to me as soon as she arrived at school. 'I think I've done it', she exclaimed breathlessly and excitedly. I looked. I smiled. I sucked air in through my teeth. 'Ah but look . . .', I began in response. Emma's expectant gaze turned to the inevitable temporary frown. This was the fourth morning in a row this little scene had been played out after I had set the problem of solving the so-far insoluble four-colour problem (drawing five distinct areas of land on a map so that each of them – when coloured – touched the others) to the class. Emma had gone home each evening determined to show it could be solved. And that she was the one that could solve it.

For some people I guess, a world without problems would be more like their idea of heaven. But problems do not just go away. Someone has to sort them out. For some like Emma, being prepared not only to use her potential and innate cognitive abilities to solve them, but also wanting to take a social responsibility for being the one to do so when others perhaps couldn't be bothered, set her well on the road to being the first-class medical doctor she is today. Without the skills and attitude to go with the knowledge, many of society's great medical, scientific, humanitarian, political, and economic challenges in the twenty-first century would not be being faced head on today, by individuals working alone and collaboratively, for better futures for all. When no one can tell you the answer, it simply has to be found.

The cognitive imperative

From a physiological standpoint, it is relatively easy to argue for problem solving as an essential adjunct to the experiences necessary for the development of our critical thinking skills, and indeed to extend our wider intellectual faculties. It is known from a neurological perspective that our brain develops and changes as a result of our exposure to different experiences. Multiple pathways for learning are a feature of the way our brain functions and adapts. The part of the brain that enables problem solving is called the cerebral cortex, and the frontal lobe of the cerebral cortex is the part concerned with controlling higher-order thinking processes. These general and specific areas of the brain mature relatively late and so are readily susceptible to environmental influences in children's lives. Consequently, activities based around problem solving that are designed to extend children's thinking processes will provide a stimulus for development which allows the construction of even more pathways for learning. The danger would appear to be in making too strong a case for a specific brain-based teaching and learning approach or programme when what is required is an openness to the inclusion of problem-solving activities within a broad and balanced pedagogy.

In terms of child development, psychologists have recognized that both the sensory stimulation and personal motivation of the learner are important elements in the successful development of children's problem-solving abilities. Early Piagetian theories suggest that these abilities may be linked to the stage of logical development a child has reached and thus that these skills cannot be greatly enhanced in young children. However, it is now widely acknowledged that logic is only a small part of our problem-solving tool kit, and so is only part of this journey. Donaldson (1978) advanced the notion of the importance of language in the selection and use of successful strategies, while Vygotsky (1978) proposed that the opportunity to share problem solving with others was also a major contributory factor in advancing such skills. The modern study of heuristics has opened another avenue of exploration, which contends that humans solve different problems in different ways through use of an adaptive toolbox of specific strategies according to the type of problem encountered, indicating that intelligent behaviour has a much less definite structure and has evolved over time. In a longer-term evolutionary and historical sense, the ability to solve problems relates closely to an individual species or a whole civilization's survival and expansion. Indeed, Wenke et al. (2005) argue that problem solving, more than any other human activity, is unrivalled in the extent to which it has shaped human culture.

Within education, the notion of a distinctive and appropriate teaching and learning environment has been found to foster learning in certain specific areas (see also Kathleen Taylor's discussion of *Environment* in Chapter 7). In particular, research has shown that a constructivist approach to pedagogy can lead to greater development of critical thinking and in turn can be seen as a vital factor in successful problem solving. As noted earlier, this should not be seen as advocacy for an off-the-shelf programme to be adopted as a panacea for all educational failings, when all that is being urged is that consideration should be given by schools and teachers to the ways in which learning is promoted within their classrooms. In particular, the adoption of teaching practices that provide opportunities for children to engage in problem-solving activities within a constructivist setting is to be encouraged.

The social imperative

Alongside the cognitive imperative there is also the need for problem solving to be adopted within social contexts. This can be seen when children are seeking to make sense of their world through the complexities of social interaction. This naturally has its most recognizable outworking in the observable behaviours of the child. On the one hand, behaviourists would suggest that a simple stimulus–response process is responsible for learned behaviours. In his social learning theory, however, Bandura (1977) suggested that observation of modelled behaviour was also a strong influence, and as he added expectations and beliefs to his ideas, social cognitive theory emerged. One key message that may be extracted from this theory is that children need to develop self-efficacy and self-regulation in order to learn to take control of and manage their own lives. The provision of authentic group problem-solving activities then allows pupils to construct knowledge through observation of and interaction with others and the real world around them.

The frequent need to work with others on many problem-solving activities also allows the development of communication skills. From the processes of thinking aloud and brainstorming ideas to the negotiation of procedures and processes through to the final presentation of proposals and solutions to others, communication is fostered and practised through this approach. Acceptance of others' ideas and compromise in decision making utilizes cooperation skills. A multiplicity of viewpoints requires development of empathy and persuasion in equal measure to reach an acceptable way forward or final position.

Another aspect of the social imperative for problem solving is the way in which independence can be nurtured. For many children, the opportunity to work on their own in a sustained manner can be an alien concept. For others faced with constant classroom demands to work with others, it can actually provide relief. At both extremes the chance to work alone can be an important experience that enables confidence in one's own abilities to grow, and is also a key characteristic of the inventive and entrepreneurial mind. Independence from the teacher can also be promoted in problem-solving settings, as the learner is not striving to reach a known answer to 'please' the teacher but is genuinely able to develop new methods and solutions of their own.

Similarly, the child and the class are not constrained by imposed social conventions and structures when engaged in the process of problem solving. Reflecting on my own context, it seems that so much of recent educational thinking, national curricula, national strategies, standards, testing, league tables, inspections, and concerns over children's behaviour has resulted in a kind of orthodoxy of school and classroom micro management. Readers will wish to consider how developments in their own schooling system have affected opportunities for imaginative approaches to learning. A problem-solving dimension to teaching and learning can enable these limitations to be addressed and allow the questions of 'why are we learning this' and 'why are we teaching this way' to be considered and perhaps answered within philosophical and reflective parameters. In this way, children have the freedom to explore issues of change, challenge, and culture in a safe and supportive environment and to allow them to apply this learning when these things become very real in their lives in the wider world of their futures.

This possibility of gaining the tools and skills needed to apply knowledge and understanding is very real and apparent through a problem-solving approach. It is an aspect of curricular learning that is often seen as weak, most frequently because the pressures of coverage and delivery and standards do not induce or even allow the kind of learning environment in which using and applying one's faculties are able to flourish. It is one thing, for example, providing superficial add-on 'calculations in words' at the end of a maths worksheet, and another, starting with a real-life child-contextual problem that allows meaningful application of previous deep learning.

What does problem solving actually look like in primary schools?

The following subsections highlight the importance of using meaningful contexts that stimulate and motivate the child, and provide illustrative examples from a range of real-life situations that have been used in primary schools. In addition, the role of the very necessary but more specifically created and engineered tasks which teach, promote, and develop the essential problem-solving skills and strategies is also examined. Examples of good and effective practice from across the primary age-range are identified and demonstrated. In each case, problem solving is the key element of the lesson that links them all together. However each, as well as being set within differing, largely subject-specific contexts, also has different facets of problem solving integral to it.

Rachel's history lesson: the solving of specific clues

A second year BA student (Burton 2010) was teaching a history lesson in which her mixed Year 5 and 6 class (aged 9–11 years) were given a challenge to find out more about the reasons for specific events in the past. A series of clues in the form of pictures, maps, music, and written documents were provided and through discussion and reasoning in groups the children had to conjecture, and justify why, certain things may have occurred. The use of a multi-sensory approach not only catered for differences in learning styles but enabled connections to be made between different types of evidence, with the children being required to make choices about the relative importance and reliability of different forms of information.

Nigel's mathematics lesson: development of skills and strategies

One of my favourite problems in mathematics relates to the positioning of a new post box (or any other needed facility) on a housing estate. By using grids linking nodes (street corners), a model can be developed to determine whereabouts, in theory, the best position would be. Minimum unit distances from each node to the post box in all possible positions can be calculated by totalling. Then, by varying and extending the size and shape of the estate, and also the number of post boxes required, generalizations can begin to be made that can then be used in real situations involving the children's own neighbourhood.

Weatherproof science: limitations of time and resources

Year 3 and 4 children (aged 7–9 years) were given the task of designing and making some winter rainwear for one of their classmates. The parameters, involving applying their knowledge of exploring the properties of different materials, were provided, as well as only a limited choice of materials. Although the task could potentially be carried out in as much detail and complexity as the children wished, the constraints of lesson time were also a factor. In this way, an element of the real-life restrictions of a design process and production line were alluded to. The children not only brought to bear their scientific knowledge and understanding but also aesthetic, economic, and physical properties of various materials.

Assembly scenarios: the obvious may not be the best solution

In front of the whole school, two volunteers – one from Key Stage 1 (children aged 5–7 years) and one from Key Stage 2 (children aged 7–11 years) – were asked to help themselves to some delicious chocolate cake from a plate. The catch was they had to eat it only by using a pair of metre sticks, doubling up as chopsticks. Inevitably, the gregarious extrovert Year 6 boy attempted all sorts of sporting manoeuvres such as sliding and flicking that resulted only in cake crumbs being liberally dispersed on the hall floor. Discussion and suggestions from the other children eventually resulted in the desired solution, where first he had to feed the Year 2 girl before she reciprocated for him.

Team building in physical education: the possibility of different and yet also most efficient solutions

Three teams of nine pirates (also known as Year 5 children) were stranded on three separate desert islands (at other times referred to as PE mats) in shark-infested waters (otherwise known as the hall floor). Help was at hand in that a small boat (a small PE hoop) had been washed up on each of their three islands, which potentially could take them to safety on the mainland before the Navy came to arrest them all. However, each boat had only room (at a pinch) for four pirates at a time. Who would manage to escape in time? And how? Each team quickly devised a plan involving multiple journeys. One team went for the minimum two in a boat each time, one the maximum four, and the other went for three. How many crossings did each require? How relatively quickly could each crossing be carried out? In practice, there are no right answers, especially if the length of the crossing, size of hoop, and number in a team is varied. But is one way usually more efficient?

Designing a car/egg carrier: creativity and lateral thinking

Within problem-solving tasks there need to be elements that enable the creative and lateral thinking characteristics to come to the fore. Classic design technology projects that allow children to combine fact and fantasy in securing a possible solution, such as designing a machine to move an egg from one place to another safely, may fit the bill. Some prefer the use of a step-by-step approach: design–plan–make–test. However, children should be encouraged to ask *what if?* Or to imagine what might be possible and see if the most outlandish ideas can be made a reality. Heath-Robinson and Professor Branestawm should be key role models, where the inventive genius and heroic failure are revered in equal measure. Unless children are encouraged to think and explore *outside of the box*, they indeed may be trapped within it forever.

Story writing: the inevitable ending – working backwards

An interesting technique to encourage children away from the inexorable 'and they all went home for tea/lived happily ever after/woke up and found it was all a dream' story endings that many otherwise delightful tales drift into through lack of time, imagination, effort or motivation, is to start at a given story ending. In many spheres of problem solving, this is a well-used strategy and really allows the learner to see things from an alternative perspective. Every consequence then suddenly has a rationale and children's creativity and logic are suddenly released and channelled into creating stories that begin to recognize the sequential but often complex nature of good narrative.

Where to site the supermarket or designing the school playground: this is real

Each of the examples in the sub-title above necessitates consideration of personal, societal, and philosophical values in their solution or evaluation of that solution. However, one should acknowledge that each is an artificial scenario in which the children as learners would readily recognize that their engagement is not at a level of critical involvement in a real-life situation that matters to them and their lives. So application of problem solving in a consequential context is both a natural progression and a necessary component in ensuring that values are related to vision. Examples of these would be where children themselves are actual stakeholders in any decisions and outcomes that are made, such as when the future may be literally in their own hands. Some they can be in charge of – for example, what they would like to see in their new school playground that the Parent–Teacher Association is planning to stock; others they could hope to influence – for example, what the arguments are for and against the new supermarket planned for their town. Only then are the inherent values translated into a vision of the future through the problem-solving process.

Pause for thought

Consider the practical examples of learning and teaching outlined above. Reflect on:

- whether the focus is on the adult as teacher or the child as learner;
- how independence and inter-dependence feature within the activities;
- how real-life and constructed situations are used to facilitate learning, and any strengths and limitations in the approaches;
- how each example may impact on the motivation of the learners;
- what cross-curricular links can be developed to enhance and/or extend each problem-solving activity.

Developing practice

To develop effective practice, we need to consider:

- the purpose and nature of problem solving as an approach to learning and teaching;
- how problem solving can be made engaging, purposeful, and manageable for learners;
- how a multiplicity of viewpoints gained through teamwork can be balanced with the development of independence and personal confidence;
- the relationship between real-life, manufactured, knowledge-based, and child-centred activity.

Conclusion

Throughout this chapter, I have sought to make a persuasive case for a problem-solving element within primary school pedagogy. I accept that it is hard to define and then to come to some shared meaning of what such an approach looks like in practice. Like many things within education, research and theory will suggest many dimensions and arguments for and against its use and effectiveness. Actual examples need seeing and experiencing; not just brief descriptions of them. This will enable the reader to adapt them into their own practice. As Alexander (2012) contends, the real danger within the education system in England currently is the insidious advance of a 'state theory of learning' and hence a prescribed pedagogy. Perhaps this is one of the biggest problems of all. However, it is possible to find solutions. As a teacher or as a prospective teacher, you are a professional. The way you teach is ultimately still in your own hands: develop your own evidence-based philosophy; try things out; examine reliable and valid educational research. Then continue to strive for a better future whatever problems need solving and whatever obstacles stand in the way.

References

Alexander, R. (2012) *Children, Their World, Their Education: Final Report and Recommendations of the Cambridge Primary Review*. London: Routledge.

Bandura, A. (1977) *Social Learning Theory*. Englewood Cliffs, NJ: Prentice-Hall.

Barmby, P., Bilsborough, L., Harries, T. and Higgins, S. (2009) *Primary Mathematics: Teaching for Understanding*. Maidenhead: Open University Press.

Burton, L. (1984) *Thinking Things Through*. Oxford: Blackwell.

Burton, R. (2010) Unpublished lesson plan. Lincoln: Bishop Grosseteste University College.

Cockcroft Report (1982) *Mathematics Counts*. London: HMSO.

De Bono, E. (1972) *Children Solve Problems*. London: Penguin Books.

Donaldson, M. (1978) *Children's Minds*. London: Fontana.

Fisher, R. (1987) *Problem Solving in Primary Schools*. Oxford: Blackwell.

Gardner, H. (1983) *Frames of Mind: The Theory of Multiple Intelligences*. New York: Basic Books.

Her Majesty's Inspectorate (HMI) (1987) *Mathematics from 5–16*, 2nd edn. London: HMSO.

Polya, G. (1945) *How to Solve it*. Princeton, NJ: Princeton University Press.

Vygotsky, L. (1978) *Mind in Society: The Development of Higher Mental Processes*. Cambridge, MA: Harvard University Press.

Wenke, D., Frensch, P.A. and Funke J. (2005) Complex problem solving and intelligence, in R.J. Sternberg and J.E. Pretz (eds.) *Cognition and Intelligence*. Cambridge: Cambridge University Press.

CHAPTER 7

Environment

Kathleen Taylor

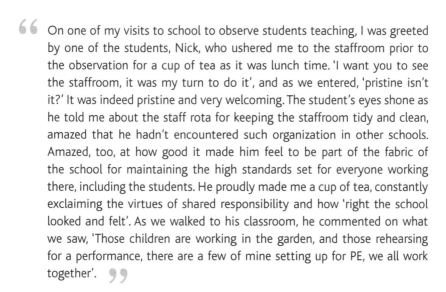

> On one of my visits to school to observe students teaching, I was greeted by one of the students, Nick, who ushered me to the staffroom prior to the observation for a cup of tea as it was lunch time. 'I want you to see the staffroom, it was my turn to do it', and as we entered, 'pristine isn't it?' It was indeed pristine and very welcoming. The student's eyes shone as he told me about the staff rota for keeping the staffroom tidy and clean, amazed that he hadn't encountered such organization in other schools. Amazed, too, at how good it made him feel to be part of the fabric of the school for maintaining the high standards set for everyone working there, including the students. He proudly made me a cup of tea, constantly exclaiming the virtues of shared responsibility and how 'right the school looked and felt'. As we walked to his classroom, he commented on what we saw, 'Those children are working in the garden, and those rehearsing for a performance, there are a few of mine setting up for PE, we all work together'.

Introduction

Perceptions about modern childhood in Britain are complex and confusing. On the one hand, parents fear for the safety of their children playing outside because of perceived increases in road accidents, abductions, bullying, and muggings, while on the other hand, keeping children seemingly safe indoors is resulting in a whole gamut of issues about children's wellbeing related to a lack of physical exercise, over-exposure to inappropriate internet use and videos, and the commercial pressures of TV advertising and programmes. Alexander discusses evidence from a wide range of sources in the Cambridge Primary Review showing some mismatch between 'heightened adult fears concerning childhood' and 'less negative attitudes from children', while recognizing the genuine concerns of children about more local issues such as safe areas to play and gangs of older children (Alexander 2010: 56).

A significant finding in the report was children having a more positive outlook if their school had involved them in tackling environmental issues together. The findings of a recent report, *The Impact of the Commercial World on Children's Well-being* (DCSF 2009), suggest a gap is developing in adult knowledge about the fast moving technological and commercial world and its impact on children, and as a consequence perceptions, usually negative ones, are reinforced rather than critically evaluated in light of evidence. However, the very speed by which the technological world moves means that most of us will be limited by a gap in knowledge, especially knowledge about its impact on our lives and in particular on children's lives. It is with these uncertainties, contemporary dilemmas, and sometimes ill-informed perceptions that parents and carers look to the school for assuredness and stability.

This chapter examines school environments in relation to twenty-first-century pressures. How will the school manage its position as a 'safe haven', and what will the 'safe haven' look like? Is there, for instance, a set of guiding principles for school environments that have stood the test of time that we can build on and use for the future? By examining the ideas of major thinkers and educationists of the past, together with those who are influencing schools today, the chapter provides a picture of the present and a possible picture for the future. One of the striking differences between the past and the present is the status of the child who, now firmly established as an equal in the fabric of the school community, has the right and the voice, for example through school councils, to contribute ideas, establish new guiding principles, and shape the schools of the future.

The chapter moves focus to the wider school environment as an instrument for learning and teaching. It addresses both learning from the environment and learning about the environment. Major issues such as sustainability, interdependence, pollution, and conservation will form a discussion about the way in which the local environment intrinsically relates to the global environment. Links will also be made between issues and guiding principles to focus attention on the significance of attitudes in developing children and school communities who, at their heart, have a love of the environment, a duty of care for it, and whose lives are enriched by it. The conclusion highlights that the chapter has been as much about discovering the qualities of a school community as understanding a school environment and that shaping the school environment and being shaped by it are mutually compatible

Democratic environments

Newcomers, visitors, and Nick (the student teacher in the vignette at the start of this chapter) act like barometers by getting a 'feel' for the school and can provide a measure of how 'right' it feels. Impressions of the school stem from the many sensory signs the school gives out both directly and indirectly. In my role as a visiting tutor for Initial Teacher Education between the university and schools, I am privileged to see many different schools in many different places. I am privileged because each time I visit a school to see students teach I feel I am being let into the future where the ideals *for* children and ideals *of* children mesh together in caring, respectful, all-embracing, intellectual, and aesthetic environments that we call school.

Such values are instantly experienced on entering a school in the school's reception area, often through the assembly singing that can be heard or the general chatter between children, teachers and parents, the photograph galleries of school staff and school councils or of recent educational visits and children's achievements, the warm lingering smell of toast from breakfast club, celebratory displays of children's artwork, eye-catching information about special causes the school is supporting, and often a video celebrating the school's ethos. These together with administrators and teachers who greet and help parents, carers, children, and visitors whilst also ensuring such things as identity checks are made, visitors log books signed, entrances and exits checked, make up a very special setting that is both inspiring and reassuring, and a joy to be part of.

Such images form national impressions of what primary schools are about because it is what we have hopefully experienced as children and go on to experience as parents and carers or workers and helpers in schools. However, what do the children see and experience? How involved are children in the ethos and design of the school or their particular classroom? Can smaller, younger children see the photographs on the wall above their heads? Do they know why they are there? Do some children merely hear conversation rather than join in? How do children not on the school council, or who haven't achieved, view photographs of those aspects of school life to which they might feel excluded? What do children arriving late feel about the smell of warm toast when they may have had none? I raise these issues for the sake of children, because it is their views and experiences that concern me in this chapter about environments. To view the school fully we have to re-vision the school through the eyes of others, especially children, because what you and I experience may not be what children experience.

To find out what children experience and make of their school environment, I would suggest, requires further radical shifts in how we view children and childhood. There is no doubt that since the United Nations Convention on the Rights of the Child (UNCRC; United Nations General Assembly 1989), children's entitlement to education, health care, good standards of living, and play have fuelled change for the better and helped break down traditional attitudes which assume children should be seen and not heard. Article 12 of UNCRC gives children the right to be listened to and an entitlement to participate in decisions that affect them. However, there is still room for more opportunities for children to be part of the decision making in schools and while school councils epitomize children's entitlement to be heard and go a long way to ensure this, there are other practical ways of involving children in decision making. Not all children want to be part of a 'school council', and not every child can be a member. In the same way the reception area might be perceived differently by different users, the school council is susceptible to the same criticism in that it might be seen as a more democratic system for some children than others. Children are quick to recognize hierarchies and equally quickly learn their place in them and for this reason I am suggesting further shifts for children's roles that equate to greater equality and democracy. For example, simply involving children, possibly on a rota basis, as part of the team responsible for maintaining the school reception area, which happens in some schools, opens up opportunities for them to contribute to the school ethos and how they want their school to look and feel for themselves and to others. In this way, children become involved in the ethos, rather than a nebulous idea that they hear adults talk about.

Children interpret the school's ethos in many ways, especially through relationships, but involving children in decision making about their school environment equally enhances their sense of fairness, inclusiveness, and social responsibility. Furthermore, involving children in decisions about the look and feel of their school and classroom offers them opportunities to discriminate between why one thing works and another does not. For example, in assembling a photo display decisions have to be made about optimum sizes of the photographs in relation to their position on the wall, content of the photographs in relation to themes, how backgrounds might compete with or distract from the photographs, spaces in between photographs that affect whether or not the display looks too busy, and most importantly, whether it provides a fair representation of the children in the school, all of which encourage children to exercise the discernment transferable to other decision-making tasks in a wider context. Advocating greater child involvement in the social uses of their schools and with respect to decorating wall spaces, Isaacs referred to the 'waste of possibilities in active co-operative effort, not to mention aesthetic training' by not including children in such tasks (Isaacs 1959: 108). Research projects such as those conducted by Dr. Catherine Burke, who has published prolifically on school architecture, pedagogy, and children's perspectives, asks among many pertinent questions, 'how we can afford to ignore, or manage away, children's part in designing learning environments for now and the future' (Burke 2003). Her words illustrate a compelling call for radical changes in the way we view children's role in their education. Designing and assembling a photograph display may seem trivial in relation to children being party to designing their school, but it is inclusion, involvement, equality, and the democratic initiative lying within it that is meaningful to not only the children but the school community.

Pointon and Kershner (2001) suggest that teachers are more inclined to involve children in display than other more complex aspects such as noise levels often associated with behaviour. Their analysis points the way to involving children more in the dynamic processes that affect the classroom culture (Collins et al. 2001: 60–1). In addition, Fielding, arguing for greater democracy in schools, advocates the idea of seeing children as fellow citizens and multilingual co-constructors of knowledge, researchers and experimenters, in the same way that Loris Malaguzzi, founder of the Reggio Emilia early years centres in northern Italy, saw children when he asked the fundamental question: what is our image of the child? The question itself makes the case for the primacy of the child within the education system or school unlike other more technical questions that might ask what works in education or what works in my school (Fielding and Moss 2011: 79). For Malaguzzi, the design of the early years education system he founded was based upon the child's perspective borne out of the region's desire to safeguard their future society from the dangers of injustice and inequality that the Reggio area suffered during the Second World War (Thornton and Brunton 2005: 3). He wanted to nurture and maintain a vision of children who could think and act for themselves (Dahlberg et al. 2007, cited by Moss 2011). Children who feel their voice will be heard and listened to and who welcome listening to others, feel safe. They are more likely to know *why* things happen in the school day rather than merely what happens, the former giving them a greater sense of security.

A democratic classroom cannot exist without meaningful talk and dialogue that supports a questioning approach. Vygotsky's ideas on the social process of children's development alerted teachers to the importance of talk for learning. Structured interventions help *scaffold*, or form a bridge, between what the child knows and what they could know with the help of another (Alexander 2004). In Reggio Emilia childhood centres, the social context exists because the classrooms are in – and part of – the community, so children have a greater opportunity to talk and interact with people. Their voice makes up the many voices in the community. As a consequence, they are equally part of the struggles within the Reggio Emilia community as its successes. Howard Gardner, reflecting upon his experiences at Reggio Emilia, captures the essence of a democratic classroom when he says 'its [where] students undergo a sustained apprenticeship in humanity' (Thornton and Brunton 2005: 14).

Pause for thought

Consider your image of the child:

- In your school, or your classroom, how do you ensure every child is listened to?
- What mechanisms are in place for children to participate in democratic decision making?
- How do you involve your children in the organization of your classroom such as furniture arrangements, groupings, equipment and resources, and display, and how does such involvement benefit them?

In their study about school buildings of the future, Leiringer and Cardellino (2011: 918) cite other research that shows natural light and ventilation, and good acoustics have a beneficial effect on motivation, learning, and achievement. Other factors such as colour and temperature also have effects on learning.

- Do you discuss lighting, air condition, seating, acoustics, decoration, and how these might be made better with your children?

Classroom environments

Case study

In one school I visited, a Year 6 child, Tanya (aged 10), was sitting with a group of Year 3 and 4 children who needed help with their number work. It was fascinating to watch her elicit explanations from the other children rather than help them answer. She was patient, encouraging, and challenging, asking: 'why have you said that?' and 'can you think of an alternative way of working it out?' She was also adept at writing comments and questions in their books to promote thinking with one child while speaking to another. At one point, gently laughing, she said to one of the children when he made a mistake, 'Oh, I used to do that, I got all mine wrong once, it's hard at first'.

The scenario involving Tanya captures the confidence the school has in its children and the value it places upon the function of teaching as a tool for learning. It expands and extends firmly based ideas in schools concerning peer reflection and peer assessment, and child-led practice such as those exemplified in the *Excellence and Enjoyment* professional development materials (DfES 2004). In this situation, teaching and learning is seen as a reciprocal act that is democratic through the equality it places on the two. It is the sort of radical shift towards greater democracy for children I alluded to in the previous section because of the opportunity it gives to children to see themselves as contributors to the learning and teaching environment of which they share in the responsibilities of maintaining its high standards.

For most of the day and throughout the school year, for both teacher and child, the classroom represents their experienced school learning environment. Surely, therefore, it should be a place that inspires the teacher to teach and learn, and the children to learn and teach. The classroom is a major element in effective teaching and learning where children not only interact with the teacher and each other but with the physical classroom itself, in that everything in the classroom has an impact on learning. If like Nick's staffroom the classroom is tidy and clean, resources are accessible and well organized with clear routes for access, and in addition the classroom has inviting points of interest that relate to children's current learning as well as change to inspire new learning and celebrate children's achievements, then this will have a positive effect on teaching and learning.

More to the point, Ridley (1998) states that 'to ignore the quality of the classroom environment not only demonstrates a lack of awareness of motivational psychology it also displays a lack of respect for the learners'. Good-quality classrooms cannot be achieved by the teacher alone; on the contrary, like the staff and children in Nick's school who all share the responsibility for maintaining the environment, so too children need the organization whereby they have roles to play in maintaining their classroom. The more autonomy the children experience in the classroom, the greater the potential for children to accelerate their all round learning. Knowing their classrooms and feeling confident in their resources is enabling for children, because in these environments it is possible for the teacher to hand over responsibility to the children, not only for maintenance but also for teaching. Children showing each other how to arrange books on the shelves or set out the role play area may seem mundane but the interaction between children is that of teacher and learner, the teacher-child enabling and facilitating learning of another child. In other words, cooperating and communicating with the single aim of making their classroom the best place to be. Extending general maintenance duties by giving children the opportunity for a makeover of their classroom invites their imagination in and may well take their practical skills to new limits. Lancaster and Broadbent describe 3- and 4-year-olds giving their classroom chairs a makeover when they described them as 'boring' and reported on the 'sheer pleasure and enjoyment' the children felt 'in designing and creating solutions to real problems and challenges'. They also said that children's 'suggestions to improve inside and outside spaces and aspects of your service delivery should be valued' (Lancaster and Broadbent 2003, Creative Design 2).

Knowing *why* things happen matters, so children involved in the day-to-day running of the school are more likely to gain a greater insight about how the school works, leading them, hopefully, to make better judgements and decisions because of what they know. There is a whole range of skills to be learned by partaking in running their school. Exercising their judgement over their school environment paves the way for their future as decision makers, designers, negotiators, and team players – in other words, life skills. Child–adult teams have great benefit. For example, working with the caretaker and cleaners provides insight about *why* to keep the classroom clean and tidy, and being part of the 'dinners' team helps children learn *why* to make good choices over food. It follows that if we are to make some radical shifts, as I am suggesting, in the way we think about children and the school, then we should consider a greater role for children as teachers, for example in planning and assessment. As part of our repertoire for teaching, we already involve children in teaching, such as demonstrating and modelling skills to others, explaining problems and solutions, conducting presentations, mentoring each other, and assessing through peer assessment, and so on. However, inviting them into the intricacies of teaching in the way we might organize for them to see, and admire, dentists, farmers, doctors, actors, artists, poets at work provides insight upon which they can build a bigger picture of why they are doing what they are doing. But, more than this, such collaboration in teaching invites them to display their best assets – imagination, innovation, knowledge about children, and their often advanced technological skills, the latter being particularly helpful if we are to ensure technological safety in our schools and that we move as technically fast as children.

Pause for thought

I am sure you are familiar with children playing 'schools' and 'hospitals'. Consider:

- whether you have seen a role-play area set out as a school for the children to play at being teachers and pupils;
- how children might be involved in the planning process;
- how the logic behind a sequence of learning objectives could be shared with children;
- whether assisting in planning helps with children's overview of their learning;
- how links throughout the curriculum could contribute to a medium-term plan and how to involve the children in planning;
- how opportunities could be created for children to mark and evaluate each others' work;
- the advantages for children assessing and evaluating their own and each other's learning.

Now take another look at the scenario of Tanya, the Year 6 girl teaching children from Years 3 and 4. Divisions between year groups had been broken down and it was the norm in this school for children, at appropriate times and for appropriate reasons, to work alongside younger and older children. In effect, the school was viewed as one whole classroom. In village schools this is often the norm, sometimes with two teachers, one working in Foundation Stage and Key Stage 1 and the other teacher in Key Stage 2. With the emphasis in schools on standards and achievement, such cross-year groupings might be viewed as brave, but some in education feel there is much to be gained. The social, emotional, and behavioural skills experienced by children supporting one another in their learning provide the foundations upon which they build a desire to learn and care for others. Implicit in the groupings is the element of care and trust, as older children see themselves as taking care and helping younger children, and the younger children trust the older children to help them. By empathizing with the younger boy who made a mistake, Tanya made him feel safe to make a mistake and also showed her self-awareness. Both attributes – empathy and self-awareness – are recognized as contributing to 'building a community of learners and creating a social environment where learning flourishes' (DfES 2004).

Philosophy of education and the classroom

Case study

Veronica, a second-year student teacher, said at her tutorial in university, 'There are things I'd like to do with my classroom but I feel as if I can't change much because I'm only here for six weeks, and I don't know how my teacher would feel'. This is the sort of thing I often hear said by a student teacher at the beginning of school placement. Invariably, if the student doesn't organize and negotiate with their teacher to put the changes in place, the teacher's comments to me on my first visit to school would usually go something in the order of, 'I thought she would have done more with the classroom, I have told her it's hers for the six weeks. I was hoping she'd sort out the resources in my cupboard and have them ready for the children. You expect something different, something new, when you have a student'. However, Veronica went on to work with her teacher and children to make changes that were inspirational, making her classroom into a rocket ship.

We owe much of our current Western philosophy of education to Dewey's ideas on democracy and education in the late nineteenth and early twentieth century. He believed democracy was a form of 'associated living and communicated experience' (Dewey 1961: 87), very evident in the Reggio community-based early education centres. He envisaged new schools moving away from the then more formal, institutionalized schools to which he objected. By providing more space for children to have the opportunities to participate in an interest that relied on cooperation, he envisaged the barriers to class, race, and national territories being broken down. Through cooperation, he said, 'children learn how their actions affect others and have to consider the action of others in giving direction to their own' (Dewey 1961: 87). Essentially, he believed democracy was characterized by greater diversity of personal capacities and shared concerns.

In the lectures Dewey delivered in 1899 – reported in Garforth's (1966) book on Dewey – he identified three aspects of schooling that clearly placed the child at the centre of education and the centre of the school. First, he advocated for schools to change from places of 'discipline' to places of 'experience' (Garforth 1966: 79). Secondly, he placed the child at the centre of their education fostering in them their social, constructive, investigatory, and expressive dispositions, which must have sounded highly revolutionary, as paramount to the governments of the time was education for the masses, and mass instruction. Lastly, he said the school must be related to the outside, 'the physical environment, the home, business and industry, the university' (Garforth 1966: 79), all familiar ideals of modern-day schools, the link with universities being especially topical, as in England many schools change to become the new Teaching Schools. In addition, he said that children should not only experience the outside through school but rather bring their outside experiences to enrich school.

It is interesting that in his last lecture of the series in describing his imaginary school Dewey equates his ideals to what they might look like in reality, which is what we all do in our own classrooms and schools. In effect, our classrooms represent the interrelationship between the design of the classroom and our pedagogy influenced by our philosophy of education. It is for this 'unsaid' reason that the expectations of a teacher, having a student teacher for school practice, like Veronica (described in the case study), is for the classroom environment to be changed. Her teacher's expectations were for her to create an inspirational classroom, one in which children's aspirations would be raised. In transforming the classroom into a rocket ship, Veronica had to consider the tensions between autonomy on the one hand and inspiration on the other. Part of her design involved moving the children's tables and chairs to form two horseshoe shapes with a control desk in the middle, an arrangement that facilitates dialogic pedagogies advocated by Mercer and Alexander, who draw upon the earlier work of the socio-constructivists Vygotsky and Bruner. (For additional discussion, see Chapter 9, *Voice*.)

Research into the architecture of schools in the USA and England suggests that many schools have been influenced by constructivist ideologies, such as those of Dewey, Piaget, and Bruner, which place the child at the centre of learning and emphasize the importance of the environment to learning by experience (Frith and Whitehouse 2009). Also, ideas of children as *artists* rather than *technicians* by providing environments where children's imaginations can thrive (Schiller 1984), linked to Modernist theories about children's creativity and led to progressive school design prevalent throughout the early to mid twentieth century.

Common to progressive schools was the central idea of learning by doing, especially evident in the philosophy of the Reggio Emilia childhood centres where the central *atelier* provides a workshop environment for children to be creative and expressive (see Chapter 3 in Thornton and Brunton 2005). In progressive schools, the dynamics of the relationship between teacher and child changed from teacher as instructor to teacher as guide, where teacher and child shared in the learning journey (Frith and Whitehouse 2009: 96). The idea of journeying together is explicit in the Reggio Emilia philosophy (Thornton and Brunton 2005: 34–5). Frith and Whitehouse distinguish progressive school design by the 'holistic development of democratic child-centred environments, with an organic functionalism right down to the door handle with consideration for child development' (Frith and Whitehouse 2009: 98).

Influential educational architects such as David and Mary Medd, often working with other Modernist architects such as Erno Goldfinger, and educationists, designed schools and classrooms that facilitated autonomous learning environments for children. One such union was between the Medds and the Professional Studies Advisory Committee at what is now Bishop Grosseteste University in the 1970s, led by the principal at the time Len Marsh, resulting in purpose-built classrooms called Primary Bases. Every piece of furniture and item within the Base were arranged and placed for their purpose and aesthetic effect and to enhance educational ideologies such as those of Christian Schiller and Alec Clegg focusing on the arts and creativity, discovery and experimentation, and learning from the natural environment.

In mid-twentieth-century schools, some purposely designed by the Medds such as the famous Eveline Lowe School in Camberwell, which Burke revealed epitomized the 'relationship between progressive pedagogy and interior design innovation and highlighted the complex link between Modernist design thinking and progressive pedagogy' (Frith and Whitehouse 2009: 97), re-designing the interiors was occurring so that furniture, tools, materials, and equipment were on show not only for easy access but as an invitation for them to be chosen and used. Other ideas about pedagogy were similarly evident in schools such as those of Margaret McMillan, who believed classrooms should be like homes (Mellor 1967), and the ideology of Susan Isaacs, who understood the child's need for activity (Isaacs 1959).

Many of the major educational philosophers gave credence to play (Mellor 1967). The more recent and substantial work of Janet Moyles in her seminal text *Just Playing* has also contributed significantly to play's higher status in primary education (see also Chapter 4 on *Play*) (Moyles 1990, 2001). However, play has not always sat comfortably within classroom organization, for example in schools where the classroom is designated for 'work' and outside the classroom for 'play'. Such physical divisions between 'work' and 'play' have contributed to ideas that one, work, is worthier than the other. A similar division may exist between infant settings and junior settings, where in the latter, play can be construed through phrases such as 'playing about', as misbehaviour rather than something constructive. How the classroom is interpreted by your children and the adults working with them, parents, and carers is very much dependent upon its look and feel, all of which brings into question how and why your philosophy of education has evolved and to what extent your classroom reflects your philosophy.

Technological equipment in schools is changing how the classroom looks. It is not wholly responsible for children being confined to sitting on the carpet but has contributed to it because of the greater amount of teaching conducted from the screen. Trends in organizing classrooms over the years, such as children not having an appropriated desk area, round tables for group work or no tables at all, have contributed to children sitting on the carpet, but just as furniture arrangements have their disadvantages so too do children sitting at a level below the screen and below the teacher. At the very least, such a position causes neck strain and for some children disenchantment, which is a result of the implied inferior position adopted, from the discomfort that occurs when sitting for long periods, and from the position they take on the carpet – sides, front or back, which is best? I am not arguing against children ever sitting on the classroom carpet; on the contrary, it is ideal for story time and circle time, and remains one of the lasting comforting and cosy memories of infant and junior schooling. Nevertheless, technology so far has not changed the predominantly sedentary state of schooling and may even have contributed to it. The post-war vision for change from serried rows of children sitting in old Victorian schools to more 'open' schools designed for play and activity remains a vision for some, especially later Key Stage 1 and 2 children where emphasis on written work as evidence for learning dominates over alternative ways of recording.

Imaginative use of the technology we have now could provide alternatives, for example, schools using digital video recordings of children conducting investigations in science for moderation rather than a written account. The iPad has the potential to release children from the confines of sitting, be that on the carpet, at desks or at computer desks, which are already regarded as redundant in many schools. However, for children to be the mobile beings they are designed to be, teachers will need to grasp the virtues of mobile technology and incorporate it into their pedagogy. While cameras and digital video cams have been in schools for many years and are mobile resources, it is only recently through advancements in pedagogy, such as children recording and viewing their lessons and learning together, developing presentations, conducting *visual and sound walks* in the early years, and so on, that technology has become more widely used (Lancaster and Broadbent 2003). It will take time for pedagogy to evolve to the new mobile technological devices (discussed further in Chapter 8, *Technology*), and for this reason I return to my earlier radical idea for involving children more fully in teaching, planning, and assessment, for it is they who will grasp the potential for learning actively through technology.

The world outside the classroom

Children learning outside the classroom need not be limited to days out – rather than an extraordinary event, should it not be part of the ordinary? Many schools have developed their outdoor areas through building wildlife areas, open-air theatres, mazes, and allotments, but due to the pressure felt by many teachers to raise standards particularly in English and maths, children continue to spend most of their time in the classroom tackling desk-based tasks. The sense of release following Standardised Assessment Tests (SATs) in schools is tangible, with many schools offering their children post-SATs exciting projects and experiences to compensate for time spent preparing for SATs.

However, some teachers believe that children learn better from the continuity of learning in and from the outdoor environment. Simple day-to-day modifications that utilize outdoor areas, such as using the outdoor theatre for guided reading, teaching maths from outdoor structures and patterns, using the wildlife area for science or as a stimulus for creating stories, offer children a world of expectation, anticipation, and imagination where all is possible. Reminding ourselves of what it is to be a child (Dewey [1916] 1961: 119) requires our remembering what it *feels* like to be a child and why those feelings are crucial to learning. I urge you to remember the feeling to imagine, and that the outdoor environment, like the role-play area in the classroom, is a place where children's imagined worlds are possible.

Using the environment outside the classroom brings children closer to environmental issues that afflict our local environment and communities, and the wider world. Noticing chewing gum stuck to pavements, litter in the hedges and roadsides or cigarette butts in heaps, all colour children's views of the world and serve as starting points for raising discussion about controversial environmental issues, such as pollution and waste disposal. Children trying to control the spread of weeds or pests on their school allotment or garden learn about the pros and cons of using herbicides and pesticides and the interdependency between plants and animals. Finding ways to better heat the school greenhouse through sustainable energy sources alerts them to the limited choices we have. Collecting and using rainwater for watering plants rather than using domestic water makes practical the issues of conservation. The point is not to ignore the issues but rather enable the children to engage with them.

> **Case study**
>
> Central to my work in collaboration with UNICEF was the environment in which I worked, and with the teachers and their children, utilizing it, valuing it, changing and improving it. In a Bosnian school where I worked with the teachers following the Bosnian war of 1992–95, my first request was that they showed me their environment, as this was where we would begin. It is hard to describe the intensity of sorrow in war-torn parts of the world but that was where we began. Through their work in the environment, a re-understanding and re-valuing of it took shape, providing a new platform for the fractured local community to work and build together. No amount of input on my part would have enabled in the same way as working with the environment enabled them.

Other such experiences in other parts of the world have convinced me that the environment is the best teacher's aid. Closer to home in Lincolnshire schools, aircraft that children's parents and relatives fly link us to Afghanistan and issues directly affecting the lives of some of the children there, the growing number of signs in other languages link us to our multicultural heritage and democratic values, as well as issues of inclusion, and as the *bread basket* of England, the weather in Lincolnshire influences food availability and prices. All of this is happening outside and, I suggest, calling us to utilize the environment for learning, to value it and where possible improve it with the children.

Furthermore, and of even greater significance and a feature embedded in the examples I have highlighted, is the opportunity for children to connect with people in their environment. Bringing children close to their environment is bringing them closer to people who live in it and the issues that connect them. Issues connect people whether through a difference of opinion or through a common goal. Awareness about issues of how to construct a better environment is encouraged by involving children, not shielding them. When children enter discussions about how to make their environment better, they are effectively thinking about how things should be, which involves them making decisions on ethical and moral grounds. Fisher states that making judgements about our environment reveals 'our duties to human beings and to other species' and that deciding on priorities involves children in concepts of 'fairness, responsibility and rights, identifying consequences and imagining alternative possibilities' (Fisher 2001: 226–7). Ignoring the world outside is not an option and although teachers' perceived pressures concerning 'outcomes', 'performance', 'standards', and 'attainment' feel restrictive, many other teachers prove the curriculum as it stands is not restricting, rather it is a matter of interpretation.

The final point I wish to make concerns 'grabbing the moment', a characteristic that Ofsted (the government regulatory and inspections body) stresses is important for student teachers. Certainly, precious moments exist inside and outside the classroom but it might be that we need to be more tuned in to what is happening outside. It is about the teacher knowing the environment through the window and being at the ready to show children what might be happening. In one school I visited, some house martins had made a nest in the eaves of the reception area and children were being taken out of class to observe. In another school, Lincoln Cathedral's resident peregrine falcon was being flown and the teacher took the children outside to see and offer explanations. Later, the same teacher told me of another occasion when the peregrine was passing prey in mid-air to its young. In another class, the teacher opened the blinds after using the interactive whiteboard, pointing out the snow pattern on the roof tiles on neighbouring houses, asking children to offer explanations as to why some had snow on and others did not. These constitute precious moments encouraging children to open their eyes to their environment, but the dilemma facing teachers is whether to interrupt the journey we had planned and take that moment's detour.

Pause for thought

Reflecting on the examples of learning in the outdoor environment, consider:

- how you might use your local environment to enhance children's learning;
- how curriculum planning might include a schedule for children learning from the environment;
- how the children in a class could become involved in issues that affect the local environment and the people who live in it;
- how you would feel about taking a detour from a lesson to involve children in seeing something significant outside.

Developing practice

To develop effective practice, we need to consider:

- how we involve children in decision making about their school environment;
- what opportunities we create for children to design their classrooms;
- what opportunities we provide for children to experience the roles of others in school, such as the caretaker, lunchtime supervisors, and teachers;
- to what extent our philosophy of education has influenced our classrooms;
- how and why we use the outdoor environment to influence learning;
- why we include issues affecting our local environment in our teaching.

Conclusion

If we agree that children should be part of the decision making affecting their environments, such as the design of classrooms and schools or issues affecting their wider environment, then we must reconsider our image of the child, and value the special gifts a child can bring. We have discussed ways to enlighten children about their environment by working alongside people in it, including teachers, as well as involving children in issues local to their school environment but which impact on the wider world. These experiences provide the necessary understanding from which they can build reasoned arguments and make discerning judgements. However, their special insights, their imagination of possible worlds, their expectations, their knowledge about other children, offer dimensions often beyond the adult vision. In any vision we have for our schools, children need to have been co-constructors of that vision.

We have also considered our own philosophy of education, as this affects our classroom and whether we consider the wider environment our classroom too. Understanding the philosophies of others, especially those who have shaped our schools, helps us to understand why schools are as they are, why one is different from another, and how the look and feel represents the philosophical influences of past educators and designers. Recognizing how our own philosophy has been shaped, and by what influences, helps us identify the principles and values upon which we want to build our own classrooms.

The vision of past educators was to release children from the confines of desk work. It would seem we still have some way to go in transforming pedagogy through situating more teaching and learning in the outdoor environment that provides the natural space in which children thrive. Children's awareness of issues affecting the environment is heightened through coming to understand and appreciate it, without which lies a future generation unprepared for what nature can do when it is neglected and spoiled. Issues in the environment connect a community together, an admirable reason for widening school perimeters and connecting with the wider world.

References

Alexander, R. (2004) *Towards Dialogic Teaching: Rethinking Classroom Talk.* York: Dialogos.

Alexander, R. (2010) *Children, Their World, Their Education: Final Report and Recommendations of the Cambridge Primary Review.* London: Routledge.

Burke, C. (2003) *The View of the Child: Designing for the 21st Century.* Presentation, University of Leeds. Available at: http://www.ncl.ac.uk/cflut/about/documents/school-buildingsCatherine.

Collins, J., Insley, K. and Solar, J. (2001) *Developing Pedagogy: Researching Practice.* London: PCP.

Dahlberg, G., Moss, P. and Pence, A. (2007) *Beyond Quality in Early Childhood Education and Care: Languages of Evaluation*, 2nd edn. London: Falmer Press.

Department for Children, Schools and Families (DCSF) (2009) *The Impact of the Commercial World on Children's Wellbeing: Report of an Independent Assessment*. Nottingham: DCSF.

Department for Education and Skills (DfES) (2004) *Excellence and Enjoyment: Learning and Teaching in the Primary Years. Professional Development Materials*. Norwich: DfES.

Dewey, J. ([1916] 1961) *Democracy and Education*. New York: Macmillan.

Fielding, M. and Moss, P. (2011) *Radical Education and the Common School: A Democratic Alternative*. Abingdon: Routledge.

Fisher, R. (2001) *Teaching Thinking: Philosophical Enquiry in the Classroom*. London: Continuum.

Frith, K. and Whitehouse, D. (2009) Designing learning spaces that work: a case for the importance of history, *History of Education*, 38(2): 94–108.

Garforth, F.W. (1966) *John Dewey: Selected Educational Writings*. London: Heinemann.

Isaacs, S. (1959) *The Children We Teach: Seven to Eleven Years*. London: University of London Press.

Lancaster, P. and Broadbent, V. (2003) *Listening to Young Children*. Maidenhead: Open University Press.

Leiringer, R. and Cardellino, P. (2011) Schools for the twenty-first century: school design and educational transformation, *British Educational Research Journal*, 37(6): 915–34.

Mellor, E. (1967) *Education Through Experience in the Infant School Years*. Oxford: Blackwell.

Moss, P. (2011) *The Municipal Schools of Reggio Emilia: A Case of Radical Democratic Education?* Presentation, Institute of Education, University of London. Cited in Dahlberg, G., Moss, P. and Pence, A. (2007) *Beyond Quality in Early Childhood Education and Care: Languages of Evaluation*, 2nd edn. London: Falmer Press.

Moyles, J.R. (1990) *Just Playing: The Role and Status of Play in Early Childhood Education*. Buckingham: Open University Press.

Moyles, J. (2001) Just for fun?, in J. Collins, K. Insley and J. Soler (eds.) *Developing Pedagogy: Researching Practice*. London: The Open University and Paul Chapman Publishing.

Pointon, P. and Kershner, R. (2001) Organising the primary classroom environment as a context for learning, in J. Collins, K. Insley and J. Soler (eds.) *Developing Pedagogy: Researching Practice*. London: The Open University and Paul Chapman Publishing.

Ridley, K. (1998) *Passion, Pedagogy and Professionalism*. South America, unpublished.

Schiller, C. (1984) *Christian Schiller in His Own Words*. London: National Association for Primary Education.

Thornton, L. and Brunton, P. (2005) *Understanding the Reggio Approach*. London: David Fulton.

United Nations General Assembly (1989) *The UN Convention on the Rights of the Child*. New York: United Nations.

CHAPTER 8

Technology

Linda Cooper

 After School One Day . . . William aged 11 years and Grace aged 8 years

4.00 pm. Grace: Hey mum, 'Cat Piano' is free for the iPad, can I download it? Can I install Hungry Cats as well, it's free too . . . Oh and while I was waiting at Maria's house [for you to pick me up] I saw she had 'How to do Origami' on her iTouch, can we have it on the iPad? By the way, Maria's favourite game is 'Moshi Monsters', which is great 'cos it is mine too.

4.15 pm. William: Mum, can I go on Minecraft please, I want to meet Dennis [on the server] at 4.30. We are building a castle [together].

5.00 pm. William: Mum, while you were taking Grace to Brownies, I was trying to download a new texture pack on my game . . . it gives me better looking blocks for building with on Minecraft . . . but when I go to download it the page takes me to another screen with adverts and it wants me to buy stuff. I know I don't want to buy it but don't know how to skip it, it is not letting me skip it, I have clicked in lots of different places. Can you come and look at it?

6.30 pm. William: Mum, I need to do my geography homework. Have you finished on your laptop so I can go to the school's VLE [Virtual Learning Environment] to see what I have to do? . . . Ah, it is geography I need to use GoogleMaps on your laptop.

8.00 pm. Grace: Can I use the e-reader to read Warrior Cats please as my bedtime reading?

Introduction

Technology pervades the life of many children both at school and at home, and the dialogue above, which was transcribed from a real conversation, illustrates the casual way in which children approach technology for play, social interaction, and learning.

This should inform our views of technology in school as a tool that can be used across the whole curriculum to offer creative, constructive, enriching, and ultimately motivating learning opportunities. It is a mechanism that facilitates a playful approach to learning and a medium in which children routinely exercise a capability to problem solve, make connections, and access higher level thinking skills. Used constructively in classroom situations, cyberspace – with its limitless possibilities and ever changing face – should free children and give them the opportunity to access their formal learning in innovative and alternative ways.

The vision set out in the previous paragraph was very easy to compose, but is perhaps harder to realize. For one thing, writing about the application of ICT (Information and Communication Technology) in the primary classroom is rendered difficult because of the pace of change, which often outstrips the pace of educational responses. For another, we need to acknowledge the fluctuating place of ICT within the curriculum. At the time of composing this text, the status of ICT in the curriculum is once again under 'review' in England. This places practitioners in a position of uncertainty regarding the direction of curriculum development and makes planned approaches to the teaching of ICT difficult. Combined with the need to keep up with the relentlessly changing landscape of available technologies and with the requirement to remain current with changes within the wider curriculum, radical swings in terms of attitudes to ICT can make teaching it feel arduous and unrewarding. Readers will want to consider how such sentiments reflect the situation in their own contexts and in the light of their own experience.

This chapter aims to take stock of the curriculum as it stands at present, in an attempt to try and make some sense of 'where' we are in terms of our technology teaching. It will also try to articulate what it is that practitioners need to teach to prepare children for their adult lives in the twenty-first century. This is, perhaps, particularly pertinent at this point in time, when the curriculum is in a state of flux. In these circumstances, practitioners have to be entirely sure of how ICT fits in with their own philosophy and their own motivation for using it, to help children progress. The chapter will emphasize skills development, engagement, and the ways in which play-like approaches to teaching ICT encourage creativity.

Pause for thought

Consider the short vignette at the start of the chapter. It depicts two children who are well versed in the use of technology.

• Compare this story with a typical evening at home when you were a child.

- How might their home experience help children when learning about technology in school?
- Would there be any potential problems for the children when using technology in school?

ICT: where are we now?

Over the last decade, schools have experienced and grappled with a series of government-led initiatives that have focused on making technology central to the child's learning experience in school. The New Labour government (1997–2010) invoked technology as a central theme in its development strategy and gave schools direct access to funding that was allocated specifically for technological development. A typical example of this was the Harnessing Technology grant, which was a three-year programme (2008–2011) to provide £639 million for schools and Local Authorities to fund some of the capital costs of specific parts of education ICT. This resulted in vast investment in updating hardware and the introduction of much needed broadband connectivity in schools. Growth was swift and complex but it did succeed in dramatically improving access to technology. At the time of the change of government from New Labour to the Conservative/Liberal Democrat Coalition in 2010, ICT policy had developed so much that it was ambitiously aiming to use technology to promote the agenda of personalization in learning, which was 'at the centre of national aspirations for education' (BECTA 2008; Miliband 2004). Educational technology based organizations like BECTA (2008) mooted that ICT would be a significant player via which the home/school partnership would be cemented. In particular, Virtual Learning Environments would offer the opportunity for 'anytime' learning whether the pupil was at home or at school.

The two recent curriculum reviews led by Alexander (2009) and Rose (2009) also sought to explore the position of technology in schools, although their subsequent proposed reforms to the curriculum dealt with this subject in very different ways.

Significantly, Rose (2009) proposed to place technology at the heart of his curriculum, stating that children should be able to converse with the most up-to-date types of technology in schools. He desired the development of digitally literate citizens who would be sufficiently skilled to operate and compete in future societies. Rose (2009) listed technology as one of his essential skills for learning and life.

Alexander (2009), on the other hand, advocated the use of technology in schools for different reasons. He emphasized the 'communication' aspect of ICT and stressed the importance of teaching ICT across the curriculum. He proposed that it is the job of the teachers to help children to approach digital media with a degree of critical awareness and discrimination, and cautioned that its delivery should be carefully judged and should be balanced to ensure the 'educational primacy of talk' (Alexander 2009: 270). From Alexander's viewpoint, therefore, ICT should be seen as an aspect of literacy that should be treated with no less rigour than more traditional encounters with the written and spoken word (Alexander 2009) and used in ways that would help promote, enrich, and extend classroom dialogue. (Further discussion on issues relating to language can be found in Chapter 9 on *Voice* and Chapter 2 on *Narrative*.)

With the emergence of the new political coalition, the fortunes of ICT have shifted once again in England. The place of technology within the curriculum is set to change significantly. In January 2012, the Education Minister announced that the ICT curriculum was to be scrapped. The existing programme of study was denounced as being 'dull and un-motivating' and ICT in schools was condemned as a mess (Burns 2012). The curriculum is to be radically revamped so that children will be concentrating on 'computer science' instead of learning to use applications as part of the current Information and Communication Technology curriculum.

This discourse suggests that ICT is currently thought to be a difficult area that needs to be 'fixed' and it is worth asking why. We shall therefore spend a little time reviewing some of the perceived problems of ICT in school and the apparent dissatisfaction with computing. Why is it that after so many years of investment first initiated by the Labour government that the ICT curriculum requires rewriting? Should we not expect schools to be leaders and innovators in the field of technology?

The complications of ICT

While there has been great momentum in the development of technology in school, ICT can still be a problematic area for practitioners. ICT, in fact, faces a unique set of multi-dimensional circumstances that are not readily encountered by other curriculum subjects.

Planning for ICT is undeniably time-consuming and this is often combined with poor subject knowledge on the part of classroom professionals, for whom media and internet technologies can appear bewildering and even threatening. This can result in teachers being reluctant to take risks and producing lessons that depend upon tried and tested solutions. Questions about the reliability of the technology, moreover, frequently make teachers feel uneasy and fear that a lesson might be at risk of failure (Barber and Cooper 2012). Ultimately, BECTA (2004) suggests that the investment of time required when planning for ICT can appear too onerous in relation to the perceived benefits to the learning experience of the children (Barber and Cooper 2012).

Another aspect of the 'problem' of ICT is essentially rooted in the fact that children are using technology in many areas of their lives, not just in school. This should potentially be viewed as a positive with those children who use technology in their own time being more able to translate this investment into quicker progression in the classroom. However, it creates a problem too, as children are likely to become disengaged with the use of technology in the classroom if their heightened expectations are met with conservative teaching responses.

There is a danger that the use of technology in the home bears so little relation to its application in school that rather than engaging and motivating children, ICT inclines children to become indifferent to learning activities. The technologies that children use in the home are often more sophisticated, engaging, and consuming than those encountered in school. Put simply, the 'ICT' lesson pupils experience might appear to be 'boring' and 'irrelevant' when set against the enjoyable, recreational, and stimulating encounters with technology at home.

Selwyn et al. (2010) explored this problem of the home/school divide and found distinct differences in ICT use. For instance, school internet use was dominated by learning-related activities and picture retrieval. Home internet use comprised online games, watching videos clips, chatting, visiting virtual worlds, and social networking (Selwyn et al. 2010). In addition, Selwyn and colleagues found that pupils reported that their least favourite out of school applications were programs that concentrated on word processing, databases, and spreadsheets, the very programs that children are *most* likely to use in school. The technologies that children are experiencing and enjoy using are often a world away from the experiences that are encountered in school.

The issue outlined above is exacerbated by several other factors. Children are coming to lessons with different levels of competence. It might be tempting to make the assumption that all children are completely immersed in technology and that ICT-mediated experiences make up much of their leisure time. Indeed, some children will be competent users of technology, in some cases having skills that exceed those of the practitioner. This can be interpreted as a potentially threatening situation for all but the most confident of educators (Puttnam 2008). However, other pupils will not have had the same access and be very limited in their experience. At the same time, other children might lead lives that are technology 'rich' but remain, in actual fact, not very competent or independent in their ICT capability.

This diversity of experiences can present a complex picture for a teacher when trying to plan a unit of work to meet the needs of all pupils. This complex situation can result in unfortunate scenarios. The teacher can often underestimate the capability of a child because they do not value the child's type of technology consumption. They might dismiss the 'game playing' of a child as being of little value and miss the complexities, challenges or creative potential supplied by the game. They simply might not see this as offering any type of educational experience and miss the fact that the child in question has demonstrated valuable skills. This results in the child being underestimated in terms of their ICT abilities, devalued, and ultimately disengaged.

The problem of the teacher simply not being aware of the ICT experienced by a child is a serious issue in the educational world. Sutherland et al. (2009) argue that teachers need to be open and attentive to what students bring to the lesson, as this can help add to the whole notion of knowledge production in a lesson; they conclude that schools should actively draw on the resources children bring into school to enable them to add to and extend the aspirations they have for them.

Prensky (2003) labelled children of today as digital natives with technology forming a major characteristic of childhood. He details some interesting data on the activities of children and states that by the time they reach the age of 21, the average student will have spent 10,000 hours playing computer games and over 10,000 hours talking on digital cell phones. The reader should also bear in mind that these figures are 10 years out of date as of publication of this book. This has led to an increasingly well-documented concern on the over-consumption of technology by children. This has struck a chord with many, the thoughts of Professor Susan Greenfield (2010) being typical. Greenfield (2010), a neuroscientist, suggests that consistent use of the technology has 'rewired' brains creating an inter-generational distinction in terms of thinking skills and approaches to learning. When reading, children now tend to skip from topic to topic in an associative mode of thinking, resulting in young people being at risk of losing the ability to gain real understanding of texts. Greenfield (2010) feels that children are only able to 'download' information and not necessarily understand it. She develops her argument by stating that online game playing could be even more dangerous in terms of development, as children could potentially become obsessed by the fight or flight arousal brought out by computer games, which could be compared on a chemical level to addiction. Although advocates of technology might consider Greenfield's (2010) view extreme, her thoughts have gained momentum, being picked up in forums such as the House of Lords in the UK.

This concern for the problems of screen addiction has resulted in some schools taking an extreme stance and disassociating themselves from technology. Selwyn et al. (2010) note how some schools view themselves as enforcing the regulation and control of young people's engagement with technology. Schools, therefore, should be used as sites where the excessive screen time of the young is tempered. Schools should instead concentrate on traditional teaching and establish themselves as ICT-free zones. This view is a far cry from the recent curriculum suggested by Rose (2009), which placed ICT at the centre of the learning experience of the child, but it does, however, illustrate well the vast array of views on the status of ICT in schools at present.

Teaching about ICT

It has long been argued whether ICT should be taught as a discrete subject or applied across the curriculum. Alexander (2009) proposed that ICT should be taught across the curriculum arguing that treating ICT as a discrete curriculum area might not be the most engaging way to develop the desired capabilities. Perhaps the most exciting way to use ICT is to enhance learning in different subjects and how this is achieved will be the substance of the next subsection of this chapter. However, in either case, whether children encounter ICT as a discrete subject, as part of a cross-curricular approach, or both, they need to address several vital areas of technological learning. It is here that we will consider what is it that children actually need to know and how to prepare them to be technologically savvy in the twenty-first century. While there is not the space in one chapter to consider all possibilities, we need to acknowledge that any new curriculum should recognize the following themes:

- Children need to be digitally participative and literate.
- They need to be able to understand 'control'.
- They need to develop 'ICT capability'.
- They need to be safe.

Digital literacy

Children need to know how people communicate in the twenty-first century. They need to be aware of the use of blogs, microblogs, wikis, podcasts, SMS messaging, collaborative document sharing, newsgroups, email, message boards, social networking sites, audio and video conferencing, and IP telephony to name but a few communicative methods. Children need to be given the skills to access digital media in a discerning manner and this involves learning techniques that are different to the more traditional forms of engagement with text. As Bazalgette (2010) outlines, being literate in the twenty-first century needs to include the ability to understand the composition of a multimodal text, and to make meaning from a non-linear arrangement of pictures, sounds, and print. Children need to be able to understand the effect of light, colour, and movement as well as to be able to interpret the order and duration of visual and aural material. They need to be equipped with the skills of identifying the sources they use and to assess the reliability, truths, and untruths of electronic media (Bazalgette 2010).

The internet has made information much easier to come by, but this is only useful if children are taught to make meaning from it by being critical in their reading. Moreover, an equally important facet of digital literacy is not only to read texts, but to participate via electronic media. Web 2.0 has given an added dimension to digital literacy. Users not only consume electronic content but can also 'produce' knowledge. Whether using a social networking site or using a Web 2.0 based educational application or even creating and maintaining a blog, children are now being offered new methods of communication that cannot be ignored. Indeed, participation of this nature offers 'intriguing layers of communicative purpose that can be realised simultaneously, with an ease that encourages experimentation, creative innovation and playfulness' (Lankshear and Knobel 2008: 258). Lankshear and Knobel (2006: 201) argue that schools should be moving to a model of 'knowledge-producing communities' where children have an opportunity to create and share work on a level not previously available. For example, prior to Web 2.0, work that children produced would normally only be celebrated within the classroom or the home/school environment. Now, new technologies allow children to participate and share their voice on a school level, community level or even on a global level. When it is considered that even as early as 2006 a typical blog search service would be tracking around 30 million blogs alone, this method of participative communication should be an essential part of the skill set that children should be offered in school (Lankshear and Knobel 2006).

Control

Control is the part of the ICT curriculum that is associated with what eventually emerges as computer science. This involves the idea of combining and sequencing instructions to control an object or appliance. For instance, at a very basic level a child might be involved in sequencing a series of instructions to control a simple floor robot. Alternatively, a child might be creating a series of instructions to manoeuvre an object in the virtual realm. Children might also be producing instructions on screen using a series of commands to control buzzers, lights, and motors that are connected to a PC from which they are working.

Teachers have traditionally found this area of the curriculum more difficult to teach. The resources can be expensive and lessons like these can take a large amount of preparation and planning. Teaching 'control' lessons can be very labour-intensive for the teacher, as it can take a while for children to become independent in this area. However, the skills that are acquired from this aspect of learning are numerous and desirable. Control requires children to break problems down into simple parts or stages, thereby creating a model or abstract representation of a real-life process. To achieve in this area, children need to think logically, sequence instructions, and analyse a process. It requires children to work via trial and error, to learn from their mistakes, and to think ahead and hypothesize. All of these attributes are very desirable learning outcomes and attributes of higher-order thinking skills (each of which can be linked to discussions about *Investigation* in Chapter 5 and *Problem Solving* in Chapter 6). Furthermore, a well-delivered control lesson is engaging, absorbing, motivating, and hopefully offers children good opportunities to experience achievement and success in learning.

Safety

All ICT teaching needs to be carried out within a safe and secure environment. Although new opportunities for learning have been created by advances in technology, particularly the internet, it cannot be denied that inherent new threats have also arisen. These 'threats' are diverse in nature. As outlined above, one threat offered by technology reveals itself in the concern that children spend too long undertaking screen-based activities, leading to behaviours that could be considered addictive. It is also reflected in the fear that children have access to unsuitable gaming content that is too graphically violent and sexually explicit. Taking a broader view, it is worth acknowledging the fact that the internet is an uncontrolled environment within which young children can become the target of unscrupulous advertising and – more disturbingly – find themselves unwittingly in vulnerable positions and subject to grooming and the predatory attentions of adults and other children who are able to conceal their true age, gender, and identity, not to mention intentions. (For further discussion of these issues, see Mason and Woolley 2012.)

The fear that surrounds the internet has been well documented (perhaps too well documented) by the media and this has served to create the impression in many parents' minds that the online environment is an inherently and inescapably dangerous place. This is further exacerbated by the feeling experienced by many parents/carers, that they lack control of their children on the internet. Parents and carers often have little direct personal experience of this domain and correspondingly little understanding of what their offspring get up to.

While the threats posed by new technologies must be part of a new curriculum, the view that it advocates should be measured and not become over-reactionary. The Byron Review (DCSF 2008) argued for this balanced view, acknowledging that although technology brings risks, this must not overshadow the great benefits offered to children. Byron (DCSF 2008) argues that while children's access to the internet should be mediated as far as possible, so as to shield them from the undesirable behaviours encountered there, it is also our job to empower children by teaching them to use technologies in a responsible manner. Instead of trying to shield children from any threatening exposure, thereby making content 'hidden treasure' that children have to access secretly, they should be made aware of the inherent risks. Children should be equipped with the knowledge and skills to know how to react if unsuitable content is discovered.

ICT capability

Children need to know when to use and apply ICT. The emergence of capable children requires them to be able to combine and apply their ICT knowledge and skills to solve meaningful problems that are encountered across the curriculum. This capability is not promoted via teaching children passive and routine operations like how to produce text-heavy Word documents. Capability is produced by sustained engagement with technology, and through the production of creative, problem-based learning opportunities that have been set by confident and capable practitioners.

Pause for thought

Return to the vignette at the start of the chapter.

- Do you think the children in this vignette are digitally and critically literate?
- Are there any issues concerning e-safety?
- Do these children show evidence of ICT 'capability'?

Creative uses of ICT

The case studies that make up the rest of this chapter aim to demonstrate how creative this curriculum area is and in so doing reveal one of the most exciting features of this subject. Practitioners should be able to spot creative and exciting uses of technology that appeal to children instead of 'contriving situations for curriculum delivery'. As Wheeler (2005: 133) notes:

> the computer is an ideal medium for creativity. On a computer screen nothing is permanent unless you wish it to be, and things can be changed as many times as children have new ideas.

In addition, the tendency for children to see technology as a playful vehicle can also be put to excellent use in the classroom. Play naturally takes away the fear of failure and frees children to take risk. Cross (2012) discusses the application of creative uses of technology by describing how to combine traditional resources with new technologies to build learning dens – she calls these creative learning experiences. Importantly, she does not deny the importance of low-tech materials like large cardboard tubes, crackly plastic sheets, and buckets of polished stones. Instead, Cross (2012) combines these with sounds, large projected images, and light to heighten the effect of an imagined environment, where children are totally engrossed in the experience. It could be suggested that an enjoyable immersion in a creative, technological experience where children are 'learning without realizing' is a desirable way to teach.

Case study

Adrian was a quiet, well-behaved Year 5 child (aged 10 years). At school, Adrian liked the lessons of science, art, PE, and ICT. His least favourite lesson was literacy. Adrian read well but preferred non-fiction texts and his favourite book was the *100 Wonders of the World*. He rarely read storybooks as they had never really hooked him. Adrian did not like speaking out in class and tried to avoid answering questions, although his teacher was usually sure of his comprehension and understanding of subject matter. His teacher was, however, struggling to get the best out of her pupil in several areas of literacy. Adrian read with very little expression and did not like to read aloud. He also gave very limited responses when it came to story creation and the stories that he did produce were often limited in detail and expression.

Adrian's teacher decided to talk this issue through with his parents on an open evening. His parents agreed with the teacher's comments about literacy but they also said that Adrian was an avid user of the Apple iPad and he was particularly keen on a cartoon creation package called 'Toontastic'. The school had been fortunate enough to recently purchase some iPads and Adrian's teacher decided to download this free 'app' and allow a group of her children to use it.

Toontastic is a virtual story creation program. It is set up to allow children to produce cartoon-like stories in a step-by-step process. The program allowed this teacher's children to create scenes for different parts of the story, including the 'set up', the 'conflict', the 'challenge', the 'climax', and the eventual 'resolution' of the story. The children were required to animate each of the scenes in order. Creating a visual representation of the story environment was simple, as the program provides a selection of ready-made backgrounds, as well as a choice of characters, with which to populate the story. The program also contains a tool that allowed the children to create their own 'props' – pictures of objects – to insert into the story if the desired items were not available. Animation was achieved very simply by moving the characters around the screen for each scene after hitting the animation button.

While they were animating, the children were able to narrate the events in the story by speaking in front of the iPad; the sound sensor recorded their voices. The children added further atmosphere to their scenes by using a range of available music clips to portray emotions at various points in the story.

Adrian's teacher observed the children using this app. Adrian was completely absorbed and led the way in helping the group to create cartoons as he was already familiar with the program. He applied himself to the creation of a story in a way that the teacher had not previously managed to achieve. Adrian helped to create a wonderfully imaginative story about an escape from a pirate ship. He had to think carefully about the sequence of events. He considered how he used the animation to deliver the intention of the story to the audience and how at the end of the story the pirates got their come-uppance so that 'good' triumphed over 'evil'. More importantly, for once, Adrian was eager to speak out in order to narrate the scenes and for the first time his teacher heard the excellent expression in his voice when bringing the characters in the story to life.

This case study shows why technology is such a useful tool. The teacher was able to spot an opportunity to use technology in a creative, playful manner resulting in several desirable outcomes. The activity was used to help promote talk as well as ICT skills. Most importantly, this activity helped to engage a child in an important area of the curriculum for which he had previously shown very little interest.

Case study

Year 1 – Google Earth Lesson
This lesson was split into two different activities. One activity explored Google Earth and looked at a birds-eye view of the local area. It required the children to spot any features, such as trees, parks, traffic lights, etc., that they recognized and use the street view to check that they were correct in their observations. This group then typed up a list of features they could find. The class teacher supported this activity and worked with the children of lower ability who had poor fine motor skills and found it particularly difficult to control the touch pad.

The second activity looked at maps of the local area, trying to find where the children's houses were and the features surrounding them. A learning support assistant supported this activity and helped children remember their road names. The children then drew pictures of the features that were near their house.

From this lesson the children went on a walk around the local area to see the features first hand. Once back in the classroom, they looked at the route via Google Earth and drew the path they had followed on the interactive white board. The main features of their local area were then plotted onto the map, requiring the children to use their findings from the previous lesson. The map and plotted features were then printed off and a copy was given to the children. They then had a map to follow and as a class walked around their local area, using their maps as a guide.

It was clear that the children had not used Google Earth before, so it was a new and exciting resource. The first lesson was important and was necessary to support them in using Google Earth and to allow them to see their local area from a birds-eye view.

Many thanks to Jasmine Brown, Kathleen Hargreaves and Lucy Hodges (Year 3 Initial Teacher Training students at Chichester University) for the above case study.

The children found using Google Earth interesting and liked using the street view feature, especially to find their own houses. Although they found it quite easy to use, adult support was needed to show the whole class how to use it in the first place.

The walk around the local area provided a context, meaning, and value to using Google Earth. The children could experience the features first hand and related the images they saw on Google Earth to what they could see on the walk. The activity was also made relevant by explaining to the children that they could use Google Earth to find the houses of their friends, which would stop them from getting lost on the way. While on the walk the children identified their likes and dislikes of the local environment, for example, they concluded that they did not like the amount of litter and dog mess that they came across. These likes and dislikes were then recorded on their own maps and such information could be used in future geography lessons.

From this case study, it is evident that an ICT resource such as Google Earth could be used to support children's acquisition of geographical skills in a very engaging manner. These very young children were able to combine outdoor learning experiences with technology to progress their understanding of this subject in a meaningful context.

Case study

Some Year 5 children (aged 9 and 10 years) were introduced to GPS (Global Positioning System) as a geographical navigational tool and were told what GPS stands for. They then discussed with a partner what it could be used for and what its function could be. In discussion the children decided that global means 'world' and that positioning means 'where you are', and that a system is like a 'device'. From this they came to the conclusion that a GPS was a 'device that told you where you are in the world'. The children then talked about coordinates and how they could be given coordinates of a certain place and then use these to navigate their way using a GPS. The geographical language that occurred in this discussion was rich and was developed from discussing the GPS devices.

Many thanks to Jasmine Brown, Kathleen Hargreaves and Lucy Hodges (Year 3 Initial Teacher Training students at Chichester University) for the above case study.

The children were shown how to use the GPS, double clicking a button twice to see the menu and using the cursor button to navigate through the menu and select options. They found it quite tricky at first, but after some support and experimentation they soon knew how to use the features. The children were asked to find the games application on the menu and go on the game called 'Geko Smak'. With this they had to use the GPS to catch the Geko on the screen, navigating their way on the field. This activity was used as a warm-up to help the children to understand and use the features of the GPS. They discovered that the device is very sensitive and therefore has to be held in a particular position.

Next, the children were shown that on the top of the home screen of the GPS there was a series of numbers called 'coordinates'. The children were quizzed about what the coordinates were. Through discussion they correctly concluded that the coordinates were an indicator for where they were positioned. Next, the children were given coordinates with a riddle to support them, for example: 'I drink, but not from a glass; I eat with ten thousand fingers. What am I? 50.87, −0.99'. The children then used the coordinates of their current position as a basis to find the given location and coordinates; by using a riddle it ensured that the activity had purpose and once they reached the correct destination there was another riddle waiting.

The children also navigated their way around the playground using an iPhone, using the 'Maps' application. They looked at their positioning by satellite and could see the markings on the playground. The children walked around the field watching their positioning change.

These activities provided ample opportunities for children to use ICT and develop their geographical language. They decided that they would use the iPhone rather than the GPS device, because 'an iPhone is easier to use, you always have it with you and it has other applications on it'. One boy said that the GPS would be good for adults to use and could also identify that a sat' nav' also used a Global Positioning System, therefore showing he was able to apply its purpose to different types of technology.

> ### Developing practice
>
> To develop effective practice, we need to consider:
>
> - the technological home/school divide;
> - the different technology capabilities with which children come to school;
> - creative and meaningful uses of ICT;
> - that children should be digitally and critically literate;
> - how children should participate in new mechanisms for communication;
> - that children should be safe when using technology;
> - in what ways children should be technologically capable;
> - how and why children should know how to 'control' equipment.

Conclusion

Think about how many times a day we now rely on technology for work and leisure – it is hard to imagine a world without the internet, for instance. In many parts of the world, technology has become integral to people's lives, and it is our responsibility to provide a fulfilling and engaging technology curriculum to our children to help prepare them to operate in the twenty-first century. Technology offers new and innovative ways for children to communicate and these should be embraced and explored as learning strategies. Technology is an exciting and creative tool that should exist alongside, and complement, more traditional types of learning to enhance the experience of the child when in school.

References

Alexander, R. (2009) *Children, Their World, Their Education: Final Report and Recommendations of the Cambridge Primary Review.* London: Routledge.

Barber, D. and Cooper, L. (2012) *New Web Tools in the Primary Classroom.* London: Routledge.

Bazalgette, C. (2010) *Teaching Media in Primary Schools.* London: Media Education Association.

BECTA (2004) *A Review of the Research Literature on Barriers to the Uptake of ICT by Teachers.* Available at: http://dera.ioe.ac.uk/1603/1/becta_2004_barrierstouptake_litrev.pdf (accessed March 2012).

BECTA (2008) *Personalising Learning in a Connected World: A Guide for School Leaders*: Available at: http://trustnet.learningtrust.co.uk/Trust/Services/ICT/ICT%20Docs/Personalised%20Learning%20in%20a%20Connected%20World.pdf (accessed March 2012).

Burns, J. (2012) School ICT to be replaced by computer science programme, *BBC News Online*, 11 January. Available at: http://www.bbc.co.uk/news/education-16493929 (accessed March 2012).

Cross, C. (2012) Why we need to bring creativity and technology back together across the curriculum, *The Guardian Online, Teacher Network Blog*, 21 March. Available at: http://www.guardian.co.uk/teacher-network/teacher-blog/2012/mar/21/creativity-technology-classroom-teaching (accessed April 2012).

Department for Children, Schools and Families (DCSF) (2008) *Safer Children in a Digital World: The Report of the Byron Review.* Available at: http://www.education.gov.uk/ukccis/about/a0076277/thebyronreviews (accessed March 2013).

Greenfield, S. (2010) Computers in school could do more harm than good, *The Telegraph Online*, 12 February. Available at: http://www.telegraph.co.uk/education/7220021/Computers-in-schools-could-do-more-harm-than-good.html (accessed March 2012).

Lankshear, C. and Knobel, M. (2006) *New Literacies: Everyday Practices and Classroom Learning.* Buckingham: Open University Press

Lankshear, C. and Knobel, M. (2008) *Digital Literacies: Concepts, Policies and Practices.* New York: Peter Lang.

Mason, S. and Woolley, R. (2012) *Relationships and Sex Education 5–11: Supporting Children's Development and Well-being.* London: Continuum.

Miliband, D. (2004) Speech to North of England Education Conference, *Personalised Learning: Building a New Relationship with Schools,* Belfast: Available at: https://www.education.gov.uk/publications/eOrderingDownload/personalised-learning.pdf (accessed April 2012).

Prensky, M. (2003) *Has 'Growing Up Digital' and Extensive Video Game Playing Affected Younger Military Personnel's Skill Sets?* Paper presented at I/ITSEC 2003. Available at: http://www.marcprensky.com/writing/Prensky%20-%20Has%20Growing%20Up%20Digital%20Affected%20Military%20Skill%20Sets.pdf (accessed August 2012).

Puttnam, D. (2008) Building schools for the future, *Futurelab Podcast.* Available at: http://media.futurelab.org.uk/podcasts/becta_talks/lord_puttnam/ (accessed March 2012).

Rose, J. (2009) *The Independent Review of the Primary Curriculum.* Available at: http://publications.education.gov.uk/default.aspx?PageFunction=productdetails andPageMode=publications andProductId=DCSF-00499-2009 (accessed March 2012).

Selwyn, N., Potter, J. and Cranmer, S. (2010) *Primary School and ICT: Learning from Pupil Perspectives.* London: Continuum.

Sutherland, R., Robertson, S. and John, P. (2009) *Improving Classroom Learning with ICT.* London: Continuum.

Wheeler, S. (2005) *Transforming Primary ICT.* Exeter: Learning Matters.

CHAPTER

9

Voice

Mike Steele

> On the rusty bench, amid the quiet chaos, sits the teacher-gardener, frowning with questions. Which soil? Which fertilizer? Shade or sun? Too early to plant out? Will continual measuring really help? This one needs a trellis. That one will grow whatever the conditions. This one is withering – mulch and wait. Nature . . . or nurture?
>
> Then, musing done, thoughts are left hovering like a kestrel, while feet slide back into wellington boots, and dirty hands reach for the hoe before weeds make themselves at home. But, now and then, like full stops meeting at an ellipsis, teacher-gardeners gather, laugh at anecdotes of daisies and daffodils, bemoaning inclement weather, and resisting pressure to exhibit prize pumpkins when the inherited plot is full of daisies. Gardening secrets are whispered over coffee, before returning to the potting shed with renewed enthusiasm.
>
> Later, rushing anxiously through a concrete jungle, the teacher-gardener comes across a solitary oak, tall and majestic, roots firmly anchored in the values of its humble beginnings. It speaks. 'Hello, remember me? I was a sapling and you protected me. I wilted and you encouraged me. Thank you.' The teacher-gardener smiles, and waits for the next acorn to fall.
>
> *Sally Reed, Class teacher in Lincolnshire*

Introduction

A voice is expressed through language and it is primarily through talk that children develop their sense of identity as members of their culture and society

(Edwards, cited in Norman 1992). We teach and learn through language in its many forms. Indeed, Barnes, writing about the importance of talk for learning, suggests that one of the most important aspects of teaching is how the behaviour of teachers as listeners and respondents sends out tacit messages to children about the role they are expected to play as learners (Barnes, cited in Norman 1992). Bruner's final point in his book *Child's Talk* (1983) makes explicit the connection between language acquisition and the child's acquisition of their culture.

Language is one of the important means by which we make sense of our world and we do so by naming it. By writing, expressing our voice on paper, we verify this world that we see in passing, and our part in it. By reading, we name the world that is beyond what we see in the here and now (Meek 1991). We also hear the recorded 'voice' of others. The skills of speaking and listening, writing and reading that we use to make the unfamiliar familiar and the unknown knowable are at the very heart of learning. In these ways, we use language to learn about what is around us and beyond, and surely that is what we understand as education.

Among the aspirations of every teacher is that they should provide illumination on language, how we use it and how it is used. This is exemplified in the vignette that opens this chapter: the power of metaphor creates possibilities for myriad understandings of the author's ideas, and allows the reader to conjecture and imagine. This image of the teacher-gardener offers a far richer perspective than a simple dictionary definition could ever afford. This is also possible by making best use of language in the classroom: illumination for knowledge or understanding is a common metaphor in our culture. It is clearly there in our naming of the philosophical movement in the eighteenth century, the Age of Enlightenment, but goes back to the Bible, if not before. The importance of light, soil, water, and tending, each offers opportunities to begin to give voice to the notion of what a teacher may be.

This chapter considers the power and potential of language in education over the past centuries and in the present. We have already highlighted the fundamental feature of language to make meaning and we will consider how this may best be used as a tool for teaching and learning. We will take account of the theoretical background that underpins our understanding of how language works in the many forms we meet in the classroom and beyond. In turn, we will look at these elements – speaking, listening, reading, and writing (all ways of expressing our views or 'voice') – as the chapter moves on to focus on the primary classroom. We will also consider the creative power and potential of harnessing speaking and listening as a means to engage children and then explore and expand their learning.

Language and society

Case study

Consider the following account of two children discussing how to deal with a lost ball during playtime at school:

Paul: Thyat not reight in e-ad thee if tha thinks he's gunna let thee av ball back. He keeps em tha knows.
Amy: We're not gunna get anyweer if wi don't ask.
Paul: Thee gu then if tha thinks tha can gerit back.
Amy: Sir, please may I go and ask Mr. Fitter if we can get the ball back off his garage roof?' (Mr. Fitter was the caretaker, and the ball had been kicked onto his garage roof)
Teacher: Certainly Amy. I'm very pleased you asked me first.
Amy: Thank you sir.
Amy: See I teld thee, now we can gu through gate proper like.
Paul: Aie, but I wunt like to be thee when tha asks Fitter.

A voice is expressed through language and language is made up of words, but language is complex: people adapt and change words; they invent new ones and new ways of using them. Young children are great experimenters with language, often creating new grammatical forms to get their meaning across. For example, in her extensive research project into children's use of story language in storytelling, Fox (1993) cites various examples of children inventing new terms in their efforts to combine their existing grammatical knowledge with the associated analogy they have in mind. So when a child says 'flannel it clean' or 'bumble it down' for write it down quickly, two examples from my own experience in school, or I'm going to 'pliers' this out' when referring to getting spaghetti out of the pan, one of the examples Carol Fox cites from the work of Clark (1982), children are experimenting and inventing ways of using language, and discovering what language can do (Fox 1993).

Pause for thought

When children experiment or play with language, they are in effect finding their 'voice' and developing their 'style'. As teachers, therefore, we need to question our responses to such inventiveness. Consider:

• What is your reaction and what would your response be to the examples provided in the preceding paragraph and in the case study of Amy and Paul?

- Have you examples of your own?
- Do you find such experimentation more acceptable in the verbal form than written form, and if so why?
- What might hinder children's inventiveness with language?

Words exchanged by people refer to their common experience. Facts, ideas or events are communicated through language and refer to a stock of knowledge that people share. But language is not a neutral medium. It is not value free but instead reflects the attitudes and beliefs of those that use it. It not only expresses a shared culture, but also in many ways embodies it (Kramsch 2003).

Language and context

How language is spoken creates different meanings and these agreed forms vary from place to place and situation to situation. This is the subject of the extract from Paul and Amy's conversation: this example of everyday conversation in a Yorkshire school's playground shows two children exchanging comments in local dialect, but adopting Standard English to address their teacher. We may consider how our use of language changes according to audience, and the ways in which our choice of words and language structure differ whether we are with friends, family or in a formal setting.

The situation is by no means unique since young children learn from an early age that different language is called for in different places, with different people, and for different reasons. Expressions of politeness are central to interaction in a society and are reinforced by its institutions, such as family, government and, as in this case, its education system. In the primary school, we certainly encourage children to be polite and adopt positive values; demonstrated by the actions of the children and the polite way in which Amy addressed her teacher. She was no less polite in her exchanges with her friend; rather, the two of them accepted the dialect 'voice' as appropriate between them but adopted a different 'voice' to meet the expectations of their teacher. Children are very adept at adapting their talk for their audience. In this way, the social mores embodied in the language are strengthened.

We employ one voice, one set of language features, to go shopping and another voice comprising a different set of language features to visit the doctor. There are words and expressions that we use quite comfortably at home that we would not dream of using in school. These linguistic registers and vocabularies, which evolve over time, draw on a shared culture with its own history and traditions. Because of this a language can take on a symbolic value as an embodiment of a people and become closely associated with personal identity.

Written language, too, is culturally defined. Different sorts of texts have their own rules and structures whether, for example, they are literature, journalism or business. But the rules are not universal; they change depending upon the circumstances. This is an area that we address explicitly in primary school when we teach children to write using different language structures – for example, stories, letters, and poems – and in different genres – for example, fairy tales, ghost stories, adventures – and each one culturally defined.

Linguists have noted for some time that language changes according to the social setting. Changes in and the varieties of language used have formed a separate academic discipline for over half a century – sociolinguistics. But language does not just change according to a broad social setting; it is subtle and can change *within* that setting. As in the playground example, a child will have a vocabulary and adopt a different register for the classroom than for interacting with peers in the playground. Sometimes this classroom language is reinforced or taught explicitly by the teacher, but often it is learnt in the same way that language is learnt out of school: by listening and attempting it in situations that the child feels are appropriate. When we look at language in this way, it seems ever changing, in a state of constant flux and metamorphosis, but paradoxically it is also a strong and solid enough structure to provide the necessary scaffolding for children to build a voice in which they can learn.

Pause for thought

An awareness of the different structures of language we use is a first step to making use of them in our teaching. Either do the following exercise on your own or pool some ideas with friends:

- List the different situations during a typical school day in which you use a distinctly different form of spoken language; for example, meeting parents/carers as children come into school, taking the register, leading assembly.
- Examine why and how your 'voice' changes in different situations.
- Are there some situations where you feel more confident? Why are you less confident in others?
- What does this tell you about the child? What opportunities do children in your class have to express themselves in different situations using different forms of spoken language?

Similarly, make a list of the different forms of written language you use in a day, what you read and what you write. Ask similar questions, especially why you feel confident in one and not others, as this will help you identify with a child facing the complexity of language.

Language and history

This section surveys how language in its many forms has been used in the pursuit of learning over the centuries in England. Humans have connected language and learning for as long as there has been language. The bard who was able to perform and retain the poems or tales of a people was much revered in oral traditions before writing was adopted. This storyteller became the historian and repository of religious and moral values as well as the entertainer and bringer of news (Grainger 1997).

Religious groups identified early the power of reading and writing as a way of reinforcing and disseminating ideas and beliefs. Judaism, for example, is a religion based on a sacred text. Christianity adopted part of this text, added to it and this became central to its beliefs. Islam, too, is a religion based around a central authoritative text. This inevitably had implications for how those following these faiths would be educated (Lawton and Gordon 2005), with a strong emphasis placed on the ability to read, hear, recite, and understand the writings at the religion's heart.

With the invention of the printing press during the sixteenth century, texts that had been handwritten and limited to devotees were now available to many more people. Not only were texts available to many more readers but the range of reading now available in printed copies extended from the ancient to the contemporary. However, those who could take advantage of this newly available literacy were limited in the 1500s to the wealthy, who could afford the newly printed books, and the religious.

With the rise in Protestantism in the seventeenth century, it was seen as the duty of believers to read the gospel, not just listen to it interpreted by a priest, and thus a clear connection between religion and mass literacy was made (Lawton and Gordon 2005).

During the eighteenth century Age of Enlightenment, scientific method and reasoned argument were placed at the heart of the learning process – both of course expressed through language – by many of the thinkers of the time. Their goal was to understand Nature, that is to say the world around us, which resonates clearly with the central argument of this chapter outlined in its opening section. Here we also have an example of using the medium of language as a tool for thought, an idea echoed by educational writers to this day.

During the nineteenth century, many writers felt that education – and greater literacy in particular – was a desirable social goal in order for a widening electorate to make intelligent political choices and a profitable investment for society. It was also realized that through appropriate texts the poor might be introduced to the new science of economics, with lessons on 'thrift, better health, the avoidance of the pawnbroker and better shopping' (Lawton and Gordon 2005: 120). Early in the twentieth century, with the emergence of the new science of child psychology, researchers began to study closely how infants acquired language. Some, like Skinner, considered it to be a behaviour learned by imitating adults, which was then reinforced by them (Johnston and Nahmad-Williams 2009). Others, like Chomsky, questioned a model that saw human beings starting as a completely blank sheet on which language was imprinted, and asserted that, on the contrary, every person from an early age has an innate inclination to learn language; that very young children possess a universal grammar in part of the brain with which they can process and respond to language (Johnston and Nahmad-Williams 2009). These theories have echoed throughout the past century among educators, thinkers, and educational policy makers and continue to encapsulate the two positions in the debate about how children learn, not just language, but anything at all. Does learning take place solely through the nurture of children, regularly reinforced by the human beings and the surroundings in which they find themselves? Or is it in a child's nature to acquire knowledge, and is the extent of their ability to do so already preordained? This issue was raised at the very start of the chapter, within Sally Reed's metaphor.

Language and the curriculum

The 1990s saw the implementation of the National Curriculum, established in 1989, in schools in England. The influences for the English language component arose out of three major reports, first the Bullock Report (DfES 1975), then the Kingman Report (1988) followed by the Cox Report (Cox 1989). English that encompassed language across the curriculum derived chiefly from the Bullock Report, *A Language for Life*. A section highlighted in the Kingman Report under the heading of 'The Teaching of Language' explained that although teaching the linguistics of a subject discipline is desirable as recommended by Bullock, similarly teaching about the English language is equally desirable, hence 'Knowledge about Language' formed major sections of both the Kingman and Cox Reports. The revised National Curriculum (DfEE/QCA 1999) chose to focus on 'communication' as a Key Skill for promotion across the curriculum, thus emphasizing the main purpose of language, stating 'opportunities for developing this key skill are provided through English in particular and through pupils' use of language across the curriculum' (DfEE/QCA 1999: 20). One can see the emphasis in the National Curriculum was for the key skill to be taught as part of the English curriculum 'in particular', an aspect concomitant with the then current emphasis on the teaching of specific features of language and literacy through guidance documentation reinforced by the National Literacy Strategy (NLS) established in 1998 (DfEE 1998).

The NLS had come about because standards in literacy had not increased according to expectations of the government, and accumulating evidence from Ofsted (2010) suggested not enough teaching of literacy was happening in schools (Beard 2000). One of the most innovative and instrumental features of the Literacy Strategy highlighted by Beard (2000) is its structured and routine approach for teachers to share and explain the objectives of the lesson with their pupils, which had not been a feature in lessons prior to this initiative. Beard (2000) draws out Ralph Tyler's understanding for educational objectives to be used as the criteria by which materials are selected, content outlined, teaching approaches developed, and assessment procedures prepared, all very familiar territory for the contemporary teacher. Other innovations included shared reading and shared writing that included teacher demonstration and modelling of reading and writing to 'illuminate' the meta-cognitive processes indicative of the skills in each. For example, skimming and scanning non-fiction, reading inference in fiction, proofreading for spelling and grammar, editing and re-drafting.

The NLS drew upon a wealth of research concerned with the teaching of English and raising standards (Beard 2000), and while the profession was critical about the prescriptive nature of the strategy and the lack of emphasis given to speaking and listening, it nevertheless set in motion many good aspects of teaching we now take for granted. With respect to the latter criticism, the NLS aimed to provide specific guidance to support the National Curriculum, which at that time stated that speaking and listening should constitute a third of the English component with reading and writing taking up the other two-thirds, each inextricably linked. It was never envisaged as taking away the statutory rights of the child; however, Standardized Assessment Tasks predominantly addressing reading and writing and not speaking and listening formed the basis of the pressure teachers felt to concentrate on their teaching of reading and writing. To address growing concerns about perceived neglect in teaching speaking and listening, a resource pack entitled *Speaking, Listening, Learning* (DfES/QCA 2003) was developed and sent to all schools, but pressures in schools meant dissemination was patchy. The resource drew upon significant research cited for further reading at the end of the handbook for teachers, including Alexander's (2000) five nations' study of pedagogy and culture that identified dialogic teaching as a way towards developing pedagogy in England; Dawes and colleagues' (2000) work on thinking together for the co-construction of knowledge; and Neelands and Goode's (1991) extensive work on drama in the classroom; as well as identifying the importance of storytelling in the classroom through such studies as that of Howe and Johnson (1992). Emphasis was also given to the assessment and progression of speaking and listening skills. This, together with calls for more creativity in the curriculum, first heralded in 2001 through the (NACCCE) publication *All Our Futures* (DfEE 2001) and followed by *Excellence and Enjoyment: A Strategy for Primary Schools* (DfES 2003) empowering schools to develop their own character, take control of their curriculum, and to be more innovative, provided a new and exciting backdrop for schools to pursue their shared ideals. Instrumental in innovations in pedagogy, particularly with respect to giving children a stronger voice in their learning, was Alexander's (2004) short paper, 'Towards dialogic teaching', where he claims from the outset that what he calls dialogic teaching uses the power of language, particularly speaking and listening, both to stimulate and extend the thinking of children and therefore also their learning and understanding. He outlines a model of learning where children construct meaning not just through assimilating and accommodating it alongside what they already know, after Piaget, but also through their linguistic encounters with others including their peers and adults, calling to mind Vygotsky's important writing in this area to develop a child's potential understanding (Vygotsky 1978; Alexander 2004). Alexander makes explicit the link between spoken language and learning and reminds us that this is central to a child's cognitive development. In doing so, he also reasserts the important link between language and thought (Alexander 2004).

Language and the primary classroom 1

> **Case study**
>
> Jacob, aged 10, recommends a book to the class:
>
> 'I really enjoyed this book because it has a good story and it is funny. Not just boys would like it. And you don't have to be a good reader to read it. I think anyone in this class could read it.'

Let us now look more closely at good practice in making use of the different aspects of language as a vital tool for learning and enabling children to express their views. We will look at the different aspects in turn: reading, writing, speaking, and listening. In a classroom where reading, for example, is valued, children talk about it. They are encouraged to do so with the teacher, other adults, and between themselves. This is very much in line with Alexander's (2004) model where talk is a tool for learning. In this classroom, if a visitor asks a question about their books, the children will answer it, as they will have learnt and practised using language of evaluation and appreciation associated with review.

The role of the teacher is central here, as he or she is likely to have been the facilitator and model for the children to learn this skill. He or she is likely to plan in time for the children to develop and practise the language of talking about reading. Time, as we know, can be in short supply in the primary classroom but an opportunity to read and talk about reading is time well spent. It might be time for individuals to read and discuss their book with a more experienced other – to echo Vygotsky (1978) again – whether it be an older child, teaching assistant, parent/ carer or helper. It might also be in groups for phonics, shared and guided reading in Literacy lessons or other timetabled activities. It might be the opportunity to sit down as a class and for children to recommend the book they are reading to their peers (as with Jacob in the case study). I suggest that in a classroom where reading is valued, a teacher might plan in time for all of these things, as such activities provide valuable opportunities for children to express their opinions, face their opinions being challenged, and in doing so find justifiable reasons to substantiate their opinions. In this way, children learn the way in which opinion is achieved and as a consequence appreciated by others rather than rejected. Speaking and listening can be used as a tool to reinforce the practice and enjoyment of reading. One need look no further than the Book Clubs that have sprung up around the UK in recent years to see further evidence of this beyond the primary classroom.

Reading and writing are closely connected; one informs the other. To give richness and variety to our spoken and written language, we have to hear and experience that language. To give structure to our writing, we have to meet, come to terms with, and learn the various written forms prevalent in our culture. One of the jobs of the primary teacher is to present, model, and teach these forms. They range widely from appropriate messages on greetings cards to the study of literary genres and should include fiction and non-fiction, poetry as well as prose. Modelling what is involved in writing is possibly one of the most powerful tools for teaching writing. It is a way of demonstrating the mental struggle that takes place when composing writing, such as decisions about why one word works better than another, how punctuation can mimic oral expressions and gestures and thus aid meaning, and how grammatical structures such as clause structure also aid meaning. Modelling writing is not solely the task of the teacher, but should be shared with the children so that they, like the teacher, through talking through their thinking while composing in front of others, can explain the meta-cognitive processes involved. Children who are confident writers are in effect empowered to make permanent their voice through writing.

Studying texts to reveal how they have been constructed is also another worthy teaching tool. Rather like a scientist examining some rare specimen or phenomenon, examining text can be equally exciting and revealing. Indeed, taking on the role of 'language detective' that we have seen some teachers adopt to demonstrate investigation and convey specific knowledge about language has the effect of motivating the children to want to find out how language works, knowing it is more powerful when it works best. Children who know how to compose their writing to best effect know too the feeling of empowerment it engenders.

One final point concerning writing is to draw attention to the artistic nature of writing rather than the mere technical aspects. Hardy (1968: 5) said that 'narrative like lyric or dance, is not to be regarded as an aesthetic invention used by artists to control, manipulate, and order experience, but as a primary act of mind transferred to art from life'. Her famous quotation is as valuable today as it was in 1968 as a reminder that at the heart of language lie the human stories waiting to be told. If this is the case, then as teachers we need to ask what opportunities we give to children to express their life stories. Rachael Paige, in her chapter on *Narrative*, explores the question in detail, but for the purposes of this chapter one cannot ignore the significance of personal stories that make up a child's 'voice' in the world.

Pause for thought

- Think about children who arrive in your classroom from other countries, and ask yourself what you know about their lives and how can they inform you.
- How might you as a teacher hear their 'voice'?

One way is to embrace the variety of ways children express themselves and their stories, for example through drawing, music, dance, and drama, and embrace their writing albeit in another language while they grapple with the new. Not to provide opportunities for children to express themselves, or to extinguish expression because we cannot understand it, is to extinguish the voice of the child. Voice extends language and is the greater entity because within it lays the basic human right to be. A teacher who interprets the artistic expression of a child's story for the child in writing to be shared and told to other children is giving 'voice' to that child.

Language and the primary classroom 2

Case study

Sarah, aged 9, looks back in her journal over the last few weeks of poetry:

'I think I have learnt that when you read a poem it is not always what it seems. So you have to read it again and again before you know what it is really about. I have learnt the 'Paint Box' with Sheila and Lisa. I have sort of learnt 'Cargoes' with Sheila. I like learning them with other people.'

Poetic forms on the page are easily discernible and therefore are not difficult to perceive for the child, or model for the teacher. But it is important to consider the idea, expressed by the poet Elizabeth Bishop, that if the sound of poetry is forgotten, a whole level of meaning is lost (cited in Astley 2002). In the best classrooms where reading and writing are valued, poetry is *heard*. Sometimes it is read aloud by individuals; children also seem to really enjoy reading poetry with friends and sometimes it is read as a whole-class activity. There is a strong connection between poetry and song; a verse in a poem is closely allied to a verse in music. They certainly can look the same on the page. In this way, poetry can also be committed to memory, often with very little effort, in the same way a child sings and the music remains in the mind (which is reminiscent of the comments made by Sarah in the case study).

Poetry is an ideal form of language to explore in guided reading. Its words are carefully chosen, often carefully patterned, and can be studied as a complete piece rather than an extract. As Sarah says in the case study, a poem is not always what it seems after an initial reading and a careful re-reading, guided by a sensitive teacher, will encourage the development of higher reading skills such as inference and deduction.

Language and the primary classroom 3

Case study

A head teacher reflects on a Mantle of the Expert project:

'What pleased me most was the engagement, energy, and excitement of everyone, the staff and the children. I liked the way that the children who normally fade into the background came forward, in character, and were listened to. I was really pleased with the quality of the work they produced and this was reflected in the SATs results, particularly in Literacy.'

Let us not forget the speaking and listening that occurs in drama that can be used highly effectively to enhance learning in the primary classroom. In *Speaking, Listening, Learning* (DfES /QCA 2003), techniques such as hot seating, conscience alley, and paired improvisation are used to go deeper into a given situation and explore the thinking and motives of participants and broaden the thinking of the children involved. Heathcote's work in her 'Mantle of the Expert' approach takes the idea of providing a situation for learning one stage further, with the group of participants creating and then operating within a powerful imagined scenario as they learn; whether it be a medieval monastery (Heathcote and Bolton 1995) or a modern media company. This scenario or context, which takes on great significance over the life of the project, is created through language, initially modelled by the teacher and then gradually adopted by the children taking part as their own (Heathcote and Bolton 1995). The idea of a context for learning fostering better understanding harkens back to the much earlier work of Donaldson (1978) and it is still a powerful and worthwhile tool for learning.

Another aspect of speaking and listening that can be employed effectively as a tool for learning is when children evaluate their own and each other's work. This can take the form of a discussion with another adult, often the teacher. As in the case of guided reading, mentioned earlier, and when establishing the context for the 'Mantle of the Expert', it is the teacher that is crucial as the model for the language to be used and gradually this language is taken on by the children and used to further their learning and understanding. Clarke has written extensively on the subject: about how this language might include sharing goals or objectives, providing feedback after a child has completed a task, recognizing next steps in their learning, and agreeing how to take them (Clarke 2001). The clear link between this sort of formative assessment and using language as a tool for learning was recognized by Alexander (2004) and it is an important part of the teaching process.

Developing practice

To develop effective practice, we need to consider:

- how we can support children in developing language so that they can express their views and 'voice';
- how we show that language differs according to context and purpose, and affirm that these different voices are valued and valuable;
- how we can support children in expressing their personal story, to help them to find their voice;
- how we model sharing views and ideas through speaking, listening, writing, and reading together.

Conclusion

In this chapter, we have considered the power and potential of language in education. There has been an emphasis on the fundamental feature of language to make meaning and how this valuable tool can be employed to explore and expand children's learning in the primary school. Attention has been drawn to the link between speaking, listening, reading, and writing. We have considered the value of poetry and particularly drama, sometimes overlooked in the curriculum, and its huge potential to engage and empower even the most retiring and reluctant learners.

A voice is built using language that is complex and powerful. It draws much of its power from the desire of every human being to make meaning: to make sense of the world – an idea recognized by many writers who have made the key connections between language, thought, and understanding. These links, when recognized and utilized in the primary classroom, can be a force for good. By helping children to build a voice using means touched on in this chapter, the teacher will be providing them with a powerful linguistic tool for their learning now in the primary school and for learning about learning in the future. We leave the last word to Michael Halliday (1993: 5, cited in Alexander 2004):

> When children learn language they are not simply engaging in one type of learning among many; rather they are learning the foundations of learning itself.

References

Alexander, R. (2000) *Culture and Pedagogy: International Comparisons in Primary Education.* Oxford: Blackwell.

Alexander, R. (2004) *Towards Dialogic Teaching.* Cambridge: Dialogos.

Astley, N. (ed.) (2002) *Staying Alive: Real Poems for Unreal Times.* Trowbridge: Bloodaxe.

Beard, R. (2000) Research and the National Literacy Strategy, *Oxford Review of Education,* 26(3/4): 421–36. Available at: http://eprints.ioe.ac.uk/1436/1Beard2000Researchandthe NationalLiteracyStrategy.

Bruner, J. (1983) *Child's Talk: Learning to Use Language.* Oxford: Oxford University Press.

Clark, E.V. (1982) The young word maker: a case study of innovation in the child's lexicon, in E. Wanner and L.R. Gleitman (eds.) *Language Acquisition: The State of the Art.* Cambridge: Cambridge University Press.

Clarke, S. (2001) *Unlocking Formative Assessment.* London: Hodder & Stoughton.

Cox, B. (1989) *English for Ages 5–16 (The Cox Report).* London: DES.

Dawes, L., Mercer, N. and Wegerif, R. (2000) *Thinking Together: A Programme for Developing Speaking, Listening and Thinking Skills for Children Aged 8–11.* Birmingham: Imaginative Minds Ltd.

Department for Education and Employment (DfEE) (1998) *The National Literacy Strategy: Framework for Teaching.* London: DfEE.

Department for Education and Employment (DfEE) (2001) *All Our Futures: Creativity, Culture and Education.* Nottingham: DfEE.

Department for Education and Employment/Qualifications and Curriculum Authority (DfEE/QCA) (1999) *The National Curriculum: Handbook for Primary Teachers in England (Key Stages 1 and 2).* London: DfEE/QCA.

Department for Education and Science (DES) (1975) *A Language for Life* (Bullock Report). London: HMSO.

Department for Education and Skills (DfES) (2003) *Excellence and Enjoyment: A Strategy for Schools*, London: DfES.

Department for Education and Skills/Qualifications and Curriculum Agency (DES/QCA) (2003) *Speaking, Listening, Learning: Working with Children in Key Stages 1 and 2.* Norwich: HMSO.

Donaldson, M. (1978) *Children's Minds.* London: Fontana.

Fox, C. (1993) *At the Very Edge of the Forest: The Influence of Literature on Storytelling by Children.* London: Cassell.

Grainger, T. (1997) *Traditional Storytelling in the Primary Curriculum.* Glasgow: Scholastic.

Halliday, M.A.K. (1993) *Towards a Language Based Theory of Learning.* Linguistics in Learning, 5, cited in Alexander, R. (2004) *Towards Dialogic Teaching.* Cambridge: Dialogos.

Hardy, B. (1968) Towards a poetics of fiction: (3) An approach through narrative, *NOVEL: A Forum on Fiction*, 2(1): 5–14.

Heathcote, D. and Bolton, G. (1995) *Drama for Learning.* Portsmouth, NH: Heinemann.

Howe, A. and Johnson, J. (1992) *Common Bonds: Storytelling in the Classroom.* London: Hodder & Stoughton.

Johnston, J. and Nahmad-Williams, L. (2009) *Early Childhood Studies.* Harlow: Pearson.

Kingman Report (1988) *Report of the Committee of Inquiry into the Teaching of English Language.* London: HMSO.

Kramsch, C. (2003) *Language and Culture.* Oxford: Oxford University Press.

Lawton, D. and Gordon, P. (2005) *A History of Western Educational Ideas.* London: Woburn.

Meek, M. (1991) *On Being Literate.* London: Bodley Head.

Neelands, J. and Goode, T. (1991) *Structuring Drama Work.* Cambridge: Cambridge University Press.

Norman, K. (1992) *Thinking Voices: The Work of the National Oracy Project.* London: Hodder & Stoughton.

Ofsted (2010) *Reading by Six.* London: Ofsted.

Vygotsky, L. (1978) *Mind in Society.* London: Harvard University Press.

10 Inclusion

Karen Elvidge

> 66 Robert, aged 8, shared his experience of an incident on the way to school. Supported by his signing assistant, he described how, that morning, he had driven past the marina and it was there that he had spotted a swan, lying motionless in the water. The other children wanted more information and he was asked what he thought had happened. His face lit up, he created his own version of a sign for a shark, 'Jaws', and made rhythmical noises associated with the film of the same name. 99

Introduction

The school that Robert attended comprised fully inclusive classes where every member of staff had high expectations of all of the children and every child was considered to be special and unique but also to have individual needs, which needed to be met to maximize the opportunities for learning, and where shared values were put into action. Robert was hearing impaired but this did not define who he was because the school valued Robert, his quirky sense of humour, his sense of fairness, and his enthusiasm for learning about natural history. He was fully accepted as a contributing member of the class community rather than being identified by a deficit label, 'The deaf child'.

Robert had been fitted with a cochlear implant, giving him some ability to process sound on one side, when facing the sound source. He had learned to speak before meningitis, at the age of 2, had left him with bi-lateral deafness. He was confident in communicating using British Sign Language and was keen to share some signs with other members of his class. Robert was confident that his narrative recount would be valued by the members of his class because of the inclusive ethos of the school modelled by all staff and understood by all of the children. In that inclusive environment, he was empowered to be a full and contributing member of the class community.

Defining inclusion

Early definitions of inclusion (Warnock Committee 1978) related to the entitlement for all children to a broad and rich curriculum within a mainstream class where this was not to the detriment of other children. In England, the National Inclusion Statement (DfE 2011) simplistically and mechanistically defines inclusion through mandating a curriculum that provides relevant and challenging learning for all children following three principles:

- setting suitable learning challenges;
- responding to pupils' diverse learning needs;
- overcoming potential barriers to learning and assessment for individuals and groups of pupils.

Inclusion is never simplistic and mechanistic and current informed debate, led in part by Baroness Warnock, continues to question whether it is in the interest of some children to include all children in mainstream classrooms.

Ainscow and Booth (2011) agree with the underpinning principles of the National Inclusion Statement, adding that inclusion is also about the self-audit of the core values and ethos of the whole school from the head teacher to the youngest member of the community and a determination to put a framework of common values into action. A truly inclusive learning environment is empirical: a living, learning, adapting community.

In this environment, the development of the school's culture, policies, and practices involves the staff, parents/carers, and children together in developing the ethos of the school, through the detail of a school improvement plan that empowers both adults and children to voice necessary changes. Working together, the school community develops a passion for social justice, global citizenship, sustainability, rights and values, and responds to meeting the diversity and needs of the whole school 'family' and 'community'. Changes in the learning environment and practice are seen as developmental, with advice from external agencies, through informed reflection on individual children's needs within the school and with an awareness of children who potentially may enter the school in the future.

Inclusion in this definition is a learning process that starts by valuing the children in terms of 'uniqueness', and provides appropriate resources to support personalized learning, rather than seeing 'needs' as problems or barriers to be overcome.

Pause for thought

Drawing on your experience and knowledge of the education system in your context, consider:

- Why might teachers be anxious about inclusion?
- Is this because many practitioners define inclusion in terms of anxiety about defined difference?
- How might a sense of the uniqueness of each individual member of the school 'family' help to address any issues or anxieties?

National student surveys in England clearly show a gap between the understanding that is demonstrated in curriculum provision in schools and the confidence of teachers evidenced in the responses of individuals, in particular those who are newly qualified as teachers, because all children are different and do not fall neatly into simple stereotypes.

This chapter promotes Doveston and Keenaghan's (2006) 4 D cycle of 'appreciative inquiry' as an approach to developing inclusion within classrooms and schools, removing the fear of difference (and associated responsibility) with developing experience. Doveston and Keenaghan (2006) define appreciative inquiry, in relation to inclusion, as action research that pro-actively learns from what is working well with real children in the context of a real classroom, rather than basing provision on assumed and stereotypical needs or assuming that one child with a labelled need will have the same needs as another child with a similar label.

Case study

Jon likes to spend his time using the computer. He prefers to work on his own and can be aggressive with other children. He has autism. William needs to follow a visual timetable and finds change to his routine disturbing. He also finds the dining hall unbearable unless he wears his white noise eliminating earphones. He flaps his hands when distressed, curls into a ball and rocks. He also has autism.

Reflecting on this example:

- Can you identify the adjustments that are necessary to include Jon?
- Can you identify the adjustments that are necessary to include William?

Both boys have autistic spectrum disorder (ASD) but different reasonable adjustments are needed to enable both to function in the mainstream classroom and in the wider school context.

Inclusion is about the practitioner appreciating *the child* before *the difference*. The case study identifies the children by the adjustment to be made and the barriers to be overcome. It says little about their interests and the qualities they bring as members of the class.

To achieve inclusion, teachers need to be informed and reflective practitioners: informed about a child's specific individual needs and learning differences, and reflective about the whole child, starting with the child to explore how to meet those differences and needs with confidence. This starts cerebrally with the language used to describe Jon. Is he 'the autistic child' or is he 'Jon'?

Developing confidence

According to Ofsted, the government regulatory and inspection body in England (2008: 11), confidence relates to a sound understanding of how to plan for progression for all children, a culture of sharing previous experience, and a knowledge of common techniques to overcome most barriers to learning. It is also about immersion in a busy classroom, discovering each child's prior life and world experience, mores and traditions, self-identity, talents, and personal circumstances and is rooted in proactively developing good relationships with all of the children and their parents and carers.

The school is the small beginning of an inclusive society, although there will arguably remain a small number of children whose needs are best met in specialist provision with targeted services. An inclusive school enables an ethos of acceptance, collaboratively with each child, as a starting point for developing appropriate learning for individuals and groups within the classroom. An inclusive school believes that every child can learn, really listens to children and their parents and carers, and has high expectations of all children's progress in learning without expecting children to fit into broad stereotypical groups, based on protected characteristics. In essence, an inclusive school is child centred, with a holistic view of learning and teaching that moves practice forward from 'Every Child Matters' (DfES 2004b) to what parents already know – that 'every child is special and precious'.

To achieve full inclusion, all teachers and practitioners need to engage in responsible, professional dialogue with more experienced colleagues and be open minded enough to take risks to try out new ways of working, or reflect on personal assumptions made that relate to personal prior life and world experience. Sometimes this will involve making errors in communication and these errors will challenge personal assumptions and stereotypes.

For example, in many classrooms teachers make gender assumptions that there are two sexes within the class, namely 'boys' and 'girls'. Progress has been made in access to resources that were traditionally defined for 'boys' or 'girls', but discrimination is still seen in teacher perceptions. For a number of children, the received definitions of 'sex' or 'gender' are less clear-cut and it is informative to count how many times a day and in how many ways an assumption of children as 'girlie-girls' or 'manly boys' diminishes the increasing number of children who have an awareness of their own difference from those stereotypes. Watch lines of children walking to assembly or washing hands for lunch: how often is the line defined as a pattern of girl, boy, girl, boy?

Self-identity relates to personal appearance, ability, gender and cultural background, and a lack of acceptance of self-identity presents a major barrier to inclusion as children self-assess their value against received social norms (Dowling 2005; Smith et al. 2003). These evaluations influence self-esteem and self-efficacy, and low self-esteem leads to lack of educational progress.

Statistics reveal that almost two-thirds of lesbian, gay, bisexual, and transsexual (LGBT) people have experienced and have been diminished by homophobic bullying in mainstream schools because of the projected stereotypes of 'boys' and 'girls'. Staff expectations within the school identify the child as different and therefore the bully's victim. The figure increases to 75 per cent in faith schools, diminishing children every day by an awareness of personal difference from the received norm. Guasap (2007) reports that half of all teachers fail to respond to homophobic language in both the playground and classroom and three in five children fail to intervene on behalf of another child. Children, therefore, become bystanders to homophobic bullying because they are not made aware of the devastating consequences for other children. It is important for all teachers to become familiar with current terminology so that distinctions are understood between biological 'sex' and socially constructed 'gender', as these terms are no longer interchangeable. 'Sex' relates to biological, physiological, and anatomical differences, whereas 'gender' refers to social expectations about behaviours, dress, and roles. For example, within the classroom, overt gender exclusion is experienced when girls are told that construction materials are 'boys' toys' or that only boys are allowed to play football. Teachers must acknowledge self-identity. Lasting emotional damage may occur when children define themselves other than as determined by their sex at birth yet feel unable to live as their preferred gender until adulthood.

A rich understanding of inclusion, starting with the child, demands a holistic and forward-thinking approach to individuality and self-identity, rather than staff being careful not to discriminate against individuals because of their protected characteristics (as identified in the Equality Act 2010). This demands deep self-reflection to recognize that the teacher's stereotypical responses can and do raise barriers to learning. The Equality Act 2010 requires that, in England, the impact of professional practice is assessed with reference to its effect on classifications of groups of people and it highlights the needs to:

- *eliminate unlawful discrimination*, harassment, victimization, and any other conduct prohibited by the Act;
- *advance equality of opportunity* between people who share a protected characteristic and people who do not share it;
- *foster good relations* between people who share a protected characteristic (such as age, gender, ethnicity).

Teachers are mandated to provide 'Quality First teaching' (DCSF 2008: 9) for all children and to track individual progress in learning, seriously and responsibly, in order to identify and personalize the necessary reasonable adjustments for individual learners. These must be social as well as physical and curriculum adjustments. Valuing people rather than stereotypes is thus at the heart of inclusionary policies. Valuing the child's self-identity grows self-esteem. A class of children that value and respect each other grows inclusion.

Pause for thought

From the case studies outlined earlier, Robert's difference was an obvious sensory loss that could be met with support from his signing assistant. Jon's needs could be met by providing him with personal space and a laptop. William's needs could be met by providing white noise earphones and a 'time-out' space when the noise became intolerable. But a child who is gender different may have needs and anxieties that are deep-rooted and less obvious. Take a moment to reflect on what these might be:

- in relation to school uniform;
- in relation to cloakroom facilities;
- in relation to seating arrangements and social grouping;
- in relation to playtime.

All teachers need first-hand experience of the joys and sorrows of working with a child or children with special needs, disabilities or gender differences to begin to develop a 'hearts and minds' awareness of what this means in practice. To this end, the Teaching Agency (2012) has produced a set of tasks to guide trainees and newly qualified teachers in informed reflective practice, so as to link the theory with the practice of working with real children rather than discussing stereotypical medical deficit labels of need and disability. This is an excellent starting point for all practitioners to action plan growth in inclusive practice through apprecia-tive inquiry.

Davis and Florian (2004) emphasize that most of what is considered to be good practice in learning and teaching pedagogy for all children, is good practice for children with special educational needs and disabilities, children from culturally diverse backgrounds, and children who are gifted and talented and/or gender different.

Inclusion necessitates reflection on the messages that the learning environment engenders for the children and the subsequent removal of images and resources that perpetuate gender, disability, and cultural stereotypes. Practitioners should further reflect on developing the environment with books and other resources that reflect positive images of difference and inclusion for the current class and for all children. Controversially, children do not see difference other than in terms of curiosity. Adults enculture intolerance because of their own learned prej-udices and ignorance. The first steps in creating an inclusive classroom requires teachers to find out:

- what each child can do;
- what each child likes to do; and
- what each child thinks they are good at.

This maximizes the opportunities for each child to show the best of what they can do and engage in personal target setting to develop the weaker areas of their work at a manageable pace.

Nind et al. (2003) suggest that striving for equal access means enabling all children and young people to participate fully in education as barriers to learn-ing are removed. For example, teachers reflect on the layout of the classroom and seating that allows all of the children to see and hear the teacher. Low-level disruption is minimized by encouraging classroom talk related to 'on-task activ-ity', instead of playground chatter. Displays are regularly enhanced and used as visual prompts and resources are labelled in pictures and words and are stored for independent access by all, including wheelchair users. Is this enough? Does it take into account the importance of dignity, self, and self-esteem as the cata-lyst to owning the learning process? Or is it simply that inclusive schools are concerned with the wellbeing of all children as part of a planned, resourced, and monitored equal opportunities policy without a need for positively valuing people?

The Salamanca Statement (UNESCO 1994, cited in Wearmouth et al. 2004) mandates members of staff, teachers, schools, communities, and education sys-tems to fulfil needs and facilitate inclusive learning and teaching. This demands an ethos of zero tolerance for bullying, discrimination, and harassment. It also requires that teachers reflect on the social dynamics of the classroom rather than focusing on difficulties, problems, and political correctness.

Dean (2000) highlights the importance of the learning environment and the whole-school ethos, providing a positive and consistent learning atmosphere that includes a variety of groupings of children. This includes: whole-class teaching, mixed-ability groups, groups organized by prior attainment, think-pair-share groups, and the setting of individual targets and clear learning objectives. It also requires an informed reflective approach by the team of professionals to ensure the effectiveness of the learning and teaching environment, taking evidence of progress from formative, summative, and periodic assessment. Corbett (2001) also highlights the role of the teacher in the identification and minimization of barriers to learning and participation and the maximization of appropriate resources. This includes valuing positive visual literacy, the use of visual cues, hand signals and prompts, class routines, the use of ICT, alternative methods of communication such as pictures and symbols, and making use of alternative ways for children to record their ideas other than through the written medium.

Learners should be encouraged to explore how they learn best and this may not necessarily be limited to a preferred learning style. As in the vignette that opened this chapter, Robert, with a sensory deprivation related to effective communication, overcomes this by using the signing assistant as a translator or as an alternative form of communication to engage in the dialogic communication of a busy classroom.

Hughes (2001) argues that multisensory learning increases the likelihood of learning being remembered, as different sensory memories are stored in different areas of the brain. Clough and Corbett (2000) agree with a multisensory approach. Teachers need to be flexible and adaptable, recognizing that learners have different ways of understanding and interpreting information that are personally unique. Mittler (2000) agrees and the TDA (2008) support the notion of flexibility in approach and the choice of learning objectives to promote progress, making links where possible to topics that are related.

Identifying barriers to learning

There are different ways of identifying barriers to learning. Historically, a medical deficit model of disability defined a child by his or her negative attributes (Table 10.1). In this model, the problem is seen as the child. Pollard (2002) discusses how in the past people were defined by their disability, seen as 'abnormal' or 'sub-normal', and sometimes were placed in institutions, often locked in, far from their local community, denied access to a full family life, to employment, and to a voice.

Table 10.1   The medical model of disability

Confined to a wheelchair	*Suffers* from dyslexia, dyspraxia, dysgraphia, dyscalculia	*Slow* learner/cognitive *delay*
Can't read	Blind	Deaf
ADHD (Attention *Deficit* Hyperactivity Disorder)	Has receptive language *problems* (*difficulty* in understanding language)	*Low* self-esteem
Suffers from diabetes	*Crippled by* cerebral palsy	Autistic Spectrum *Disorder*

Sometimes this model is used as an excuse to label people and sort them into neat categories so that services can be targeted to meet needs: 'the SEN child', 'the deaf child', the blind child, 'the EAL child', or defined by their gender dysphoria. The disability, cultural difference, giftedness or gender difference is seen to be the child's problem and a reason, or excuse, why this child is unable to access the curriculum. This model prevails in a society that acknowledges physical 'crutches' such as ramps and Braille yet condones *social exclusion*, denying young people the right to plan to live where they want to, assuming that in late adolescence the child will return to the family home as a consumer of services. It precludes independence and a sense of normality.

Pause for thought

Consider:

- Have you heard children referred to by their *medical deficit* label? If so, where did you encounter this?
- How did the use of such terms make you feel? Has this made you want to challenge perceptions and see the gifts that the child has before the deficit?
- How might an educator's understanding of inclusion affect a child's experience and the experience of others?

In the preferred 'social' model of inclusion (Table 10.2), the practitioner starts with a knowledge of each child, of their individual needs, gifts, likes, and dislikes, and the level of achievement of each child, and reflects on the totality of the classroom experience of the child, which may include barriers such as those highlighted in Table 10.2.

Table 10.2 The social model of inclusion

Poor acoustics in the classroom	Teachers giving long and detailed instructions	Young children expected to sit on the floor for lengthy periods
Lack of texts or recordings to engage with at the right time for the child	Homework being given in a rush at the end of a lesson	No lifts, ramps or stairs to access parts of the environment
Lesson pace too fast or too slow	Totally print-based curriculum; lack of access to personal laptop with spell-checker and speech to print software	The print-based or didactic approach to the curriculum affords the child few experiences of success

Adapted from Cross (2002; cited in TDA 2008).

The practitioner, rather than the child or parent/carer, takes ownership of the barriers to learning for a child (Doveston and Keenaghan 2006), particularly in terms of social inclusion, and reflects on ways of minimizing those barriers by:

- *Discovery*: the teacher identifies a social barrier and looks for positive examples of ways of overcoming the barrier through discussion with the child and class. The teacher listens to the children and reflects on the *circles of inclusion* that affect the child. Circles of inclusion involve noticing when a child expects to communicate with adults such as doctor or teachers rather than with peers.
- *Dream*: the teacher visualizes the positive outcome and shares this with the class, encouraging the class to share ways of achieving the desired outcome. This may involve setting up additional *circles of friends* or groups of children who agree to include the child in their social group to ensure that child has friends and communicates with other children. Optimism is important here.
- *Design*: co-constructing the alternative approach, highlighting the advantages of change. For example, the teacher's role may be to meet with the circle of friends and the focus child for around 20–30 minutes a week to solve problems in the early stages. Successful circles will often become largely self-sustaining and provide support for the focus child without the need for regular adult input. When there is careful planning and real commitment from the facilitator, results from the process are seen very quickly.
- *Destiny*: the class and the teacher work towards achieving change.

For example, Robert needed to learn to communicate in writing. In addition to the difficulties experienced by all young children, he had to overcome differences in word order with British Sign Language, such that his preferred signing language would structure his thinking as 'Car, the red one', and traditional English sentence order would be 'The red car'. By identifying the barrier noticed by the signing assistant, discussing this with the child and valuing all attempts at word order, collective strategies to overcome difficulties could be trialled. By planning Robert's work with photographs, communicating through the signing assistant, and sharing ideas at the table with his peers and then using a series of quick drawings as a writing frame, Robert was able to think of sentences with a response partner and correct them for writing in Standard English. He could rehearse the sentences in his head and then meet the writing objectives with the other children. Robert, rather than the teacher, was in charge of choosing the strategies that would work best for him. This avoided the risk of practice that might unwittingly emphasize difference or deficit in the classroom. As above, the inclusive ethos enabled his lively sense of fun to enrich the classroom community.

Similarly, discussion with Robert's parents during a home visit identified that the front door bell was connected to the house lights. When a visitor pressed the bell, the house lights went off. A child who had wondered why there was always someone at the door when his mother went to it, yet no one at the door when he checked, was enabled to develop this concept only when he was able to understand the bigger picture blocked by sensory deprivation. Valuing parental input, the teacher was able to adopt an appreciative inquiry reflection related to classroom practice. Incidences were identified when Robert was unaware of how the other children knew to line up, stand up, sit down or respond to the teacher. The light switch was then used as a strategy for getting the attention of the whole class. Flicking the lights off and on attracted the attention of all of the children in that class and the signing assistant gave Robert information about the specific meaning of the intervention; but this strategy would not necessarily work for all children with hearing loss as it was rooted in exploration of his previous life and world experience.

ICT can be a valuable and visual tool. Nind et al. (2003) support the idea that ICT can be used to make existing practices more efficient and to develop concepts that rely heavily on language definitions. ICT and media applications are accessible and readily available resources to enhance the learning experiences of all children, particularly in terms of visual literacy.

Working in school involves working with other adults as part of a team and working with the parents and carers of the children as defined in the teachers' standards in England (DfE 2012). It involves maintaining the active support of parents and carers (DfES 2004a) establishing what learners already know, building on past experiences, and identifying and developing skills. This necessitates 'creating a learning culture' encompassing the conditions necessary for learning in school as a whole-school ethos. But the ethos can start either with the senior management team or through the example set by one class of children. From the example of Robert, staff, parents, carers, and children may develop a shared understanding of the values and ethos of a facility designed to promote learning and inclusion for all, meeting the entitlement to a broad, balanced, and rich curriculum.

'Special Needs' is a term that has developed with use to include children with long-term (more than one year) conditions that may impact at any age. However, this idea of fluidity is useful when considering Robert's story of the swan. By putting in place systems to minimize his disability and enable him to recount his news, Robert's interest in natural history could be shared. He was able to play a full and active social role in lessons and therefore his self-esteem was high and he was able to make progress, in a mainstream classroom with his social peers. Therefore, it is useful to interrogate the strategies and motivation that lead to Robert's inclusion. First, an ethos of inclusion through appreciative inquiry of the positive attributes that Robert brought to the classroom, including his laughter, his sense of humour, his determination, and his love of rhythm and drumming. Secondly, partnership with parents: valuing their experience of working with Robert. Thirdly, an initial circle of friends introduced by the teacher that blossomed into acceptance of Robert's difference by all of the children. Fourthly, use of his preferred communication style and time to think and plan in flexible groups that sometimes included his friends and sometimes included working in ability groupings that were different for different subjects or curriculum areas.

Ofsted (2006) highlights the need for high standards in schools and high expectations of *all* children: with high self-esteem and self-confidence fundamental to the class and school community. This includes:

- Effective target setting, within the curriculum or personalized programme, as part of a whole-school policy on assessment and planning learning. Best practice includes developing ways of challenging progress for different pupils, using their ages as starting points, as well as the time they had been receiving specialist support.
- Tracking pupils' personal, social, and emotional development systematically and questioning rigorously whether pupils were making the best progress they could in the areas of greatest need. Based on their knowledge of individuals, staff frequently judged that pupils made very clear and rewarding progress.

Case study

An inclusive learning environment starts with social mapping. The teacher needs a large grid and three different coloured pens. The teacher asks each of the children to name their two best friends in the class, the two people that they would ask for help with their work and the two people that they think are the best behaved.

The teacher then plots the results onto the grid (as shown in Figure 10.1) and immediately identifies that there are children within the class who will fail to thrive unless the teacher takes immediate action to develop their social inclusion as well as meeting their learning needs.

Name	Susan	Robert	Peter	Saleha	Darren	James	Amandeep	Kathryn	Harpreet
Susan				XO*				XO*	
Robert with hearing impairment						XO*			
Peter	XO*			O*			X		
Saleha with EAL	XO*							XO*	
Darren with learning differences			XO*			X*			
James		XO*	XO*						
Amandeep with EAL			X	O*					XO*
Kathryn	XO*			XO*					
Harpreet with EAL	XO*	X					O*		

Key: X = best friend, O = the person the child would go to for help with their work, * = the role model for behaviour

Figure 10.1   A teacher's record of social mapping

The map is for the teacher's eyes only. Note that the teacher can see straight away that Darren has no one who sees him as an important friend, no one asks him for help, and no one identifies him as a role model. On closer observation at playtime, the teacher might find that Darren is alone in the playground, standing quietly and watching the other children engrossed in their playtime games despite there being playground monitors and a 'bus stop' for children to pick up others without playmates.

Robert relies on his signing assistant for support but plays with James. Susan, Saleha, and Kathryn are on the high achievers' table. Saleha speaks four languages including English, while Harpreet and Amandeep both speak Urdu as their first language and English as an additional language. They both go to each other for support in discussing concepts in their first language and meet socially to go to the Gurdwara for additional training in Sikhism and in the values and beliefs expected of them within their cultural group; values that will not be the same for all Sikhs.

Reflect on this case study example. Consider:

- Which of the children may have high self-esteem?
- Which of the children have chosen their best friends as role models?
- How might you develop this understanding further and ensure that all of the children develop high self-esteem?
- If you were the teacher, how would you include Darren?
- Would you set up a circle of friends for Darren and, if so, who would you choose to be part of the circle?
- What support would you expect to give the class to ensure that Darren is included?
- What curriculum lessons lend themselves to children discussing friendship and inclusion?

Developing practice

To develop effective practice, we need to consider:

- how labels are used in schools and other learning settings (how are labels used to refer to a need or a 'deficit' and how can the emphasis be changed to focus on the child?);
- how our own experiences affect the ways in which we relate to others and respond to similarity and difference;
- our response to the term inclusion (do we see it as positive and liberating?);
- whether a school ethos focuses on meeting the letter of the law or minimum requirements, rather than aiming to maximize the positive learning experience of each child;
- how communication with a child and their parents and carers can help us to appreciate who a child is in greater depth.

Conclusion

Removal of the barriers to learning and barriers to belonging is not passive: it is the responsibility of the class teacher, working in partnership with children, colleagues, and parents/carers, and must be viewed as an active process owned by the whole class and community.

Effective learning and personal development can only take place in schools and other settings where children feel safe, secure, and valued. Society is not homogeneous: every person is unique and special. Heterogeneity is the norm (as is also discussed in Chapter 11, *Beliefs*) and children can be supported in appreciating and valuing difference as a part of daily life. This is a means of addressing 'isms' and 'phobias' (Cole 2008), including classism, disablism, racism, sexism, and homophobia. Helping children to appreciate both difference and similarity is an important part of helping them to encounter the world, and one another, in positive ways and to prepare them for the diverse, varied, and unique people they will meet throughout life. It is also an essential part of helping them to value how special they are themselves.

References

Ainscow, M. and Booth, T. (2011) *Index for Inclusion: Developing Learning and Participation in Schools.* Available at: http://www.eenet.org.uk/resources/docs/Index%20English.pdf.

Clough, P. and Corbett, J. (2000) *Theories of Inclusive Education: A Student's Guide.* London: Paul Chapman.

Cole, M. (2008) Introduction, in M. Cole (ed.) *Professional Attributes and Practice: Meeting the QTS Standards*, 4th edn. Abingdon: David Fulton.

Corbett, J. (2001) *Supporting Inclusive Education: A Connective Pedagogy.* London: RoutledgeFalmer. Available at: http72.3142.35/dxreader/jsp/eprint/PrintAllPages.jsp?id=18 (accessed 5 April 2012).

Davis, P. and Florian, L. (2004) *Teaching Strategies and Approaches for Pupils with Special Educational Needs: A Scoping Study*, Research Report 516. London: DfES.

Dean, J. (2000) *Improving Children's Learning: Effective Teaching in the Primary Classroom.* London: Routledge.

Department for Children, Schools and Families (DCSF) (2008) *Personalised Learning: A Practical Guide.* Nottingham: DCSF.

Department for Education (DfE) (2011) *National Curriculum Inclusion Statement.* Available at: http://www.eduation.gov.uk/schools/teachingandlearning/curriculum/b00199686/inclusion (accessed 1 February 2013).

Department for Education (DfE) (2012) *Teachers' Standards.* Available at www.education.gov.uk (accessed March 2013).

Department for Education and Skills (DfES) (2004b) *Every Child Matters: Change for Children in Schools.* London: DfES.

Department of Education and Skills (DfES) (2004a) *Excellence and Enjoyment: Learning and Teaching in The Primary Years. Introductory Guide: Supporting School Improvement.* Surrey: DfES.

Doveston, M. and Keenaghan, M. (2006) Growing talent for inclusion: using an appreciative inquiry approach into investigating classroom dynamics, *Journal of Research in Special Educational Needs*, 6(3): 153–65.

Dowling, M. (2005) *Young Children's Personal, Social and Emotional Development*, 2nd edn. London: Paul Chapman.

Equality Act (2010) Norwich: The Stationery Office. Available at: http://www.legislation. gov.uk/ukpga/2010/15/data.pdf.

Guasap, A. (2007) *Homophobic Bullying in Britain's Schools*. Available at: http://www. stonewall.org.uk/documents/the_teachers_report_1.pdf (accessed 8 June 2012).

Hughes, M. (2001) *Strategies for Closing the Learning Gap.* Stafford: Network Educational Press Ltd.

Mittler, P. (2000) *Working Towards Inclusive Education: School Contexts.* London: David Fulton.

Nind, M., Rix, J., Sheehy, K. and Simmons, R. (2003) *Inclusive Education: Diverse Perspectives.* London: David Fulton.

Ofsted (2006) *Inclusion: Does it Matter where Pupils are Taught?* An Ofsted report on the provision and outcomes in different settings for pupils with learning difficulties and disabilities, July 2006. Available at: http://www.ofsted.gov.uk/publications/index.cfm?fuseaction=pubs.displayfileandid=4235andtype=pdf (accessed 31 May 2011).

Ofsted (2008) *The Framework for School Inspection.* Available at: http://www.ofsted.gov. uk/resources/framework-for-school-inspection (updated December 2012).

Pollard, A. (2002) *Reflective Teaching: Evidence-informed Professional Practice.* London: Continuum.

Smith, P.K., Cowie, H. and Blades, M. (2003) *Understanding Children's Development: Basic Psychology.* Oxford: Blackwell.

Teaching Agency (2012) *SEN and Disability Skills: Resources for One-Year ITT Programmes.* http://www.education.gov.uk/schools/careers/traininganddevelopment/b00201451/sen-skills/sen-resources/1yr-itt-sen.

Training and Development Agency for Schools (TDA) (2008) *Special Educational Needs and/or Disabilities: A Training Resource for Initial Teacher Training Providers: Primary Undergraduate Course.* London: TDA.

Warnock Committee (1978) *Special Educational Needs: The Warnock Report.* London: DES.

Wearmouth, J., Glynn, T., Richmond, R.C. and Berryman, M. (2004) *Inclusion and Behaviour Management in Schools.* London: David Fulton.

CHAPTER

11

Beliefs

Eunice Kimaliro and Richard Woolley

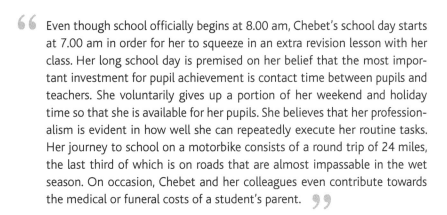

66 Even though school officially begins at 8.00 am, Chebet's school day starts at 7.00 am in order for her to squeeze in an extra revision lesson with her class. Her long school day is premised on her belief that the most important investment for pupil achievement is contact time between pupils and teachers. She voluntarily gives up a portion of her weekend and holiday time so that she is available for her pupils. She believes that her professionalism is evident in how well she can repeatedly execute her routine tasks. Her journey to school on a motorbike consists of a round trip of 24 miles, the last third of which is on roads that are almost impassable in the wet season. On occasion, Chebet and her colleagues even contribute towards the medical or funeral costs of a student's parent. 99

Introduction

Beliefs can be a thorny issue. They are an aspect of life that can be difficult to quantify or substantiate; at times they are rooted in sources or experience that are open to question from others; they can inspire a passion that engenders discussion, debate, tension or disagreement. For some, belief can be a fluid state, evolving over time in the light of reflection on experience and deepening understanding; for others, it can lead to entrenchment and separation, even isolation.

This chapter helps to explore how our professional beliefs can affect our practice as teachers. It considers how beliefs can underpin and enrich our practice by supporting a sense of vocation and a desire to serve others within society. It also considers how we can relate to those with beliefs different to our own and explores strategies to support relationship building with others.

Beliefs can stem from a range of sources. These can be philosophical, political, sociological (including being rooted in our background and upbringing), religious or spiritual. Some of them may find expression through involvement with formalized organizations or groupings; others will be more personal and individual. As professionals, it is essential that we consider how our belief systems affect the ways in which we see the world and influence our relationships with others. This is important if we are to aspire for all children to learn and achieve (DfEE/QCA 1999). Our beliefs will inform the values that we bring to the classroom (these are explored in more detail in Chapter 13, *Values*).

This chapter considers how teachers' beliefs about their role, identity, and status can impact on the education made available to children and young people. Whether a teacher feels valued and respected, and has a sense of professionalism that allows them some freedom to design both the curriculum and the learning environment, plays an important part in the formation of their philosophy of education and ability to work in creative and imaginative ways.

Beliefs can be a sensitive subject because of the assumptions associated with their origins, forms, and impact on one's judgement, yet everyone holds certain beliefs. They are deeply personal, frequently unsubstantiated and, on occasion, even superstitious in nature. Borg (2001: 186) defines a belief as:

> A proposition which may be consciously or unconsciously held, is evaluative in that it is accepted as true by the individual and is therefore imbued with emotive commitment; further it serves as a guide to thought and behaviour.

Some scholars attempt to make a distinction between knowledge and beliefs; the latter may be less demanding in evidence and yet more compelling in action. Griffin and Ohlsson (2001: 364), for example, see knowledge as 'the representation of a proposition' and belief as 'the representation of a truth value associated with a proposition'. Furthermore, they make a distinction between knowledge-based and affective beliefs, stating that individuals may be more reluctant to change their affective beliefs even when presented with sound evidence. Some beliefs are acquired in a manner that does not encourage debate, but can be challenged in the face of life-changing experiences. Their intensely personal nature makes them an intrinsic part of our identity and therefore a subject of interest to those seeking to advance discourse on teacher identity and education change. Left unstated and unexplored, teacher beliefs may continue to militate against proposed improvements or innovations (Kuzborska 2011).

The nature of beliefs

The understanding that some beliefs are subconsciously held means that they may be so deeply entrenched that an individual may not always be aware of how they influence their judgement until forced to justify them in the face of contrary beliefs. In seeking to understand the contextual construction of a teacher's identity, therefore, it would seem prudent to acquire knowledge of some of the beliefs that underlie their practice. Similarly, without a sound understanding of teachers' professional identity, it is difficult if not impossible to introduce effective educational change (this is an area to which we return later in the chapter).

A person intuitively maintains an internal hierarchy of beliefs and, logically, it is more difficult to change the beliefs that are central to the individual's understanding of who they are. When core beliefs change, in the light of newly acquired understanding, a door of opportunity is opened for the individual's self-evaluation of lesser beliefs (Raths 2001). In this chapter, the experiences of teachers and pupils from different contexts are examined in an effort to provide reflection upon teachers' beliefs and identity and also provide insights into dealing with diverse beliefs in a learning environment.

In many cultures, there was a time when each community was highly homogeneous with a propensity towards shared beliefs and values. In such a context, it was possible for individual teachers to hold the same core values and beliefs as the communities in which they worked. Their role, in part, was to consolidate that which had already been introduced to the child by family members and society at large. It should also be noted that the teachers themselves probably had their own beliefs inculcated in a similar manner. There was thus little conflict between what a child learnt within family and the school environment. However, with changing community compositions and modern communication and travel, a child today may be plunged into a plurality of beliefs from family and neighbourhood even before joining school. Some of those beliefs may affect what is considered knowledge and ways in which knowledge can be obtained. Others define the nature of human existence and forms of interaction, which in turn have implications for teacher/student relationships. Student beliefs also impinge on what students feel at liberty to disclose in a learning environment.

Our own beliefs

Beliefs can be founded in a range of sources. As educators, we have a beliefs base that informs the ways in which we practise. Theorists who have developed schema relating to child development may have affected our thinking, whether we respond positively or not to their ideas. For example, some teachers' practice has been informed significantly by the work of Vygotsky (1978) and Bruner (1986), whose social-constructivist approaches support the view that we learn best in community, from one another and alongside others with different talents and skills.

Others will hold beliefs about the nature of the world and its beginnings and purpose. Whether these stem from a belief in a supreme being who created the world and its people, or an affirmation that nature is precious and the substance of the world needs to be cared for and used in sustainable ways for all living things to flourish, these passionately held views will affect the way in which we approach caring for children. Similarly, our political views will impact on the ways in which we interpret policy, whether stemming from local or national initiatives.

Whatever our own personal beliefs, it is not the role of the educator to indoctrinate learners into accepting the same beliefs. Rather, it is our role to develop and enable reflective and thoughtful individuals able to make their own choices. However, this does not mean that our learners should be presented with a values-neutral experience, for some human values are non-negotiable. For example, it would be abhorrent to present a spectrum of racist and anti-racist views to children and allow them to choose from the options. This raises an interesting question: how can we enable our learners to develop into responsible, caring, empathetic, and respectful citizens without manipulating them in this process?

Beliefs, the classroom environment, and the role of the teacher

Case study

In his classroom, Jamie has a brief set of guidelines for positive behaviour:

- We use words in kind ways and use quiet voices.
- We keep our hands and feet to ourselves.
- We try our best.
- We use resources carefully.

The range of issues contained within these short points touches on issues of care for the environment and the world's resources, sustainability, personal comfort and safety, and maximization of our abilities. The inference is that we do this together in community, benefiting from the mutually beneficial contributions of others.

The changing classroom environment poses a number of questions for the teaching profession. How does a teacher fulfil their moral purpose (Fullan 1993) in a heterogeneous environment without contravening or undermining the rights of the diverse pupil population within their care? Is it healthy for these beliefs to be shared, discussed or explored in class? Is it part of a teacher's role to pass on the specific beliefs acceptable to the dominant culture? What are the likely consequences of ignoring conflicting beliefs? What role can a teacher play in helping pupils to cultivate a healthy relationship with diverse beliefs?

As a young student living in a heterogeneous community, Martin Luther King summarized the dilemma that some pupils face today: 'We are prone to let our mental life become invaded by legions of half truths, prejudices and propaganda' (Carson et al. 2007: 124). What is taught, how it is taught, and where the teacher is positioned in what is taught helps learners cultivate a healthy inquiry into what is held as truth. Determining the difference between truth, half-truth, propaganda, and prejudice calls for a willingness on the part of the teacher to subject their own beliefs to sustained scrutiny. The hallmark of postmodernism is society's ability to maintain a healthy suspicion about beliefs held and how they were arrived at. Martin Luther King saw the role of education as an opportunity to 'discipline the mind for sustained and persistent speculation' (Carson et al. 2007: 122). If this is the purpose of education, then the central role of a teacher is to lead students towards persistent and open interrogation of their beliefs in an environment free from bigotry.

Kuzborska (2011) states that teachers' beliefs influence their roles and further suggests they are instrumental in their choice of 'goals, procedures, materials, [and] classroom interaction patterns'. The opportunities provided by a teacher, and the resources and activities that they reject, indicate a great deal about that teacher's values and beliefs.

Case study

Ongoing research in a Kenyan primary school shows that there is a noticeable difference between approaches used by lower and upper primary teachers. Lower primary teachers have a deep belief in allowing pupils to physically interact with locally made teaching and learning materials, while upper primary teachers are of the belief their students are now of an age to follow a more academic regime. Fewer teaching aids are incorporated into lessons – except in science – and are replaced with question and answer discussions. The lower primary teachers firmly believe their role is to socialize pupils into school routines, help them to acquire basic numeracy and literacy skills and learn the language of instruction. There is a seismic shift among upper primary teachers, as they believe their key role is to help as many pupils as possible to transit to the best secondary institutions. These two opposing beliefs naturally have implications on the respective teachers' choice of learning approaches and classroom activities. Raths (2001: 1) suggests that:

'Teachers and teacher candidates have strong beliefs about the role that education can play, about explanations for individual variation in academic performance and about rights and wrongs in the classroom.'

Whereas group work and paired work are a regular part of lower primary lesson planning, they are infrequent in the upper primary where teachers are apt to focus the students' attention on preparation for the national examinations. Their perceptions of rights and wrongs are tied in with beliefs of what has worked in similar contexts.

Consider:

- how these teachers' beliefs about the nature and purpose of education might affect their approach to learning and teaching;
- the possible strengths and limitations of the changing approach from lower to upper primary school;
- how this example compares with your own experience of primary schools and other learning settings.

Beliefs about teacher identity

Data gathered from young people considering teaching as a career provides some insight into how pre-training candidates view the role. During 'Routes into Teaching Summer Schools', a three-day residential experience combining an introduction to education theory with practical experience with children, students aged 17–18 years reflected on their intended profession through the development of a series of Kenning-style poems outlining what a teacher is. The results are interesting, as they suggest what has been inferred about the role during the young people's eleven years of compulsory schooling within the education system in England.

Pause for thought

Consider the two poems below, written during the 'Routes into Teaching Summer Schools':

Poem 1	Poem 2
Apple eater	Storyteller
Board writer	Classroom communicator
Harmless threatener	Mood lifter
Book reader	Good listener
Lame joker	Knowledge expander
Strict shouter	Enthusiastic educator
Soft speaker	Circle timer
Whistle blower	Supportive shoulder
Lesson planner	

Consider:

- What beliefs about the role of a teacher do the poems suggest?
- Are the statements mainly positive, negative or neutral?
- How do these key attributes of being a teacher compare with your own view?

All the poems developed during summer schools over a period of three years (with over 75 students) have been combined to form a Wordle (a word cloud or pattern). This highlights the most common words suggested by the participants overall (Figure 11.1).

Figure 11.1   Teacher poem *Wordle*

The relative size of each word indicates its frequency of use. There is a clear focus on storytelling (which is probably the result of the emphasis of the summer school activities). Drinking coffee, being a role model, and imparting knowledge feature significantly. The latter suggests that the students see teachers as being providers or purveyors of information, rather than facilitators for learners who discover for themselves (themes also explored in Chapters 1, *Curiosity* and 14, *Vision*).

Create your own thought shower of words that you view as relevant to being a teacher. These words will indicate the importance you place on elements of the role, and indicate some elements of your own philosophy of and vision for education.

The comments arising from the Kennings have the clarity and a freshness that can only emanate from current witnesses of teachers' work and practices. The fact that the students are actively considering teaching as a career might explain why for the most part their comments are complementary, but there are succinct messages for present-day educators. On the basis of these observations, it is possible to conclude that these students believe a teacher to be a patient, caring, hard-working, knowledgeable, organized individual capable of presenting a range of planned activities that sustain interest and promote learning. There is also recognition of the teacher's pastoral role, the value of which is often overlooked. It is evident from their comments the students consider teaching to be both a professional and vocational career. In their eyes, an ideal teacher should not only have the knowledge and mechanics of the profession but also encompass the person skills that will develop the individuality of each child. This requirement is strongly illustrated by their choice of words: *approachable, carer, attentive listener, supportive shoulder, confidence booster, parent, mood lifter, talent nurturer*, and *motivator*. It is enlightening to note that of 93 comments, 25 pertain to the vocational aspect of teaching.

Overall, the students' responses to the Kennings show some balance between the perceived positive and negative aspects of being a teacher. Only 5 per cent of them mentioned being a role model, while 7 per cent referred to drinking coffee or eating apples (alluding to the traditional idea of the teacher being given apples by grateful children). Nineteen per cent considered teachers to be caring, committed or inspiring, and 12 per cent a thinker or learner: you may wish to consider this relatively low response, given the facets of the role implicit to the chapters of this book. Other areas included behaviour management and dealing with difficult situations (13 per cent), a didactic approach to knowledge transfer (7 per cent), and the way in which a teacher is expected to dress (i.e. smartly or wearing a tie) (3 per cent). Significantly, only 5 per cent of responses included any reference to the use of humour, and not all these were positive (for example, 'lame joker'). You may wish to consider whether the appropriate use of humour is one of the most significant capabilities that the teacher can have in their skills set.

Seeing as these students hold teachers as role models, it can naturally be assumed those who progress into the profession are likely to emulate the practices of their teachers. On the other hand, students recognize that teaching can go wrong. The Kennings indicate that a teacher can also turn out to be a *power-seeking, classroom-dominating, nagging,* and *student-wrecking* individual. Is it possible for initial teacher education to prevent a trainee from degenerating into this kind of a teacher? It is hoped that since the students identified these likely negative aspects and still want to be teachers that they would avoid replicating them. Such views raise the question of what the students have learned or deduced about being a teacher from their own experience of schooling, and what they believe about the aims and purposes of the role to which they aspire.

Research on teachers' professional identity recognizes the multifaceted nature of identity (Beijaard et al. 2004). The individual who is also a teacher has other roles in other places that predispose them to a variety of identities and attendant beliefs. Understanding how '[w]e define ourselves and others in the light of our social identities across many different kinds of contexts in which we find ourselves' (Vryan et al. 2003: 371) should cause a teacher to pause and reflect on the array of different identities learners might hold. Their beliefs emanate from a range of sources, including home, peers, print, and electronic media, and all find their way into the classroom and have a bearing on subsequent interaction with people and learning materials.

Contextual and cultural influences will have a profound effect upon a child's beliefs about the nature and purpose of education. As previously mentioned, the world has moved from homogeneous communities to a heterogeneous plurality of beliefs and the child is often caught in the midst of this multiplicity of beliefs. This raises the possibility of a mismatch between a teacher's beliefs and those of the pupils. In some communities in Kenya, for example, a child is taught at home that it is disrespectful to look directly into an adult's eyes in conversation, but in school, the direct opposite is expected and if not forthcoming the child is assumed to be shifty, dishonest or lacking in confidence.

Teachers' professionalism

The perception of teaching as a profession places certain expectations on the teacher's manner of engagement with the students and the policy envionment. It calls for an examination of beliefs long held in the light of professional expectations. However, debate on whether or not teaching is a profession (Etzioni 1969) and the interpretation of professionalism impact on the depth of teacher preparation and the revision of belief systems. Despite the lack of consensus on the intrinsic meaning of professionalism, the term itself conjures up images of an altruistic, self-disciplined, efficient individual in a privileged position and in possession of expertise (Boyt et al. 2001; Wilkins 2010). The attitudinal and behavioural aspects of the professional worker, particularly in their code of ethics and standard of performance, are frequently highlighted and are intended to build confidence in their practice (Boyt et al. 2001; Helsby and McCulloch 1996). Although every occupation requires knowledge and skills, a profession is thought to require a higher or specialized level of knowledge that enables its practitioners to make decisions grounded in established theories (Day et al. 2007; Young 2007).

Evans (2008: 8) defines professionalism as a 'collective commonality of approach to and execution of key roles and responsibilities and activities that constitute the work undertaken by the profession'. To ensure such commonality, professions uphold certain criteria through which these key roles are structured and professionals equipped to discharge them. Whitty (2006) uses the example of the following criteria originally developed by Millersons (1964, cited in Whitty 2006):

- skills based on threoretical knowledge;
- education and training in those skills certified by examination;

- code of conduct oriented towards the 'public good';
- a powerful, professional organization.

While elements of these criteria still hold true today, professionalism is generally portrayed as evolving through historical periods which change its meaning and expression accordingly (Young 2007). Its interpretations are affected not only by historical events, but also by different political and institutional voices (Day et al. 2007). Teachers in England may reflect on the period between the 1950s and 1970s, when they were unquestionably regarded as professionals (Wilkins 2010). During that 'golden period of professionalism', they had 'the freedom to decide not only how to teach, but what to teach' (Whitty 2006: 3). Today in England, a National Curriculum identifies what is to be taught and the emphasis is no longer solely on pre-practice training, but on teachers' life-long learning. Perhaps one of the biggest changes to the profession is the reduction of teachers' autonomy and the shift of control from the individual to educational management structures outside the profession (Evans 2008). The new forms of teacher professionalism move us away from teacher autonomy and elitism towards a meeting of standards appropriate to the new working climate, which, unfortunately, attracts suspicion that teaching is being deprofessionalized (Newkirk 2009).

The emerging models of teachers' professionalism are seen to embrace either 'managerial' or 'democratic' forms (Sachs 2001), which has consquences for the construction of teachers' professional identity. Sachs portrays managerial professionalism as leading to an enterpreneurial identity focused on efficiency and accountability, while a democratic professionalism gives rise to an activist professional identity (Sachs 2001) deeply rooted in justice and social equity. She argues that a democratic professionalism encourages collaboration and cooperation between teachers and other stakeholders, diminishing the illegitimate domination of certain individuals or groups over others. Whatever form of professionalism is embraced, O'Connor (2008) emphasizes that *caring for students* is an important part of teachers' professional work and identity.

Pause for thought

In an ongoing research project on teachers' professional identity in Kenya, pupils across the upper primary school spectrum were asked to state their expectations of school and how their teachers were helping them to attain these aspirations; their responses are summarized in Table 11.1.

Table 11.1 Kenyan pupils' expectations of school

What I want from school	How my teacher helps me	Why I am in this particular school
Preparation for the future	Teaches us until we understand	Quality education
To be important in society	Loves us	We understand the things that we are taught
To gain knowledge and skills (e.g to read and write)	Disciplines us	High discipline
	Teaches us to respect parents	Teachers who guide
		Its performance in examinations
To get an education	Teaches us good morals	Teachers work hard and help you to understand
Not to be ignorant	Teaches us how to maintain ourselves	Pupils are hard working
To be taught what to do		They teach on Saturdays and Sundays; they leave their home and come to teach us
To understand	Helps us to be aware of HIV/AIDS	
To be prepared for employment	Helps us to avoid sex	Teachers teach well
	Teaches us to understand	Teachers do not discriminate
To be able to judge for ourselves		If you feel disturbed, teachers can help
To help out parents	Teaches us how to read	You can go and disclose problems to the teacher
	Makes me love the subject	It improves
	Helps me to control my life	Good morals
		Because of knowledge
	Understands that some people are very poor	The environment
		It is near home
	Teaches us	We learn well
	Removes ignorance from us	We do well in sports and class work
		We eat in school
		Enough teachers
	Disciplines us to remove ignorance	We have a big field
		We have enough toilets
		Teachers discipline us to remove ignorance from us

An analysis of the first column in Table 11.1 illuminates a number of beliefs shared by children in the sample. They believe a school education prepares them for the future with a direct link to employment and a better quality of life. They perceive education to be a source of transformative power with the possibility of the educated becoming important people in society. Education is also believed to equip a person with the necessary skills for discernment. As most of these children come from a background of subsistence farming and large families struggling to make a living, they believe acquiring an education will enable them to lift their parents out of the poverty trap.

Because most of the teachers are now living in the same area, they have an acute awareness of their students' and community's expectations, and the increased consciousness of global recession puts additional pressure on the teachers to help their students – whose parents are also their neighbours – succeed. Teachers' beliefs are shaped by cultural influences, by classroom observations to which they have been exposed (Shinde and Karekatti 2012), their own experiences, and isolated incidents in the course of their careers. (Such critical incidents are discussed further in Chapter 12, *Reflection*.) In the sample school, the teachers' own experiences of working with an economically marginalized rural community with high expectations of their children heavily influenced their identity and practice, hence the emphasis on testing and extra tuition in the upper classes. It is interesting to compare the support that the pupils identify the teachers offering with the roles and attributes of teachers identified by the prospective teachers from the UK Summer Schools.

The idea that teaching can be transformative is important. However, as the responses from the Summer School participants suggest, sometimes the transformation can be negative as well as positive. We may each have encountered teachers who inspire us, and others who we hope never to be like; some of our teachers nurtured and challenged us, others belittled and demoralized us. The idea that teaching is a vocation, something that we feel called to do, is an important concept. Whether through a particular belief, someone who inspired us, or wanting to make a difference to the world and the communities around us, there are many different reasons for wanting to teach. Similarly, the notion of *service*, which has perhaps been less popular in recent decades, suggests that the act of engaging with learners can nurture, challenge, inspire, provide care, and make a difference to the lives of children and young people.

Case study

Consider the case of teacher Chebet in a rural primary school in Kenya, introduced in the vignette that opened this chapter:

Chebet is a young, single teacher with six years of post-training experience. She initially trained as a Certificate Primary school teacher but is now pursuing, at her own expense, a Bachelor's degree in Education through a part-time programme at the University of Nairobi. She believes that her contribution to education change and her prospects for promotion are dependent upon her level of certification. To her, knowledge received and transmitted through eligible persons and institutions equates to power.

For Chebet, education is an investment. In the same way she anticipates her higher qualifications will improve her standing and financial position, she in turn believes the invest-
ments her pupils and their parents put into education will bear results. A case in point is
of privately educated students from the district, whose parents paid a lot of money for
their primary education, who went on to the best educational institutions, thus securing themselves a place in the right networks, and who now are in high-profile positions
as a direct result of their elite educational journey. Though economically deprived, and
lacking in the advantages that private education provides, including a reduced teacher/
pupil ratio, adequate learning resources and home support, Chebet believes that with
sacrifice and tenacity her students can also qualify for the limited places in the best
high schools. To ensure their success, Chebet and her colleagues have devised a routine
that is expected to give her pupils the extra mileage in teacher support. She constantly
reminds them of consequences that can befall them if they do not strive to fulfil their
part or drop out of school prematurely. Former pupils who are in higher education or
professions are cited as role models. Chebet continuously encourages her pupils to sacrifice all else (e.g. football, drama, sports) in the interests of their study – childhood pleas-
ures supplanted by examination glory. Similarly, Chebet's school advocates for children
in examination classes to be spared from the additional burden of income-generating
labour on neighbouring farms during peak agricultural seasons. Bearing in mind the poverty of the catchment area, the school in this instance is asking the parents to make a
huge sacrifice in the cause of education. In addition, despite the national free primary
education policy, parents are expected to contribute additional levies to cover the cost
of school infrastructure, school meals, and external examination papers. The fact that
parents comply with all these requests serves to reinforce the belief that the whole community believes not only in education but in the strategies the school puts in place to
deliver it. Chebet is aware of her responsibility in the scheme of things.

She has a profound trust in the curriculum and the national examination system and
as a result her teaching methodology with the upper primary classes is geared towards
assuring success in the Kenya Certificate of Primary Education Examination (KCPE) for
her pupils.

As a teacher of Social Studies, which incorporates Geography, History, Civics, and Christian Religious Education in an examination class, Chebet has devised an action plan that
includes simultaneous syllabus coverage and revision. Fortnightly, the candidates are
exposed to a full-length examination paper that covers the syllabus from previous years
and that of the current year. Despite the fact that coaching and extra tuition are discour-
aged by policy, Chebet sees such an arrangement as vital to her pupils' success. Using the
test paper as an entry point, she devotes the extra tuition time for clarifying and con-
solidating specific syllabus content according to her pupils' needs. The regular timetabled
lessons she allocates to teaching the syllabus specified for that year are reflected in her
schemes of work. Most of these lessons follow the practice of teacher-led question and

answer sessions, where she channels pupils' attention to specific concepts in the depth she considers appropriate.

Because of the range of the syllabus, Chebet believes as a professional teacher her task is to devise a way in which key elements of the syllabus can be comprehensively covered in the shortest possible time. With this as her aim, there is little room in her lessons for discussions or deviations outside her predetermined content. In her lesson preparation, she identifies the approved textbook that most comprehensively covers the topic and, as a further safeguard, consults other teachers who have successfully taught the same content. On account of her past pupils' achievements in her subject in KCPE, the present students trust her judgement implicitly.

Chebet believes a teacher is sandwiched between students' needs and curriculum requirements. Whereas the curriculum may require her to move at a certain pace, her pupils' level of comprehension may dictate differently. As individual student's needs may affect their school attendance, Chebet realizes she has to plan for such contingencies and makes every effort to ensure each pupil covers the key elements of the syllabus. This requires considerable personal sacrifice on her part and a great deal of extra coaching in addition to her day-to-day workload of lesson planning, marking, updating records of work, and student counselling.

Chebet firmly believes that she has a duty to mould her pupils' character. This arises from the belief that her own school played a major role in her development and values. Despite the fact that her pupils come from different ethnic communities, Chebet believes that her pupils' achievements are not determined by origin but by the opportunity availed them. She has seen successful pupils from different communities. She sees school assemblies as opportunities to foster social values such as honesty, integrity, and neighbourly concern. Her lessons are filled with reminders of acceptable behaviour during and out of class. Her belief that discipline is a prerequisite for good performance means that she sets a high standard and expects it to be maintained – pupils must be punctual, work has to be handed in on time, personal and classroom cleanliness has to be observed, and pupils are to accept reprimands in the spirit in which they are given.

In her dress, her outlook, and expectations for both male and female pupils, Chebet projects a progressive face of the teaching profession, but she is a bit of a dichotomy in that she treads a cautious path with regard to the curriculum and the methodology she uses. This may be attributed to her relative inexperience in the teaching profession or the fact that as a product of her context she has an innate understanding of the community's wishes and their perception of success and how to achieve it. The community expects a teacher to attend class, instil discipline, give extra time to teaching both on the weekends and holidays, and relentlessly examine what is taught, in short get their child through the KCPE and on the road to success. In this regard, Chebet fulfils their expectations entirely, even though she realizes her present methodology is contrary to current thinking.

Chebet's case illustrates Beijaard and colleagues' (2004: 125) observation concerning the role relationships play in teachers' understanding of professional identity:

> What counts as professional then is related to ways in which teachers relate to other people, students, colleagues, parents … and the responsibilities, attitudes and behaviours they adopt as well as the knowledge they use which are more or less outside themselves.

Chebet manifests her professionalism through her association with the school's parents/carers, teachers, and pupils. The question that begs an answer is the sustainability of her beliefs regarding education in the light of twenty-first century challenges, which Kelly et al. (2008: 1) summarize as follows:

> We are educating current students for jobs, pathways and life worlds that are still in formation – some that have yet to come into existence. This challenges longstanding curriculum directions that have their roots in modernist traditions where boundaries of knowledge were assumed to be known and the skills needed for the future learning and work taken as identifiable and quantifiable.

How can teachers, then, make possible the dreams that are to shape tomorrow's pathways, if their understanding of education is limited to the definitions of yesterday's theorists and a narrow interpretation of its purposes? Teachers' beliefs can promote or inhibit the realization of these pathways. Whereas educational planners in Kenya seek to provide pathways for post-primary transition, teachers in contexts similar to Chebet will continue to measure their pupils' achievement on the basis of attainment at the highest educational levels. For them, education is seen as a source of power and the more certificated education one has, the greater the power to change one's life. Learners under their care will not be content with the option of a non-academic talent or technical achievement. Similarly, a successful shift from teacher-centred classroom practices to learner-centred practices as now advocated by policy makers in Kenya will depend largely on teachers' beliefs about the new purpose of education and how they see their role within it.

Developing practice

To develop effective practice, we need to consider:

- how we acknowledge and value pupil diversity, need, and aspiration in our classroom/setting;
- the extent to which our personal beliefs and philosophy of education impact on our professional approach/practice;

- how outside influences (such as government policy) support or challenge our views about the ways in which we teach;
- what we believe the aims and purposes of education to be, and how this affects our beliefs about the role of teacher;
- what motivates us to teach: is it a sense of vocation or service, a desire to make a difference to the world, our community or individual lives, or are there other motivating factors?

Conclusion

This chapter has considered how our beliefs, and particularly our beliefs about being a teacher, can affect our approach to the role. Whether we feel that we have some autonomy to design and deliver the curriculum, or whether we feel pressured and driven by initiatives and strategies from outside our schools, makes a huge impact on how we feel about the role of teacher and its possibilities.

We have considered views from young people and professionals from different parts of the world. Our context affects how we view the aims and purposes of education, but at the same time there are universal values that can be shared by teachers in diverse places. These relate to the fundamental value of people, the need to value the thoughts and words of children, and a belief in the importance of the whole child (an area to which we shall return in Chapter 14, *Vision*). Many such values are enshrined in the United Nations Convention on the Rights of the Child (United Nations General Assembly 1989).

We have discussed the concept of teaching as a profession, and begun to consider what this means. Our final thought is the nature of that term: *profession*. At its root is the idea that it relates to someone who professes. If teaching is – and is to remain – a profession, then it is essential that we have a clear sense of our philosophy of education, with clear beliefs and values that support our work and enable us to translate all that is asked of us into best practice.

Acknowledgements

With thanks to the primary school pupils and teachers who participated in research in the Trans Nzoia East District in Trans Nzoia County, Kenya. Also to Bev Tomblin, Veronica Oxley, Lizzy Sumner, and all the Student Ambassadors for their support in running the 'Routes into Teaching Summer Schools' at Bishop Grosseteste University, UK, and to the participants who contributed their poems to the research project.

References

Beijaard, D., Meijer, P.C. and Verloop, N. (2004) Reconsidering research on teachers' professional identity, *Teaching and Teacher Education*, 20: 107–28.

Borg, M. (2001) Teachers' beliefs: key concepts in ELT, *ELT Journal*, 55(2): 186–98.

Boyt, T.E., Lusch, R.F. and Naylor G. (2001) The role of professionalism in determining job satisfaction in professional service: a study of marketing researchers, *Journal of Service Research*, 3(4): 321–30.

Bruner, J. (1986) *Actual Minds, Possible Worlds*. Cambridge, MA: Harvard University Press.

Carson, C., Luker, R. and Russell, P.A. (2007) *The Papers of Martin Luther King Vol. VI (1948–1963)*. Berkeley, CA: University of California Press.

Day, C., Samsons, P., Kington, A. and Stobart, G. (2007) *Teachers Matter: Connecting Work Lives and Effectiveness*. Maidenhead: Open University Press.

Department for Education and Employment/Qualifications and Curriculum Authority (DfEE/QCA) (1999) *The National Curriculum: Handbook for Primary Teachers in England (Key Stages 1 and 2)*. London: DfEE/QCA.

Etzioni, A. (ed.) (1969) *The Semi Professions and Their Organization: Teachers, Nurses, Social Workers*. New York: Free Press.

Evans, L.M. (2008) Professionalism, professionality and the development of education professionals, *British Journal of Education Studies*, 56(1): 20–38.

Fullan, M. (1993) Why teachers must become change agents, *Professional Teacher*, 50(6): 12–17.

Griffin, T.D. and Ohlsson, S. (2001) Beliefs versus knowledge: a necessary distinction for explaining, predicting and assessing conceptual change, in J.D. Moore and K. Stenning (eds.) *Proceedings of the Twenty Third Annual Conference of the Cognitive Science Society*. Mahwah, NJ: Lawrence Erlbaum Associates.

Helsby, G. and McCulloch (1996) Teacher professionalism and curriculum control, in I. Goodson and A. Hargreaves (eds.) *Teachers' Professional Lives*. London: Falmer Press.

Kelly, G., Luke, A. and Green J. (2008) What counts as knowledge in education settings: disciplinary knowledge assessment and curriculum, *Review of Research in Education*, 32(1): vii–x.

Kuzborska, I. (2011) Links between teachers' beliefs and practices and research on reading, *Reading in a Foreign Language*, 23(1): 102–28.

Newkirk, T. (2009) Stress control and deprofessionalizing teachers, *Education Week*, 29(8): 24–5.

O'Connor, K.E. (2008) 'You can choose to care': teachers' emotions and professional identity, *Teaching and Teacher Education*, 24: 117–26.

Raths, J. (2001) Teachers' beliefs and teaching beliefs, *Early Childhood Research and Practice*, 3(1). Available at: http://ecrp.uiuc.edu/v3n1/raths.html (accessed August 2012).

Sachs, J. (2001) Teachers' professional identity: competing discourses, competing outcomes, *Journal of Education Policy*, 16(2): 149–61.

Shinde, M.B. and Karekatti, T.K. (2012) Pre-service teachers' beliefs about teaching English to primary school children, *International Journal of Instruction*, 5(1): 69–86.

United Nations General Assembly (1989) *The United Nations Convention on the Rights of the Child*. New York: United Nations.

Vygotsky, L. (1978) *Mind in Society: The Development of Higher Psychological Processes.* Cambridge, MA: Harvard University Press.

Vyran, K.D., Alder, P.A. and Alder, P. (2003) Identity, in L.T. Reynolds and K.N.J. Herman (eds.) *Handbook of Symbolic Interactionism.* Oxford: Alta Mira Press.

Whitty, G. (2006) Teachers' professionalism in a new era. Paper presented at the *First General Teaching Council for Northern Ireland Annual Lecture*, Belfast, March.

Wilkins, C. (2010) Professionalism and the post performative teacher: new teachers reflect on autonomy and accountability in the English school system, *Professional Development in Education*, 37(3): 389–409.

Young, M. (2007) What are schools for?, in H. Daniels, H. Lauder and J. Porter (eds.) *The Routledge Companion to Education.* London: Routledge.

12 Reflection

Lindy Nahmad-Williams

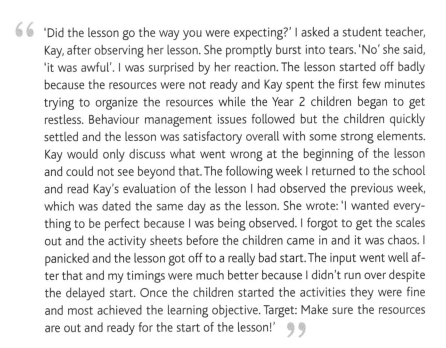

" 'Did the lesson go the way you were expecting?' I asked a student teacher, Kay, after observing her lesson. She promptly burst into tears. 'No' she said, 'it was awful'. I was surprised by her reaction. The lesson started off badly because the resources were not ready and Kay spent the first few minutes trying to organize the resources while the Year 2 children began to get restless. Behaviour management issues followed but the children quickly settled and the lesson was satisfactory overall with some strong elements. Kay would only discuss what went wrong at the beginning of the lesson and could not see beyond that. The following week I returned to the school and read Kay's evaluation of the lesson I had observed the previous week, which was dated the same day as the lesson. She wrote: 'I wanted everything to be perfect because I was being observed. I forgot to get the scales out and the activity sheets before the children came in and it was chaos. I panicked and the lesson got off to a really bad start. The input went well after that and my timings were much better because I didn't run over despite the delayed start. Once the children started the activities they were fine and most achieved the learning objective. Target: Make sure the resources are out and ready for the start of the lesson!' "

Introduction

Reflection is central to teaching and learning. To develop as teachers we must have time to think, reflect, evaluate, and analyse to move our practice forward and engage in the cycle of learning. The process of reflection is affected by a number of elements: our expectations of ourselves; the situation; our knowledge and understanding; our emotional reaction; and most importantly, time to think. Reflective thinking can vary from an immediate reaction to a situation to a more in-depth critical approach that takes account of a range of perspectives. This chapter considers what the term 'reflection' means in practice. It considers why reflection is important in teaching and learning and strategies to encourage and develop a reflective approach. It also considers how to promote a culture of reflection, involving teachers and children, to maximize the potential for learning.

Defining reflection

In its simplest form, reflection involves thinking about a personal experience to help to inform future action if a similar experience is repeated. The process of reflection transforms our thinking and affects our practice. When teaching, this may involve thinking about a lesson taught, considering strengths and areas for improvement, and adjusting future teaching based on these considerations. Although this seems fairly straightforward, reflection is a complex process. It can have many layers and can take place immediately after an experience or be returned to on a number of occasions to deepen the level of reflection. The result could be a slight alteration in practice or a profound change in our teaching philosophy.

The notion of reflection has been developed, debated, and critiqued by many theorists and writers and this section of the chapter considers some of the most influential. Dewey (1897) highlighted the need for a cycle of reflection to re-construct experiences in a systematic way. Kolb (1984) developed this idea with his cycle of experiential learning. The four elements of Kolb's cycle involve:

- personal experience (concrete action);
- thinking about that experience (reflective observation);
- considering how we might do things differently next time to improve the outcomes (abstract conceptualization);
- trying the new way of doing things to see how it works (active experimenta-tion).

This way of thinking is very systematic and can be a useful way of summariz-ing the reflective process, but in reality it is more complex than this cycle might suggest.

Schön (1987) recognized that real-life experience is often unpredictable and complex and, in addition to reflection-on-action (as demonstrated by Kolb's cycle), he referred to reflection-in-action whereby you have to think on your feet to respond to the unexpected. For example, a teacher may begin a lesson assuming the children will have certain prior knowledge and understanding about the sub-ject. As it becomes apparent that they don't have this knowledge, the teacher will quickly have to abandon what was planned and address this lack of understanding before moving on. This could be described as 'reflection-in-action', although some would argue that this is misuse of the term reflection, which can only happen after the event. Moon (1999), who is critical of some of Schön's work, suggests that we make decisions 'in-action' based on previous reflection of our experiences. In other words, the reflection does not occur during the action but occurs earlier in the cycle and impacts the way we respond to unexpected events.

Both Moon (1999, 2008) and Amulya (2003) recognize that reflections can vary in depth. The immediacy of Schön's reflection-in-action does not allow for an in-depth examination of our actions but could be described as a high-speed, surface reflection. This is then followed by a longer process of analysis and critical reflection, which helps us to understand our actions and develop our future practice. Referring back to the example, the teacher recognizing that children did not have the expected prior knowledge would later ask questions about why that assumption had been made, what happened when the children didn't understand, how it was addressed at the time, other ways to deal with the situation, how to ascertain children's prior knowledge and understanding, and how this would affect approaches to planning in the future.

Smyth (1991) provides a slightly different model of reflective practice, involving:

- describing the event;
- analysing it;
- thinking about how to do things differently;
- using this reconstruction to try out a new approach.

The first part of the model, description, is important. For some this may appear a low-level activity. Students will be well aware of tutors' assertions to move away from description and develop analytical skills when involved in academic writing. However, the process of describing the event, in other words telling the story, is the first step towards understanding what happened, why it happened, and how things can be changed. The significance of narrative is explored in other chapters (see Chapter 2, *Narrative*, in particular) and it is a highly important element of reflection.

Smyth (1991) does not refer to the emotional response as an integral part of the reflective process, yet because reflection relates to our own experiences it is hard to detach our emotions. In fact, it could be argued that the emotional response is an integral part of reflection. Moon (1999) believes that emotion cannot be separated from the process of reflection, although she does say that deferred reflection helps to reduce the emotional impact and increase objectivity (Moon 2008). Gibbs' (1988) model includes 'feelings' as one of the first aspects of reflection. It may well be that the gut reaction to an experience, whether positive or negative, is the first step towards reflective evaluation.

Pause for thought

Consider the short vignette that opens this chapter.

- Why did Kay react the way she did to the question?
- What are the differences between the written evaluation and her reaction straight after the lesson? Why are there differences?
- Consider what her evaluation of the same lesson might have been at the end of her placement.

Head, heart, and hands

Reflection could be thought of as a purely cognitive process but as it involves personal experiences with emotional connections, it is also an affective process. Teaching is a creative endeavour that is constantly evolving. Teachers themselves are influenced by their cultural backgrounds, their values, their beliefs, and their experiences. We cannot detach the process of reflection from the individual and the people with whom that individual interacts. To this end, reflection can be viewed as encompassing three core aspects: the head, the heart, and the hands.

This holistic idea of learning and reflection may be attributed to the work of Pestalozzi (1746–1827) and Steiner (1996), whose educational approaches were based on the inter-connectedness between head, heart, and hands. Sergiovanni (1992) refers to 'the head' as the aspect that makes meaning; 'the heart' as the aspect that relates to our values and attitudes; and 'the hands' as the action that may occur as a result of meaning making and attitudes. These three aspects could also be described as knowing, believing, and doing. All three are needed for in-depth critical reflection but teachers may start at different places. For example, a teacher may do but not understand, or know but not believe. When engaging in reflection, teachers need to consider and question their knowledge and under-standing, their attitudes, and their actions. It is a holistic process that should have a transformational effect, not always in action, but certainly in understanding. If we want children to be inquirers, active constructers of meaning, and engage in critical thinking, then those of us who teach them must hold the same values and be involved in the same processes.

Different types of reflection

Having attempted to define some of the characteristics of reflective practice, this section considers the different ways we can reflect on an experience. Three of the key types are an overview, a critical incident, and an area of focus. These three types demand different levels of reflection from the immediate, surface level of reflection to the deepest level of critical reflection.

'How do you think your lesson went?' is a question often asked of students during placement. They are being asked to reflect on the whole lesson immediately after they have finished teaching and often the response can be quite meaningless: 'okay', 'I think it went all right', 'the children did what I wanted them to do'. At the same time, they are trying to read the observer's facial expressions for affirmation that the lesson was successful. If we really want to encourage reflection, the lesson has to be taken apart and re-constructed to provide a more meaningful overview. This can be done at quite a surface level: what went well; what didn't go so well; what I could do to change things for next time. It could also be analysed section by section, almost using a timeline to focus on each step of the lesson. Another approach is to identify and reflect on different aspects of the lesson, such as behaviour management, time management, transitions, assessment opportunities, differentiation, and so on. As the overview becomes more focused, the reflection becomes deeper. Grimes (2006) refers to the significant role of an experienced practitioner to facilitate the reflection through careful and sensitive questioning. This relates to Vygostsky's (1978) Zone of Proximal Development, where the expert other enables development that may not be possible if the individual is a solitary learner. Even the most experienced practitioners may need to engage in dialogue with another person to deepen their level of reflection, and the importance of dialogue is returned to later in the chapter.

A critical incident is any significant experience that prompts the reflective process, which in turn may change the way we view things and alter our practice. The term 'critical' suggests a very serious incident but it is only critical in the sense that it prompts us to critically evaluate our practice (Tripp 1994).

Case study

Amy was in her first year of a teaching degree. She was doing her placement in a class of Year 2 children (aged 6–7 years) and noticed that one child, Janey, looked rather unkempt. When she asked the teacher about her, she was told that Janey was living in a children's home because she had been removed from her parents' home. Her parents were regular drug users and had neglected Janey who had been removed for her own safety. Amy was shocked, as she came from a loving home and all her friends were from similar backgrounds. This incident prompted Amy to reflect on her assumptions about society and childhood. She realized that she could not assume that all children had the same privileged background as her and that children in any one class came from a range of backgrounds with differing home life experiences.

The case study above did not result in an immediate change in Amy's practice but did involve Amy reflecting on her knowledge and understanding based on her own narrow experiences. Her view of the world and the society in which she lived changed and that in turn had an impact on Amy's development as a person and as a teacher.

A simple experience can initiate a significant change in practice, but it is only through reflecting on that experience that defines it as a critical incident. It is how the incident is interpreted. The first step is that of 'noticing' (Boud 2001). For students and inexperienced teachers, the critical incident is often one that induces an emotional reaction, which emphasizes it, and promotes the notion of 'noticing'. It can then be reflected upon after the incident, when the emotions are less raw, and analysed. More experienced teachers may also notice smaller, less emotionally charged incidents that could affect their practice. For example, a teacher may notice the way another colleague communicates with a child who is finding learning difficult. After reflection this may prompt the teacher who observed this exchange to alter their approach to a child with similar problems in the class. Once the critical incident has been noticed, the reflective process truly begins.

Pause for thought

Consider your own philosophy of teaching.

- Do you remember a critical incident that has had an impact on your developing philosophy?
- If so, what made it a critical incident?
- If not, think about the factors that have influenced your philosophy.

The third most common type of reflection is focused on a specific area. This is often used when a person has identified a particular aspect of teaching that needs developing. It may be that a student teacher and mentor have decided on a target related to one aspect of teaching, such as timings or transitions. Using one of the reflective models referred to earlier in this chapter is particularly useful in this type of reflection. It may be based on a lack of confidence or experience in teaching a certain type of lesson. For example, students often mention PE in their early years of teacher education because the organization and space used in PE are so different from those in lessons taught in the classroom. This often induces anxiety and a feeling that things will get out of control. Suddenly the routines of the classroom are no longer there and actions that are not allowed in the classroom, such as running, are positively encouraged in PE. The reflective process may start before the first ever PE lesson is planned and taught. Instead of reflecting on a previously taught PE lesson, reflections may be based on PE lessons observed, with consideration given to organization of resources and equipment, management of the children, and lesson structure. Once the lesson is planned and taught with these aspects in mind, the reflective process begins again in relation to the personal experience of teaching PE.

Pause for thought

Identify an area of practice that you need to develop. Consider the following questions:

- Why have you identified this area?
- What strategies could you use to improve it?
- How will you know if your practice has improved in this area?

The key to success is that we understand the purpose for identifying our area of focus, which will enhance deeper and more meaningful reflection. The result should be that it has an impact on our professional development, not just in a practical way, but also in our thinking and understanding. For example, a first-year student teacher, Kirsty, told me how the simple act of doing a downward movement of her hands when saying 'hands down' to the children was far more effective than just saying the words. This technique had been shown to her in a lecture. When we discussed this further, Kirsty began to reflect on the significance of both verbal and non-verbal communication. She talked about the importance of facial expressions and body language and also began to consider how to support children with speech and language difficulties. The significance of effective communication, not just in the way we use words, began to formulate in Kirsty's mind. When observing Kirsty in her final placement in the third year, I noticed how well she provided for a child with autism and communication difficulties in her class. She had a visual timetable, used key pictorial symbols, and used a range of non-verbal signals to supplement verbal utterances. Kirsty could have accepted this 'hands down' as a simple technique in her first year and given it no further thought. However, because she reflected on why this technique worked, it had a significant impact on her practice.

Strategies to encourage reflection

The importance of dialogue and collaborative working is emphasized in many of the chapters in this book, and it is an important feature of reflective practice.

Discussing our practice with others can help us to clarify our own thinking. Other people can provide an alternative perspective that allows us to consider different possibilities and develop new ways of thinking (Johnston and Nahmad-Williams 2009). We can talk about our practice with other more experienced colleagues and with our peers.

Mentoring and coaching is not necessarily the expert/apprentice model but has the explicit purpose of supporting the development of practice (Stammers 1992). Mentoring can involve a more experienced member of staff offering advice and guidance to a less experienced colleague or student teacher. York-Barr et al. (2006) suggest key characteristics to this relationship, including good listening skills by partners, a clear purpose, and being open minded to new ideas. It should be a reciprocal partnership, each learning from the other. Although the obvious learner is the less experienced colleague, the mentoring process should also encourage the more experienced colleague to reflect on his or her practice.

Group mentoring or peer discussion is an approach that involves colleagues at the same level gathering together to discuss professional issues. The fact that there is no power relationship can help promote a more honest and open exchange of views. Peer discussion can help to expand ideas, support problem solving, consider ideas for the future, and help to develop reflective practice (York-Barr et al. 2006). There are clear advantages to this approach, most notably emotional support. Sharing problems with others can allow us to see things more objectively. The well known phrase 'a problem shared is a problem halved' highlights the potential of talking things over with others to help find solutions and lessen the emotional load that can cloud our judgement. Jindal-Snape and Holmes (2006) conducted research that highlighted some of the advantages of peer support but concluded that professional development was more likely when a more experienced practitioner was involved in mentoring. Both types of mentoring have their advantages and both are strategies to support reflective practice.

Written evaluations are common practice in teacher education. They provide evidence of reflection and also allow students to see how their learning and practice has developed over the course of the placement. Daily and/or weekly evaluations are common ways of recording reflections during placements. If these are thought of as onerous tasks that add to the workload but have little value, they will serve no useful purpose. We need to view reflection as an integral part of the teaching and learning cycle. Few would disagree that planning, teaching, and assessment are integral but we need to ensure reflection is also included: reflection on our practice and reflection on children's learning. Many students find that talking about their practice is much easier than writing about it. Using a simple format that keeps the evaluation succinct and focused can help. Headings such as 'positive points', 'areas for development', and 'targets' can be less time consuming and more useful when evaluations need to be written on a regular basis.

A more narrative approach can be used in reflective journals, learning logs or diary entries. The importance of describing events and acknowledging the emotional response can be therapeutic and are a significant part of reflection. They help us to make sense of our experiences and develop our learning (Boud 2001). This relates back to the value of viewing reflection as a combination of our heads, our hearts, and our hands. Keeping a log of our experiences also allows us to look back and 'reflect' on our reflections. Looking back enables us to acknowledge our feelings at the time but gives us the benefit of hindsight and further experience to extend our learning.

Case study

Students on a BA (Hons) in Primary Education with QTS are encouraged to keep a learning journal throughout their three years of study. Tutors suggest that some of the entries should be a follow-up activity after a taught session. Other entries are written whenever students feel they have experienced something significant to their learning. These could be related to school placement experiences or university-based sessions. At the end of the first year, the students choose four entries from their learning journal to expand and comment on to evaluate their learning over the whole year. In their final year, the students write their teaching philosophy and analyse what has influenced the development of their philosophy. Entries from their learning journal from throughout the three years are included. The initial learning journal entries are made immediately after any relevant experience. The secondary reflection takes place after one year and then again after three years. This enables students to understand the effect of time, as suggested by Moon (2008), on the personal view of an issue to promote in-depth, critical reflection.

With the advance of technology, the use of digital video recording is another way to aid reflection. Very few people enjoy watching themselves on video but it gives us the opportunity to see ourselves as others see us. Filming a lesson and then watching it enables teachers to see their own practice and children's learning. It also gives the teacher and mentor observable evidence to talk about, and different parts of the lesson can be re-played to allow for more detailed analysis. When watching a student watching herself on video, words were not really needed. I could see from her facial expressions (after the initial shock of seeing herself had worn off!) when she saw something she was pleased with or something she would want to change.

This section has considered a number of strategies to encourage reflection: discussions with an experienced mentor or peer discussions; formal, written evaluations; reflective journals; and the use of digital video recording. These have all been focused on the reflections of the teacher. Let us now consider how a culture of reflection can be promoted in the classroom. This includes the children reflecting on their own learning.

Promoting a culture of reflection

Assessment for learning is a commonly used term that involves the teacher and the child working collaboratively to assess the child's learning and set targets for development. This in turn informs the teacher's planning and enables the child to engage fully with the assessment cycle. I have often been in classrooms where children are asked to indicate their own assessment of their learning or understanding with thumbs up, down or wiggling horizontally. This is usually immediately after the teacher's input or at the end of independent activities. Another strategy I have seen is children colouring in a symbolic representation of 'understood', 'understood but needs more practice' or 'not understood' in their books at the end of the lesson. This reminds me of the students who are asked to comment on the success of their lesson immediately after it has been observed. Although it gives a snapshot of their feelings at that time, can we really call that reflection? We must also ask ourselves if the children understand fully what we are asking them to assess.

If we consider aspects that have been discussed so far in this chapter, all of these apply to children: the head, heart, and hands approach; dialogue with peers and with the teacher; listening to one another and learning from one another; supporting each other with problem solving; time and space to think; and different ways to record reflections. Schools adopt a number of approaches that support the reflective process. Circle time allows children to express their views or feelings in a 'safe' but also very public environment. School Councils give children the opportunity to discuss issues that they feel are pertinent to them, but only a chosen few are actually members of the Council. Some classrooms have 'feelings' trees or other similar strategies, but again this is very public. As teachers, we need to consider how we can encourage all children to reflect, including more private reflection.

Facilitating speaking and listening skills, using Bloom's taxonomy of questioning (Bloom et al. 1956) – which involves different levels of thinking from recall and understanding to creative and critical thinking – and Alexander's (2004) dialogic teaching approach will help to encourage children to engage in deeper and more critical reflection. Listening to children and showing them that you have listened empowers children. When I was teaching Reception aged children I decided to re-arrange the classroom. I was going to do it in the Easter holidays but thought I would ask the children how they wanted the classroom arranged. We reflected on how the classroom worked in its current arrangement. The children raised issues that would never have occurred to me. For example, apparently the construction area was not big enough to enable the children to build the structures they wanted to build. We produced a plan for the new layout and made modifications based on suggestions. Together we rearranged the room and trialled its effectiveness. After the trial period, we reflected on how well the new arrangement worked and made minor modifications. This approach involved listening to each other, problem solving, time to reflect, and dialogue with peers and the teacher. The children were empowered and by listening to them I knew the classroom environment suited their needs.

Children can also keep learning logs or journals. These do not have to be written accounts. They could include drawings, photos, colours, and form to express feelings and thoughts. Children can look back at these and reflect on their feelings at the time they made the journal entry and how they feel now. They could make timelines showing when they learnt something significant and what they want to learn next. Teachers will often keep portfolios of children's work as evidence of their learning over a period of time. These pieces of work can be chosen and be reflected on periodically by the children themselves, and their comments about how they feel about their own progress can be added to the portfolios. All these strategies encourage reflection at a far deeper level than the immediate thumbs up, thumbs down approach so often seen in classrooms. They also empower children and develop a community of enquiry, which promotes critical thinking and deep reflection as central to education (Claxton 2002; Fisher 1990; Lipman 2003).

Developing practice

To develop reflective practice, we need to consider:

- how much we reflect on our own practice;
- what strategies we use to promote our own reflection;
- how good we are at 'noticing' what is going on in our classrooms;
- whether we give ourselves time to reflect more deeply on our practice and return to previous reflections for secondary reflection;
- how we promote a culture of reflection in our own classrooms;
- how we show children that we value their reflections on their own learning.

Conclusion

This chapter has explored the nature of reflection and reflective practice. The process of reflection has been defined through the use of various models, including the key elements of action: describing the action, analysing the action, considering improvements, and trying out the improvements. The importance of emotional response is emphasized, with reflection being seen as a holistic process that involves the head, heart, and hands. The initial emotional response to an experience is often the prompt to begin the reflective process and the power of this should not be underestimated. However, deferred reflection or secondary reflection – that is, standing back and waiting for the emotional response to dissipate – allows for a deeper, more objective approach.

Dialogue has a significant part to play in reflection. It allows us to rehearse the experience, consider alternative viewpoints, clarify our thoughts, and enhance our learning. Talking with peers and with more experienced professionals emphasizes the reciprocal nature of collaborative reflection, which allows all parties involved to learn from the experience. The use of learning logs and journals promotes internal dialogue and a personal response to specific events. It also enables us to track our learning and view our emerging philosophy as it evolves from reflection on a range of experiences.

If we agree that the reflective process is integral to learning, it is paramount that children are also encouraged to engage in reflection. We must promote a culture of reflection in our classrooms by giving children time to think and providing a range of experiences that encourage critical thinking about themselves and their learning. We can only do this with conviction and commitment if we are reflective practitioners ourselves and constantly strive to move our practice forward.

References

Alexander, R. (2004) *Towards Dialogic Teaching: Re-thinking Classroom Talk*, 3rd edn. York: Dialogos.

Amulya, J. (2003) *What is Reflective Practice?* Cambridge, MA: MIT Press.

Bloom, B., Englehart, M., Furst, E., Hill, W.H. and Krathwohl, D. (1956) *Taxonomy of Educational Objectives: The Classification of Educational Goals. Handbook I: Cognitive Domain*. New York: Longman.

Boud, D. (2001) Using journal writing to enhance reflective practice, in L.M. English and M.A. Gillen (eds.) *Promoting Journal Writing in Adult Education*. San Francisco, CA: Jossey-Bass.

Claxton, G. (2002) *Building Learning Power*. Bristol: TLO.

Dewey, J. (1897) My pedagogic creed, *The School Journal,* LIV(3): 77–80.

Fisher, R. (1990) *Teaching Children to Think*. Hemel Hempstead: Simon & Schuster Education.

Gibbs, G. (1988) *Learning by Doing: A Guide to Teaching and Learning Methods*. Birmingham: SCED.

Grimes, R. (2006) *Reflection in Legal Clinic*. Available at: http://www.ukcle.ac.uk/resources/personal-development-planning/example1/ (accessed May 2012).

Jindal-Snape, D. and Holmes, E. (2006) *Investigating Methods for Enhancing Reflective Practice Used by Educational Psychology Students and Practitioners*. Dundee: School of Education, Social Work and Community Education, University of Dundee.

Johnston, J. and Nahmad-Williams, L. (2009) *Early Childhood Studies*. London: Pearson Longman.

Kolb, D.A. (1984) *Experiential Learning*. Englewood Cliffs, NJ: Prentice-Hall.

Lipman, M. (2003) *Thinking in Education*, 2nd edn. Cambridge: Cambridge University Press.

Moon, J. (1999) *Reflection in Learning and Professional Development*. London: Kogan Page.

Moon, J. (2008) *Critical Thinking*. London: Routledge.

Schön, D.A. (1987) *Educating the Reflective Practitioner*. San Francisco, CA: Jossey-Bass.

Sergiovanni, T.J. (1992) *Moral Leadership: Getting to the Heart of School Improvement*. San Francisco, CA: Jossey-Bass.

Smyth, J. (1991) *Teachers as Collaborative Learners*. Buckingham: Open University Press.

Stammers, P. (1992) The Greeks had a name for it …, *British Journal of In-Service Education*, 3(2): 76–80.

Steiner, R. (1996) *The Education of the Child and Early Lectures on Education*. New York: Anthroposophic Press.

Tripp, D. (1994) Teachers' lives, critical incidents and professional practice, *Qualitative Studies in Education*, 7(1): 65–76.

Vygotsky, L. (1978) *Mind in Society: The Development of Higher Psychological Processes*. Cambridge, MA: Harvard University Press.

York-Barr, J., Sommers, W., Ghere, G. and Montie, J. (2006) *Reflective Practice to Improve Schools*. Thousand Oaks, CA: Corwin Press.

13

Values

Richard Woolley

> 66 Ali, aged 4, is playing in the role-play area of his reception classroom. The focus for the week is family celebrations, and the children have visited the local church to learn about weddings. An array of clothes and other artefacts have been provided for the children to explore. While Ali is trying on the bridesmaid's dress, his teacher notices and calls across the classroom telling him that he needs to choose an outfit that a boy would wear. 99

Introduction

As teachers, we each have a range of values that influence and inform our philosophies of education. For most, if not all of us, these will include respect for the individual, tolerance, an appreciation of the role of community and society, a sense of dependence upon others, inter-dependence with those in a range of places around the globe, and an understanding of love, care, friendship, and thankfulness.

The current focus on children's rights and the importance of the voice of the child makes an exploration of values fundamental to any consideration of the aims and purposes of being an educator: how such rights can be enacted and linked to a developing sense of responsibility and how the child's voice can be both projected and heard in ways that are genuinely welcomed and acted upon. This chapter will outline aspects of the United Nations Convention on the Rights of the Child (United Nations General Assembly 1989) and consider how these apply both to a classroom setting and the development of a whole-school ethos. This contributes to the process of helping children to develop a unique and individual sense of self, of building self-esteem, and taking on a role within their class, school, and community. It was central to the Every Child Matters agenda (DfES 2004) (a key part of education policy in the UK in the first decade of the twenty-first century) and to the

establishment and maintenance of wellbeing and good mental health. It is fundamentally connected to the development of positive and healthy relationships with
others, which in turn necessitate both self-care and mutual respect.

Expressing values

What we value is sometimes reflected in the things that we do, but it can also be
evident from what we do not do. The ways in which we organize our classrooms,
the resources we make available, how we respond and listen to children, parents/
carers and colleagues, and our use of language, all contribute to the expression
of values. For example, a review of the texts we use with children will show how
diverse and inclusive we feel society to be. Do we include different types of family, those from various ethnic and cultural backgrounds, people with a variety of
abilities and disabilities, and positive gender role models? How do we do this in a
natural way that shows aspects of daily life, rather than an issues-based approach
that segregates or marginalizes others? It is essential that we consider whether
stereotypes are present and/or reinforced in our classrooms.

Research suggests that student teachers are particularly concerned about
how parents and carers will react if schools address issues relating to values
in a way contrary to their own personal views (Woolley 2010). The students
identified three areas as being of particular concern: tacking racism, addressing relationship issues and sexuality, and learning about different religions and
beliefs. Thus it is important to have a sense of what we are seeking to achieve
as educators – and what the purpose of education is – to establish a rationale
for inclusive practice.

Case study

As a child I remember the singing game *The Farmer's in His Den*, in which the farmer
stands in the centre of a circle of children and chooses a wife, who then chooses a
child, with subsequent participants choosing a nurse, a dog, and a bone. All the children
then pat the bone and the song restarts. I remember the feeling of embarrassment on
being chosen to be the bone (and not wanting to be patted by the crowd) and also
the awkwardness of the gender combinations that children chose for the farmer/wife
relationship. It was not uncommon for a boy to choose another boy, particularly as the
participants wanted to favour their friends.

Consider:

- how the process of being chosen or not chosen during the game might impact
  on a child's self-esteem;

- how children might be encouraged to ensure that all are included during the game and encouraged to choose beyond their immediate circle of friends;
- whether the implied hierarchy of roles in the song might have any impact on the participants.

This example of a game for young children raises a variety of issues. The activities that we choose to include in our classrooms communicate a range of messages to children; sometimes these are intentional but at other times they are not. Working out how you fit into the group, developing a sense of gender identity, forming friendships, and making comparisons between self and others, are all areas that children encounter on a regular basis. Feeling accepted and coming to understand that others can be different in a wide variety of ways are both key elements of maturing into a confident individual. Being enabled to participate in activities, and learning that your ideas and questions are welcomed, are elements that contribute to becoming an active citizen. Such involvement needs to be underpinned by a sense of being valued accompanied by having personal values which enable positive interactions with others.

Claire (2001: 1) identifies seven strands that make for active citizenship:

- Empowerment
- Empathy
- Identity
- Diversity
- Ethics
- Action
- Vision.

These are not areas that can be taught *per se*. Rather, they can be nurtured through exploration and engagement with ideas and issues. The area of values, central to this chapter, is implicit to each element. Readers will want to consider whether additional elements should be added to the list as they work through the chapter.

Pause for thought

Consider the vignette at the start of this chapter.

- How might the teacher's reaction affect Ali or stimulate a reaction from other children?
- Might this situation prove embarrassing or humiliating for Ali?
- Did the teacher need to react in any way, and if so what might an appropriate response have been?

Participation

The United Nations Convention on the Rights of the Child (United Nations General Assembly 1989), the first legally binding international instrument to incorporate the full range of human rights – civil, cultural, economic, political, and social – was ratified by the UK Government in 1991. Of all its elements, perhaps the most significant principle is that children should have the opportunity to express a view on matters of concern to them, and to have that view taken seriously. Mike Steele explored the importance of children's voice in Chapter 9. In this chapter, the issue is to consider how their voice can be heard and taken into account in ways that show that their views are both valued and valuable.

In recent years, there have been moves to develop children's involvement in the life of a school through enterprises such as School Councils. If an aim of the curriculum is to prepare children for adult life, then helping them to develop an understanding of democracy and democratic processes is important. Not only does this prepare them for future life, but it can enable them to be active citizens in the present. The Crick Report (QCA 1998: 44) outlines eight key concepts that children should understand by the end of compulsory schooling:

- Democracy and autocracy
- Cooperation and conflict
- Equality and diversity
- Fairness, justice, the rule of law, and human rights
- Freedom and order
- Individual and community
- Power and authority
- Rights and responsibilities.

Each of these applies to the ways in which we relate to one another and to the world around us. From the early years, children are considering how they fit in and learning to live alongside the various others with whom they find themselves within their local school community. Learning environments are probably the first place where children encounter a significant number of others who differ from them in terms of social, family, economic, and cultural backgrounds. While one may choose friends, classmates are a given. Supporting children as they seek to cooperate with this diverse group is an important part of their socialization and helping them to develop into thoughtful and respectful citizens.

For some children, the values that they encounter at school will differ considerably from those with which they have become familiar in their home. As a class teacher, I have encountered situations where a parent has advised a child to respond to aggression with aggression, or to 'Hit him first, before he has the chance to hit you'. Children are generally resilient and flexible, and able to understand that they sometimes inhabit two worlds – that of the home and that of school. The idea that some words and behaviours are not acceptable within the school environment can be understood and acted upon. However, this brings into question the extent to which the impact of the socializing aspect of school can help children to develop a set of values that will have an enduring effect as they grow and mature.

In recent decades, schools have sought to nurture children's self-esteem by avoiding the use of a red pen to mark work, putting dots on work rather than crosses, and removing competitive sport: all intended to help children to feel a sense of success, or at least a lack of failure. I have engaged in all these actions myself with the best of intentions. However, this raises the question of how this prepares children to face a world in which failure exists, and how it presents opportunities to learn how to deal with the realities of life in a competitive and sometimes unfair world. There is no easy solution to this issue. However, whatever approach we take to such matters, the fact remains that each child in a classroom is a unique individual, worthy of respect, affirmation, and nurturing. This may sound idealistic, but I suggest that it is an ideal for which it is worth striving.

Facilitating learning

We now turn to consider three educationalists, from diverse settings around the world, who grappled with the idea of facilitating children's learning and considered the value of skills development with learners.

Paulo Freire (1921–1997)

Freire was a Brazilian educator who rejected the notion of *banking* knowledge and the associated focus on didactic teaching traditionally found in many classrooms. He did not see children as vessels to be filled with knowledge, but rather as capable of developing the skills to acquire knowledge. He believed that learning should develop both individuals and communities (including families and school communities) through action and activity. His most famous work is *Pedagogy of the Oppressed* (first published in 1968 in Portuguese) in which he argues that humans develop through the process of learning: through action-reflection (an area explored further by Lindy Nahmad-Williams in Chapter 12). Learners should be enabled to reflect on the process of learning and on their own context in order to develop a range of skills that will equip them to develop both themselves and the world around them. Freire believed that the power of education, particularly through developing literacy, could empower people to question and to challenge the constraints of the society around them (Freire 2007).

Carl Rogers (1902–1987)

Rogers was an American educationalist and psychologist whose focus was on facilitating freedom for individual learners. His stress on human relationships as a means of achieving learning (Rogers 1969) focuses on the importance of *learning how to learn* and *learning about learning*. For Rogers, the important thing is the ability to learn, which provides skills that will last and develop further throughout life, rather than on imparting knowledge. Within this philosophical outlook, the focus is on experiential learning in which the teacher becomes a facilitator, rather than the provider of information. This supportive role enables dialogue to develop, the sharing of questions, and the exploration of ideas. This does not mean that the teacher is deskilled or marginalized in the process – quite the opposite. The teacher has to become highly skilled in facilitating learning, enabling children to share ideas and to talk them through in order to deepen understanding.

Janusz Korczak (1878–1942)

Korczak (born Henryk Goldsmit) was a doctor, educationalist, and children's author from Poland. He committed much of his life to nurturing children in the orphanage for Jewish children that he ran, exploring ways of developing their self-confidence and skills of living in community (Lifton 2005). He initiated democratic processes within the orphanage, including a children's court in which the residents (including Korczak himself) were held to account for their actions. His writing reveals that this was not an easy or straightforward process, and foreshadows the work on citizenship and pupil voice that developed much later in the twentieth century (Joseph 2007; Korczak 2003). His work influenced the later development of the UN Convention on the Rights of the Child (United Nations General Assembly 1989). A key element of Korczak's philosophy is that children are not the citizens of the future, but the people of today.

All three of these educators have a focus on enabling children to become active participants in the learning process, rather than being the passive recipients of knowledge. Facilitating their thinking, questioning, and inquisitiveness is key to this process: it enables them to be active in the present, while developing skills that will continue to develop into their futures. Such ideas are fully resonant with the ideas of Robert Grosseteste, outlined in Chapter 1.

It is clear that the world in which our children will live as adults will be hugely different from that in which they have grown up. To reflect on my own experience of primary school, there were no computers (not even in the school office) and the head teacher would not buy a television, as he felt that we probably watched it too much at home. We did listen to the radio on occasion, to children's stories, music programmes or lessons on dance. The technological world that I now inhabit was not anticipated. (Chapter 8 on *Technology* explores these issues further.) The same will be true for the learners currently in our classrooms: we cannot anticipate how the world will change during their lifetime, but a curriculum that focuses on developing skills and the self-confidence to question and to explore can prepare children to face whatever lies ahead. Freire would add that such abilities equip people to challenge injustice, to question the status quo, and to work towards greater freedom:

> A Freirean critical teacher is a problem-poser who asks thought-provoking questions and who encourages students to ask their own questions. Through problem-posing, students learn to question answers rather than merely to answer questions. In this pedagogy, students experience education as something they do, not as something done to them.
>
> (Shor 1993: 26)

Education that broadens the horizons of the learner, helps them to question systems and processes, and gives them more choices in life is education in its truest sense. As Mike Steele has already explored (in Chapter 9), a system that is founded on teaching to the test and meeting the demands of a highly prescriptive curriculum works against such principles.

Enabling participation

Hart (1992) proposed a 'Ladder of Participation' to help to scaffold the empowerment of children. While this structure provides a useful metaphor for participation, it should not be seen completely in linear terms, as this might limit the choices available to those wishing to involve children in decision making. It may be better to view the five positive elements as different facets of good practice. For example, the ladder infers that child-initiated and directed participation is the ultimate aim, but this may not be an appropriate approach in all circumstances; in some situations, adults may need to take charge to keep children safe or to protect them from excessive pressure.

Hart's Ladder of Participation

Degrees of participation

8. Child-initiated, shared with adults
7. Child-initiated, but directed by adults

6. Adult-initiated shared decisions with children

5. Children are consulted but informed

4. Children are told what to do but informed

Degrees of non-participation

3. Tokenism

2. Decoration

1. Manipulation

This ladder can relate to decision making about the menu for school meals or how to spend money raised for new equipment for the school playground. It can also be used to enable engagement in child-directed learning, as outlined at various points throughout this book. At various times children ask, 'Why do I need to learn this?' Such a question is less likely if the learning is driven by the child's own inquisitiveness and curiosity. The response, 'Because it is on the syllabus', is unsatisfactory and suggests that what is being learned is not so much valued as required through imposition.

Learning environment

Kathleen Taylor outlined the importance of the learning environment in Chapter 7. Here it is key to consider how that environment communicates what we value within our classrooms and learning spaces. Ensuring that children feel welcomed when they arrive in our setting communicates the fact that we consider them special and appreciate their presence. Making sure that a room is ready for learning when the children arrive, having well-organized, good-quality resources, and preparing activities ready to engage children from the start, all show that we value the children's arrival. These may be small touches that some teachers take for granted, but poor organization or a lack of careful structure to the start of the day may not only have the potential to undermine the security that children feel in our care, they also suggest that what is about to take place has not been our main priority. We cannot know what children will have experienced prior to their arrival, although sometimes we may suspect: Have they eaten breakfast? How smooth was their journey to school? How have the demands of siblings taken the attention of their parent/carer? Have they slept well and had a restful night? So many factors can impact on a child's readiness to learn. These will mainly be beyond our control; however, it is within our control to ensure that the transition into school is supported and as positive as possible.

Similarly, carers and parents can also be made to feel welcome, although for some the process of getting children ready for school before heading off to the other commitments of the day will be stressful. Opening the classroom a few minutes early and encouraging parents/carers to read with and settle their children can be one way of both providing a welcome and creating the opportunity for short supportive conversations. Laura, a teacher of a Year 3 class (children aged 7–8 years), explains that:

> While some parents read quietly with their children, I take the opportunity to catch one or two of the adults – to make a positive comment about what happened the day before. Mentioning that a piece of homework was particularly good, that a child had been helpful, or even asking about a poorly grandparent all help me to make a connection with the parent. This is particularly helpful if, sometime later, I have to discuss a more difficult issue. It is not ideal to meet a parent for the first time when there is a difficult issue to resolve.

Such care and concern helps to develop the overall ethos and atmosphere of a school, expressing a set of values that set a standard for appreciating all stakeholders. Gregory (2000: 447, drawing on Gilligan 1993) outlines six elements that contribute to an ethic of care, and thereby, I argue, the development of both individuals and communities: acquaintance, mindfulness, moral imagining, solidarity, tolerance, and self-care (to which I add my own interpretations: Figure 13.1).

These six areas (Figure 13.1) provide a framework to support an exploration of the values we wish to develop with children. Gregory (2000) suggests that these facets provide the *soil* in which both personal and communal growth can take place through the development of mutual care. Personally, I prefer the word *respect* to *tolerance*, as it sounds less begrudging and more proactive. The framework stresses both the need to value oneself (not being self-less, but rather caring for oneself) in addition to appreciating those with whom one interacts. This is an important value to consider, as we will all have come across people who are so busy caring for everyone else that they neglect themselves. This is reminiscent of the maxim to *Love your neighbour as yourself* found in the Christian Bible (Gospel of Mark 12:31), which is sometimes wrongly read as being to love your neighbour instead of – or more than – yourself.

Transitions

Key to showing children that they are valued, and further developing an ethic of care, is the need to support them when they face major changes and transitions in life. These can be key times when adult support is crucial: as adults we may not

Acquaintance
Developing contact with others
Noticing their existence
Naming and communicating with them
Noting the impact of our contact with them

Mindfulness
Awareness of how our conduct affects others
Developing respect for others
Giving attention to others
Appreciating their uniqueness
Concerned with equality

Moral Imagining
Developing empathy and altruism
Thinking about what it might be like to be in someone else's position

Solidarity
Helping others to achieve their goals
Commitment to working on behalf of others
Mindful of others and their circumstances

Tolerance
Working towards non-discrimination
Working for inclusiveness and appreciating others' needs
Developing respect

Self-care
Being able to articulate one's own needs and wants
Caring for oneself
Negotiating with others
Appreciating that I am special – and that we all have a valuable contribution to make

Adapted from Woolley (2010)

Figure 13.1   Elements contributing to an ethic of care

have experienced the exact circumstances faced by a child, but we have far more experience of change and uncertainty than they do. We can thus seek to scaffold their experience.

Life is full of transitions. Whether it is moving home, changing school or job, developing new friendships, maturing and growing older, or coping with loss, we all face some degree of change on a regular basis. Some changes are more traumatic than others; some are long term or permanent. For children this can cause anxiety, particularly as they may not have prior life experience on which to draw as they prepare for or experience change. At other times, transition and change provide the opportunity for celebration: for the changing seasons, religious festivals or rites of passage. *The Transitions Reading Resource* (Morris and Woolley 2011) published by Bishop Grosseteste University College Lincoln identifies a wide range of resources to help children face change.

Any significant change in life can bring a sense of loss and feelings of grief. While some of these situations cannot be anticipated, some change can be predicted or expected. The move from one class or school to another provides one such example. Teachers can prepare children for such change and help them to face transition with confidence. Facing loss is a difficult area for many teachers and other members of the children's workforce to address with children. Yet children frequently face loss – the loss of a friend, the death of a pet, the separation of family members; loss and grief are implicit to the human condition and to life experience (Morris and Woolley 2011).

Often, the time when resources and support are needed the most are the times when we are least able to access them. To ensure that children feel supported and valued at these times, it is necessary to provide materials in advance of any need. Sometimes it is most appropriate to discuss change, loss or grief with a class of children at a time when none of the children are facing them in an immediate sense. Using children's stories, role play, persona dolls, and other discussion-supporting techniques, we can help children to explore their views and understanding and to begin to develop their skills.

Case study

Sara has been discussing bullying with her class of 7- and 8-year-olds, following a couple of incidents in the playground. Using two picture books she has been able to consider issues without focusing on the actual events in school, with the intention of discussing general issues rather than specific cases known to the children.

She used *Trouble with the Tucker Twins* (Impey 1991) in which a boy called Mick claims to feel poorly. While he likes school, he feels apprehensive about attending because he does not like the Tucker twins. They may not be tall or tough, but there are two of them. Wherever Mick goes, they seem to be there causing annoyance. When Mick returns to school, he finds that one of the twins is not in attendance. The other twin is miserable without him. Mick ends up offering support. He comes to realize that the twins are not as unpleasant as they seemed.

Sara also used *Is it Because?* (Ross 2004) in which a boy asks his dog 'Is it because … ?' Is it because of all his flaws and failings that Peregrine Ffrogg is a bully? Or is it because he is jealous? This lovely book, written in rhyme, focuses on the weaknesses of the bully, before revealing that he is a bully. It effectively undermines the bully's power and ends with the affirmation that the boy is confident that he has friends and a loving dog – things that the bully does not have. This book considers possible root causes of the problem and uses humour (particularly in the illustrations) to make a difficult subject accessible.

The example of Sara provides one illustration of how a teacher can explore values with children through the use of fiction. While it can be easy to over-simplify issues, or to suggest that difficulties are easy to resolve, if we are to value the experience of children, it is important not to ignore some of the complex and sometimes painful situations that they encounter. Enabling children to rehearse possible responses within the safe and supportive setting of the classroom will not make facing life's challenges simple, but it can scaffold the children's learning so that they are better equipped than might otherwise be the case. In addition, show-ing that we care about the issues around them indicates that we take them seri-ously and may help them to appreciate that they are not the only ones facing such difficulties.

Inclusion

As Karen Elvidge discusses in Chapter 10, in recent years the term *inclusion* has taken on a political meaning in schools in the UK. For some, it has come to rep-resent the idea that all children, wherever possible, should be educated within mainstream schools. This has included a range of children with special educa-tional needs and disabilities. There are cases where the specialist support needed by children is beyond that which a mainstream school can offer, and so I would argue that there is a significant and important part to be played by a parallel system of special schools. In some instances, the appearance of inclusion is no more than that, with some children being educated in separate groups, or individually, within the same building as other children. One may question whether this is effec-tively inclusion. However, there is a wider understanding of the term that considers the broader range of needs and differences within the population. The six equal-ity strands that have developed over past decades help to highlight such areas: age, disability, ethnicity/'race', gender, religion and belief, and sexual orientation. Some of these areas may be more visible at times that others. However, a parent's disability, a child's family background or family religious practices are not always immediately apparent. Being committed to creating an inclusive ethos where all members of the school community are valued is an intention that encompasses the aim of making sure that the specialness of each individual is acknowledged. Fundamental to this is Cole's (2008) notion of *isms and phobias* (see also Cole 2006), which include classism, racism/xeno-racism and xenophobia, sexism, dis-ablism, homophobia, and Islamophobia. Teachers and other child-care profession-als need to be aware of isms and phobias in order to create classrooms founded on equity, and understand the value of pupil voice and the principles of democracy. These areas relate back directly to the idea that society is heterogeneous, rather than homogeneous, as discussed in Chapter 11.

What do we value?

There is a maxim that questions whether we only value what is measurable, and whether we can actually measure what is valuable. This is, perhaps, one of the great conundrums of education. If education is about enabling children to be competent in reading, writing, and mathematics, then perhaps we can measure the outcomes. However, if it is also about learning about care, kindness, respect, and mutual understanding, then the outcomes become more qualitative and therefore more subjective. At a time when the school curriculum in England is in a state of flux, it is worth noting the two fundamental aims that have underpinned it for over a decade: that all children should learn and achieve, and that their social, moral, spiritual, and cultural development is of importance (DfEE/QCA 1999).

Pause for thought

Consider the aims of the National Curriculum for England outlined above. If you were designing curriculum aims for your local school, what three key points would you include? Consider:

- How measurable are your aims?
- What might a visitor to your school see that would show the aims are being achieved?
- How important is it to be able to measure success, and how might practical constraints (like time) affect what can be measured?
- What is your view on the validity of formal standardized testing versus teachers' professional judgement? Can the two be complementary?

Schools are under great pressure to evidence pupil progress. It may be argued that such evidence is important if the first aim of the curriculum has been for all children to learn and achieve. However, such pressures can lead to an imbalance where teaching is more about achievement in the test than the ongoing development of the child. This is to put the ideas in a stark and simplistic way, but the point is important and the pressures on teachers and school leaders – as well as on children – must not be underestimated.

Children's values

Children encounter values and beliefs from a range of sources, including in the home and via print and electronic media. As teachers we have the opportunity to help them to question the views that they encounter, so that they can form their own opinions and develop their own world-views. We can also explore a range of possibilities, so that children appreciate that choices are available to them. Research suggests that when some children share a sense of their inner selves (which may be termed 'the spiritual'), they often encounter disinterest or disbelief among adults (Adams 2009). This leads to silence and, ultimately, to a loss of a sense of the spiritual. It is important to consider how to appreciate children's ideas in ways that enable them to be heard and to consider how this can be possible if our own views contrast with those of the child.

Popular beliefs held by children may include that Father Christmas and the Tooth Fairy exist. It may be that as adults we do not share these views, but we probably allow children to enjoy their thoughts and appreciate that at some point they will change their minds. However, when it comes to seeing angels, hearing the voice of a recently deceased grandparent or having an imaginary friend, we might find it harder to accept the child's perception. Research suggests that when adults dismiss children's explanations of such experiences, the children realize that their 'experiences' are not valid in an adult's eyes and stop speaking about them. In due course, they lose this sense of otherness, having learned that it is not of value (Adams 2009).

Values and difference

Helping children to appreciate similarities and to celebrate differences between people are key elements to enabling them to accept and value those around them. Understanding that although we may differ in terms of, for example, gender, race, ability or age, we all deserve to be respected and valued is an important part of nurturing the values that stand against bullying, stereotyping, and prejudice. This is not always an easy task and children may come to our schools and settings with preconceived ideas developed in the home. Helping them to understand that school is an inclusive and supportive place where all are valued is essential in creating a place in which all are enabled to learn and achieve. It is important to note that celebrating difference does not remove the need to challenge inequality.

The Ajegbo Report on diversity and citizenship in the curriculum (DfES 2007) highlights the need to consider diversity in a broad sense, including difference between those within groups often seen as homogeneous (e.g. White British). Indeed, I suggest that it is more appropriate to consider society as *heterogeneous* – that is, made up of myriad diversities, some of which may overlap. Being female, black, young or heterosexual does not infer a shared experience with anyone else identifying with one of these labels, and to complicate matters further each person has a number of different overlapping identities. In addition, the experience of social class, wealth/poverty alongside the context in which you live adds significantly to the way in which you experience life and develop beliefs and values. We should not see difference as unusual, but as the norm.

Pause for thought

Consider an occasion when the differences between children caused division or awkwardness in your setting:

- What strategies did you use to resolve the situation?
- Was your approach didactic (telling the children why difference is special) or dialogic (enabling the children to discuss difference and to consider their responses to it)?
- Are there differences between children that you find difficult to accept because of your own values, beliefs or world-view?

Developing practice

To develop effective practice, we need to consider:

- how the way in which we organize our classroom shows that we value those who use it;
- what opportunities we create to welcome children's family members into our setting;
- whether our language, displays or other resources reflect the diverse nature of society;
- how we understand the term *inclusion* and how it fits within our philosophy of education;
- how we regard the role of teacher, and how being a learning facilitator is a part of this;
- how education can open up possibilities for children and empower them for both the present and the future.

Conclusion

This chapter has explored values from a variety of perspectives. First, there is the sense of valuing the stakeholders within a learning setting and being able to appreciate their differences. Secondly, there is the value of education and a consideration of what we are seeking to achieve when educating children. Thirdly, there is the area of helping children to develop their own values in a way that is not prescriptive: allowing them to internalize and own those values for themselves. These are not easy areas and the role of the teacher, as facilitator, is not always successful. However, having a clear sense of what we are seeking to achieve with children is important, and aspiring to help them to become the best that they can be, as caring, empathetic, and respectful human beings, is an aspiration worth embracing.

Rogers' notion of being a learning facilitator underpins much of the content of this chapter, coupled with the Freirean concept of education as empowering individuals. The third educationalist that we considered was Janusz Korczak. After his orphanage was closed and the Jews consigned to the ghetto in Warsaw by the Nazis, he continued to care for the children and to provide for their needs (Lifton 2005). When the ghetto was closed, it is said that he had the opportunity to escape (due to his fame as a children's author) but chose to stay with the children, who numbered around 190. Accounts tell that he marched with them – head held high – keeping them positive and showing remarkable care as they were taken to the train that transported them to the extermination camp at Treblinka. His story is unknown by many working in contemporary educational settings, but his legacy lives on in the United Nations Convention on the Rights of the Child (United Nations General Assembly 1989).

Enabling children's learning is a concept that runs throughout this book and is fundamental to helping them to become autonomous and self-motivated individuals. While much of the chapter has been about how we model and nurture values, a final consideration is how we value education in itself and for its own sake. Education is a means to an end in many cases, but learning to learn and appreciating the fundamental value and joy of learning can be an end in itself.

References

Adams, K. (2009) The rise of the child's voice; the silencing of the spiritual voice, *Journal of Beliefs and Values*, 30(2): 113–22.

Claire, H. (2001) *Not Aliens: Primary School Children and the Citizenship/PSHE Curriculum*. Stoke-on-Trent: Trentham.

Cole, M. (2006) *Education, Equality and Human Rights: Issues of Gender, 'Race', Sexuality, Disability and Social Class*, 2nd edn. Abingdon: Routledge.

Cole, M. (2008) Introduction, in M. Cole (ed.) *Professional Attributes and Practice: Meeting the QTS Standards*, 4th edn. Abingdon: David Fulton.

Department for Education and Employment/Qualifications and Curriculum Authority (DfEE/QCA) (1999) *The National Curriculum: Handbook for Primary Teachers in England (Key Stages 1 and 2)*. London: DfEE/QCA.

Department for Education and Skills (DfES) (2004) *Every Child Matters: Change for Children in Schools*. London: DfES.

Department for Education and Skills (DfES) (2007) *Diversity and Citizenship (Ajegbo Report)*. Nottingham: DfES Publications.

Freire, P. (2007) *Pedagogy of the Oppressed*. New York: Continuum.

Gilligan, C. (1993) *In a Different Voice: Psychological Theory and Women's Development.* Cambridge, MA: Harvard University Press.

Gregory, M. (2000) Care as a goal of democratic education, *Journal of Moral Education,* 29(4): 445–61.

Hart, R. (1992) *Children's Participation: From Tokenism to Citizenship.* London: UNICEF International Child Development Centre.

Impey, R. (1991) *Trouble with the Tucker Twins.* London: Viking Books.

Joseph, S. (ed.) (2007) *Loving Every Child: Wisdom for Parents.* Chapel Hill, NC: Algonquin Books of Chapel Hill.

Korczak, J. (2003) *Ghetto Diary.* London: Yale University Press.

Lifton, B.J. (2005) *The King of Children: The Life and Death of Janusz Korczak.* Elk Grove Village, IL: American Academy of Pediatrics.

Morris, J. and Woolley, R. (eds.) (2011) *The Transitions Reading Resource.* Lincoln: Bishop Grosseteste University College. Available at: www.bishopg.ac.uk/trr.

Qualifications and Curriculum Authority (QCA) (1998) *Education for Citizenship and the Teaching of Democracy in Schools: Final Report of the Advisory Group on Citizenship (Crick Report).* London: QCA.

Rogers, C. (1969) *Freedom to Learn.* Columbus, OH: Merrill.

Ross, T. (2004) *Is it Because?* London: Andersen Press.

Shor, I. (1993) Education is politics: Paulo Freire's critical pedagogy, in P. McLaren and P. Leonard (eds.) *Paulo Freire: A Critical Encounter.* New York: Routledge.

United Nations General Assembly (1989) *The United Nations Convention on the Rights of the Child.* New York: United Nations.

Woolley, R. (2010) *Tackling Controversial Issues in the Primary School: Facing Life's Challenges with Your Learners.* London: Routledge.

CHAPTER

14 Vision

Kathleen Taylor and Richard Woolley

> 66 My personal philosophy of education is something that is ever changing due to different experiences that I have had and through spending increasing time exploring the whole school agenda. It is rooted in my firm belief that every child needs to be given opportunities to succeed no matter what their ability or what background they may come from. I believe in teaching an engaging and interesting curriculum tailored to individual needs to ensure that all children make progress, whether it be vast and accelerated, or achieving small steps that in context equal huge milestones. Working in a Catholic School has helped me to readdress my philosophy of education. I see first-hand how providing children with the morals and values to help become good citizens of the world has an impact on their growth as individuals. There is no denying that academic progress is of course important, but I firmly believe that the emotional, cultural, and social development is equally as important and is something that should permeate everything that is done in school.
>
> *Emma Turner, class teacher, Lincoln* 99

Introduction

We associate philosophy of education with history because it is the philosophies of those who have gone before that influence us today. Knowing their perspectives on life and the universe, and in particular education, helps form our own perspectives of education. We don't necessarily come to know the thoughts of earlier educators through reading; rather, the process is more subliminal, often coming through from tutors in university, teachers in school, speakers we hear, and politicians. Developing our own philosophy of education is a dynamic process indicative of the human disposition to search out connections and relate one thing to another, often happening subconsciously. Why should we be aware that a particular practice we have observed and admired might have its origins in the 1700s? In other words, through practice we see the legacy of education philosophies, and with them as our backdrop develop our own philosophy of education for the present and the future.

Central to philosophy of education is the child and his or her development physically, intellectually, emotionally, and socially. Pedagogy, which means our practice in the classroom, affects all these aspects of child development and is an area extensively discussed and argued over by past and present educationists, continuing its high-status position in political debate about education. Fielding and Moss argue that our progressivism legacy for democratic radical education, which places the child at the centre of learning where learning is experiential, is not sustainable under neoliberal ideals focused on 'material and instrumental gain' (Fielding and Moss 2011: 68). Although progressivism and neo-liberalism appear at first sight to have things in common, such as 'choice, ownership, empowerment and personalisation', they differ because neoliberal ideas depend upon 'regulatory mechanisms', and it is these measures we feel in school may repress our progressive ideals (Fielding and Moss 2011: 69). Alexander also highlights the regulatory mechanism of testing and assessment, and especially the move to publish test data in performance tables from 1997 in England, as 'detrimental to children's and teachers' attitudes and self perceptions, and constrained primary pedagogy' (Alexander 2010: 37). Essentially, the one constant that remains amidst the philosophical turmoil is teachers who battle through for the sake of the children in their care.

Vision for teaching

Pursuing a career in teaching involves tenacity, dedication, and an overriding attitude to get on with the job. While the 'slings and arrows' fly around in the political arena, children arrive at school year in and year out to be fascinated, intrigued, and ready and designed to learn. Teachers believe in their children, they know and understand their children, they are ready to teach in whatever political climate prevails. In these attributes lie the philosophies of thousands of teachers. However, when the pressures bite deep, it helps to know why we are doing what we are doing, and while we may not cherish planning and assessment as much as teaching, it provides a demonstration of our thinking and our judgements that grounds our ideals for children within the statutory curriculum. Planning and assessment are powerful agents for validating our pedagogy.

Reasons for becoming a teacher often include: (1) wanting to make a difference to children's lives and society, (2) working with children, and (3) a love of learning.

Embedded in each are deeper ideas that reveal a developing philosophy of education, and character. In the first lie notions of intention, ambition, and purpose, revealing a determined character and one who wants to contribute to the child's life and community. In the second lie ideas about caring, enabling and empowering, and a real interest in childhood and the whole child. The third reveals an expectation to learn for oneself while facilitating and enjoying the learning of others. These are noble reasons, ideas and characteristics, and prevalent in those who want to teach, which says a great deal about the teaching profession. But, how might these reasons and ideals develop in a more complex and depersonalized society? One way is to examine our beliefs and *articulate* our purposes within the school and the classroom (Ridley 1998).

Our experiences as a teacher shape and mould our personal philosophy of education. Some experiences – more critical than others – challenge our beliefs; growing a philosophy is not easy. Indeed, teaching is sometimes construed as ideologically dangerous and why at times pedagogy is threatened. Therefore, our early questions about why we want to teach change to why we teach the way we do. Reflecting upon our teaching helps us to answer the question. We know when teaching is worthy and when it is a matter of expediency, and at times there will be a need for the latter; rather than overlook it, examine it, identify the reasons, they may well be justifiable, not every lesson will live up to your ideals. Within your philosophy lies you, your strengths and weaknesses, your ambitions and needs, your good times and bad times – getting to know these is all part of your evolving philosophy. Personal philosophies are about realities as well as ideals and beliefs; one cannot build a philosophy on a false pretext, philosophy is about understanding what is true.

Articulating philosophy

We move now to consider some statements of education philosophy written by those with whom we have worked over past years: students, colleagues in partner schools, and visiting lecturers. These snapshots of their vision for primary education provide insight to the human face of developing education philosophy.

Case study

Consider the following two personal statements of education philosophy, alongside that of Emma at the start of this chapter:

'As a primary school teacher, our job is to educate the whole child and to prepare them to become a valuable member of society. Much of this is not through the academic side of education but through the values instilled into children, a job that we as educators now fulfil.

We believe that education is about igniting passions and interests and showing children that they can achieve anything regardless of their background. It is about identifying the strengths of each child and then nurturing them so that they can achieve their full potential. In essence, it is opening the door to a world of opportunity.'

Ruth Wheatley, class teacher, Lincolnshire

'I firmly believe that it is in the earliest years of a child's life that their entire future begins to take shape. The attitudes and values they develop at this time determine the path they take through education and ultimately into society beyond. As a primary school teacher therefore I am profoundly aware of the tremendous responsibility upon me to nurture the children in my care to enable them to reach their potential and become thoughtful, responsible adults.

At times, this task can seem overwhelming but it is achievable through following key principles. I endeavour to foster a desire to learn by equipping children with the skills of research and enquiry, enabling them to make exciting discoveries for themselves – so much more engaging than simply being given the facts. I also believe it is important to demonstrate genuine enthusiasm in the classroom as this appears to be contagious and is quickly adopted by the whole class. In my experience, having high expectations as a teacher will achieve good results; however, a slight adjustment in perspective and persuading children to have high expectations of themselves, accomplishes so much more, not least of which is in the degree of self-worth. Once pupils have the desire to learn, the skills which enable them to do so and the confidence to aim for the highest possible levels, the one element remaining is that of assessment (and by that I don't mean teacher assessment). Encouraging children to assess their own and others' work provides them with a deeper insight into the success of the piece and develops a better understanding of improvements that can be made. This self-realization is more powerful and has greater effect than any comments made by a teacher.

With pupils taking so much responsibility for their own learning, what then is my function? I see myself as a role model and a guide, asking the right questions to move on thinking and empowering children to achieve their goals.'

Karen Hamilton, class teacher, Nottinghamshire

Reflect on:

- the core values that underpin each statement;
- how these values compare with your own developing views about the aims and purposes of primary education;
- how the child features in each statement, and what this infers about the relationship between learning and teaching.

Considering the vision that others have for the roles of learning and teaching provides us with opportunities to learn more about our own values. There may be elements within these statements of philosophy that we have not considered before, some that chime with our own values and hopes, and perhaps others that cause us to take time to pause to reflect more deeply. Such statements can provide a window, a structured and framed opening, into the understanding of others. At times, it is possible to gaze through a window and to see new possibilities, to have new or renewed perspectives. Occasionally, we catch a glimpse of our own reflection in the window (Style 1996) and can consider our own beliefs alongside those of others. Such windows can bring opportunity for new thinking or to reinforce existing thought. Similarly at other times, such framing can provide a mirror – enabling us to reflect on our own practice and experience. The next philosophy statements provide the opportunity to consider educational change and the sense of being on a journey of reflection and envisioning in our roles as teachers.

Case study

'One of my presentations is called "Valuing your school". The title is deliberately ambiguous, designed to provoke thinking and discussion. The word "value" has multiple meanings. Schools usually have an "aims and values" statement. This characterizes and demarcates principles, policy, and practice. Schools should evaluate their work and their worth in these terms – using "value" judgements – as well as using external measures.

These values are especially important at a time when some are asserting the notion that schools have a duty to define and preserve the status quo and to maintain "traditional" or "received" values. If schools hold true to their own values, they can retain ownership and give a moral purpose to their curriculum rather than surrender to external imposition and political imperative.

In a fast-changing world, children need to look forward as well as to look back and for our society to progress we need children who will question and challenge our ideas and ideals. We need children who will debate and reason; talk as well as listen; hypothesize and experiment. If they do this from a secure sense of values, we know that the future is in safe hands.'

Mike Smit, Lead Adviser, North Yorkshire

'Schools too often appear to function around the organizational needs of adults and are distracted from core purpose by externally initiated educational change.

I aspire to one principle: a broad experience joined up and built around an accurate assessment of learning and emotional needs. Where all children are moved skilfully from where they are, to the realization of more than was ever thought possible.

An exceptional ability to identify a child's strengths and potential, a deep understanding of barriers to learning and progression and positive relationships are fundamentally required to enable this to happen.

Throughout the learning journey, assessment is built upon in a flowing, coherent, interdisciplinary and experiential way; with shared understanding of process, guidance and intervention within learning. Adult and child are both decision makers and drivers, engaged in a positive learning dialogue, both written and spoken. Both are reactive to learning and pupils become effective problem solvers and meta-learners, confident in talking their learning. They demonstrate expertise, built upon an understanding of how their barriers have been overcome. From the baseline, it becomes clear where skills, understanding, concepts, and knowledge have developed. Achievement and success are recognized by all and seen as rewards in themselves.'

Paul Martin, head teacher, Lincolnshire

Reflecting on both statements in this case study, consider:

- how each writer sees education as transformative, and what the impact of such transformation may be;
- how each writer considers the importance and impact of change within the education system;
- what each writer hopes for the children with whom they work.

The next two statements share a focus on the Arts, creativity, and the impact that education can have upon learners. Consider how these views reflect some of the key issues and themes raised throughout this book.

Case study

'As a teacher of 34 years, I have long been haunted by the idea attributed to Mark Twain that he never let his schooling interfere with his education.

Endless statutory dictums from successive governments and their ever changing Secretaries of State have only compounded my fears that most of our education does indeed happen beyond the boundaries of our schools. Often left feeling impotent and unable to make the positive difference to children's lives they deserved, I have regularly asked myself what should primary education seek to achieve?

As a head teacher, I had a clear aim in mind, that each child should leave us liking themselves, liking others and being liked by others. I set myself the challenge to shift the emphasis in our curriculum from memorizing endless facts (many of no true value) to employing memorable practitioners who provided the children with memorable experiences that would stay with them and influence them positively throughout their lives.

I hoped that during their time with us we would contribute to and develop in them seven important C's:

- Curiosity
- Character
- Confidence
- Communication
- Caring
- Contentment
- Condition (physical wellbeing).

Most of all I hoped that as children left us, they would look over their shoulders with sadness at the departing and in the coming years look back and say, "the days at my primary school were some of the happiest of my life".'

Neil Griffiths, children's author and champion of Storysacks

'The Arts provide a means of investigation that aids the process of learning. Observing, questioning, testing, analysing, and recording encourage the development of deeper perceptions and form a model of how to learn. An object that is drawn needs to be thoroughly observed. A musical composition expressing the stages of a river, or the behaviours of a molecule explained in dance, enable links to be made across subjects that reinforce and deepen learning. They provide an extra dimension that allows some children to understand and succeed where they otherwise might not. The Arts enable children to look at a topic from a range of perspectives, and bring their own authentic point of view to bear upon it. When the right circumstances are created, extended periods of work, in-depth study, resourcefulness, self-motivation and well-crafted responses can be achieved: work to be proud of and life-enhancing skills. The Arts provide a means of giving children ownership of their learning. Such children come to school excited about the day ahead and keen to be involved in the day's activities: they are not passive recipients of "education", because they have had the opportunity to develop their own work ethic and accept the responsibility and self-discipline that this involved.'

Chris and Denise Gudgin, former head teacher and deputy head teacher, Lincolnshire

Consider:

- how these visions for primary education reflect your own values and aspirations;
- whether you have seen elements of such practice in the schools that you have attended and worked in;
- how you think the children in these schools may be affected by the vision and aspirations of their teachers and what windows of opportunity may be created.

Naturally, the statements recorded in the case studies have evolved over time and will continue to develop as further learning takes place from experience, policy, and theory. Each teacher faces the challenge of interpreting their values and vision for primary education in the light of the expectations placed upon them by a range of stakeholders. All teachers continually interpret their own values and vision in the light of a range of external drivers: whether it be government policy and strategy, the expectations of parents/carers, the vision of school managers, leaders and governors, or the enthusiasm and imagination of the children in their care. This is not always an easy task, but to engage in such a reflective process opens up possibilities for professional learning, growth, and development.

In common with each chapter within this book, the philosophy statements outlined here are rooted in reflection on the interaction between practice (and thereby personal experience) and theory (the thinking, practice, and research of others). Teaching is an interactive profession in which no two days are ever the same. This is a part of its challenge and also its appeal and necessitates a commitment to reflection in order to keep moving forward in enabling children to learn and grow.

The authors of this book all share a tremendous privilege: to have worked with those embarking on a career in teaching and to have been able to learn alongside them as they have sought to interpret theory and practice, policy, and research. This process presents great challenges, for each school community and each child is special and unique with particular needs, possibilities, and life experiences. To interpret a school and class curriculum in the light of one's own values and vision presents challenging and creative opportunities. Presenting learners with opportunities to explore, investigate, interpret, play, and reflect; drawing upon art, literature, and music; introducing key concepts in mathematics and science all have the potential to nurture a child's natural curiosity and foster a love for learning. The process may not be perfect, but the possibilities created through such a shared journey of development are immense. To be a part of such a learning process is an honour: to maintain momentum within such a process requires professional dialogue with colleagues in order to sustain stamina and take forward vision. While we are acutely aware of the challenges that being a teacher can bring, we also know that having a developing set of beliefs about professional identity and practice – an evolving educational philosophy – provides a framework within which we can explore solutions.

Developing values and vision for primary education

The very ingredients of our job – learning, knowledge, and understanding – lie at the heart of philosophy with philosophers over the centuries arguing for their true meaning. We can learn much, not from finding the meaning, which is elusive, but how meaning is found, as this is the activity of a teacher. The early philosophers – and here we are thinking of Socrates, Plato, and Aristotle – were teachers; Plato was Socrates' student and Aristotle's teacher. They taught and learnt through *dialectics*, which is the 'free give and take of face to face discussion' (Barrow 1976: 42). The idea of dialectics is to test the logic of ideas through questioning. Familiar territory, we would suggest, for many teachers, who use dialogue to scaffold children's learning (see Alexander 2004; Bruner and Haste 1987; Mercer and Littleton 2007; Vygotsky 1978). Engaging in dialogue to reach meaning demonstrates learning; the alternative is to tell the child the meaning. Dialogue rejects blind unquestioning acceptance. Talking with colleagues is important for testing out the logic of your own ideas about teaching – it happens often in staffrooms. Much of the conversation we hear in staffrooms invariably concerns teachers making sense of their teaching, and children's learning and attitudes. Making sense of your own learning and attitudes as well as those of children deepens insight of yourself as a teacher and learner, so that questions normally directed to deepen your understanding of the child can also serve to deepen understanding of yourself. Often such searching forms a dialogue in the mind where your evolving philosophy of education lodges. Your philosophy of education in action is trial and error, in your efforts to make sense of why you are doing what you are doing.

Children make mistakes and we make mistakes. As teachers we are interested in mistakes, misunderstandings, and misconceptions; they intrigue us, we want children to explain so we can see how their mistake has been made and their misconception has formed. They affect all aspects of school life from relationships to calculation errors. Recognizing mistakes, as part of our philosophy of education, is important because it grounds ideals into the reality of fallibility from which we all suffer. Mistakes vary by degree – some are more difficult to address than others, some can be quite serious whereas others are trivial and part of the course, some we expect. Again it is not the mistake but rather how we deal with the mistake that matters.

One of our oldest oral stories, that of *Gawain and the Green Knight*, helps explain how best we deal with mistakes (retold by Hastings 1981 and Morpurgo 2004). The story lays bare human fallibility, and indeed complexity, through Gawain. Most importantly is his realization, and finding self-awareness through his mistakes and the trusting, generous, and forgiving nature of King Arthur. It is a story played out many times in a school day and does not need further explanation other than that we can find ourselves in either of the character's shoes.

Perhaps the story sets the scene for a brighter aspect to our philosophy – that of passion, an aspect of Gawain's character at the beginning of the story. We often hear passion talked about in schools and we all know the passionate teacher who we wish to emulate. However, passion in the teacher is built upon firmer foundations: our knowledge and understanding of pedagogy, our sense of professionalism and our values, without which passion would be hollow. Upon those ingredients our visions for the future have the chance of coming to fruition. Passion drives us to create the future for teaching, our knowledge about pedagogy helps us explain our vision, our professionalism ensures we achieve our goals, and our values demonstrate the qualities and characteristics we wish to bring to teaching. Philosophy of education is an active concept, not ancient and static, which we see in action in our schools every day. While it embodies the past, it is active in the present, and it is your philosophies that drive teaching forward to make possible those better futures we wish for our children.

References

Alexander, R. (2004) *Towards Dialogic Teaching: Rethinking Classroom Talk*, 3rd edn. Thirsk: Dialogos.

Alexander, R. (2010) *Children, Their World, Their Education: Final Report and Recommendations of the Cambridge Primary Review*. London: Routledge.

Barrow, R. (1976) *Plato and Education*. London: Routledge & Kegan Paul.

Bruner, J.S. and Haste, H. (1987) *Making Sense: The Child's Construction of the World*. London: Routledge.

Fielding, M. and Moss, P. (2011) *Radical Education and the Common School: A Democratic Alternative*. Abingdon: Routledge.

Hastings, S. (1981) *Sir Gawain and the Green Knight*. London: Walker Books.

Mercer, N. and Littleton, K. (2007) *Dialogue and the Development of Children's Thinking*. London: Routledge.

Morpurgo, M. (2004) *Sir Gawain and the Green Knight*. London: Walker Books.

Ridley, K. (1998) *Passion, Pedagogy and Professionalism*. South America, unpublished.

Style, E. (1996) Curriculum and window and mirror, *Social Science Record*, Fall: 35–8.

Vygotsky, L. (1978) *Mind and Society*. Cambridge MA: Harvard University Press.

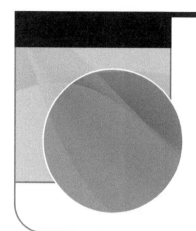

Index